pects of
Computer Supported Tasks

Cognitive Aspects of Computer Supported Tasks

YVONNE WÆRN

University of Stockholm

JOHN WILEY & SONS
Chichester · New York · Brisbane · Toronto · Singapore

Copyright © 1989 John Wiley & Sons Ltd.

Reprinted October 1991
Reprinted January 1993
Reprinted December 1993

Library of Congress Cataloging-in-Publication Data:

Waern, Yvonne
  Cognitive aspects of computer supported tasks.

  Biblography: p.
  Includes index.
  1. Human-computer interaction.   2. Cognition.
I. Title.
QA76.9.H85W34 1989   004'.019   88-33929
ISBN 0 471 91141 0

British Library Cataloguing in Publication Data:

Waern, Yvonne.
  Cognitive aspects of computer supported tasks.
  1. Man. Cognition, related to artificial intelligence
  I. Title
  153.4

ISBN 0 471 91141 0
ISBN 0 471 93066 0 (pbk)

Printed and bound in Great Britain by
Antony Rowe Ltd, Chippenham, Wiltshire

Contents

Glossary

This glossary consists mainly of terms which may be interpreted in different ways by psychologists and computer specialists. A few other central concepts have also been included.

The asterisks (*) refer to other terms in the list.

Algorithm. A set of rules which can be followed in order to derive a single, deterministic solution to a problem. In computer science an algorithm refers to the method behind a particular computer solution to a problem. In psychology, algorithm refers to any formal method for solving a problem, e.g. formal logic, or probability calculations. Algorithmic methods are sometimes contrasted with "heuristic"* methods, both in computer science and psychology.

Analogue/analogy/analogical. An analogue system or process resembles the real world it represents in a one-to-one correspondence. In computer science it is often used as opposed to "digital" or "computational" systems. In psychology the word "analogical" refers to a problem-solving approach which is not formal, but which takes another similar problem (or situation) as a starting point.

Application system. The computer program which performs the actual task. In system design it is often separated from the interface* to the user.

Artifical intelligence (AI). A term used for the science and practice of designing computer programs to solve problems which, when performed by human beings, are regarded as requiring "intelligence". The programs may attempt to simulate human problem solving to a greater or lesser extent. The methods used in AI include symbolic programming, propositional calculus and algorithmic* or heuristic* search.

CAD (Computer aided design).
"Computer aided design is an activity in which design engineers, draughtsmen and drawing assistants use specialized interactive computer systems to assist them to formulate and solve technical design problems and to communicate the resulting problem solutions. The communication usually takes the form of drawings and part lists, but may also consist of computer-readable data for use in automated manufacturing, e.g. by numerical control machines."

(Wærn, K-G., 1988a, op.cit.)

Chunk. A unit of integrated knowledge in long-term memory*, which is used to define the size of working memory*.

Cognition (Cognitive). Used here to refer to processes concerned with acquiring, storing and using knowledge, i.e. attention, perception, learning, memory, and problem solving.

Cognitive ergonomics. A science aimed at developing knowledge about the interaction between human information-processing capacities and limitations and technical information-processing systems.

Communication. An exchange of information between two partners. Here mostly used in the context of human–computer communication. This communication consists of inputs from the user and outputs from the system.

Communication component. The conceptualization of the rules for communication between system and user, i.e. the syntactics required and the design of the interactions.

Computer system. The total system of hardware, application software and user interface. Here referred to as "system".

Computational approach. Used to describe problem solving based on a finite set of rules. In psychology it can be contrasted with the "Analogical approach".

Conceptual component. The conception of the task and the concepts used to describe the task by the system.

Database. A complex arrangement of programs and data for storing and retrieving large amounts of information.

Declarative knowledge. Knowledge about facts.

Design model of the system. The conceptualization of an application system ascribable to one or more system designers (not always conscious or intentional).

Design model of task. The conceptualization of the task to be performed by a computer system stemming from the system designer (usually consciously).

Expert system. A complex program, aimed at solving a problem which requires expertise, usually in interaction with a human user.

Heuristic. A rule for problem solving which is based on the semantic characteristics of the problem rather than on its abstract characteristics. A heuristic approach does not guarantee a solution to the problem as an algorithmic approach does.

Information. This terms has two meanings. One, the technical connotation, indicates a reduction of uncertainty. The other, the everyday meaning, indicates a gain in knowledge.

Information-processing psychology. A theoretical approach to cognitive psychology which is based on the assumption that human cognitive processes can be described as operations on symbols.

Interface. A mechanism, system, or entity which mediates between two partners in a communication. Here only used in the context of the human–computer interface. A human–computer interface consists of the system designed to handle the communication between the application system and the human user.

Knowledge. This word is not very well defined in either psychology or computer science. A definition fairly well suited to the use of this term in connection with "knowledge systems" is: "Knowledge is justified true belief." In the present book the word is used in this way as well as in its intuitive everyday sense.

Knowledge state. The information about a problem which is available to a problem solver at a given moment during problem solving.

Knowledge system. The general term for systems which are able to solve problems requiring knowledge or expertise, either in interaction with humans or alone.

Long-term memory. The long-term storage of human knowledge. The content consists of declarative* and procedural knowledge*.

Mental model. A subjective representation of a more or less complex situation. Usually the term refers to some declarative knowledge*. See also "model"*.

Metacognition. Used in cognitive psychology to refer to "cognition of cognition". Metacognition covers the control of cognition in both planning and evaluation.

Metacommunication. The information to the user about the rules and procedures involved in the communication between computer system and user. Metacommunication includes online manuals and help and error messages within the system, as well as documentation outside the system. Tutorials about the system (inside and outside the system) are also regarded as metacommunication.

Model. A representation of something. In the context of computer systems, models are usually characterized by an owner and a target. See also "design model"*, "mental model"*, "user model"* and "user's model"*.

Operation. A single action which changes a state of affairs. Can be used either to denote an operation performed by the computer system or by a human user. In the psychological approach to human–computer interaction the term refers to a user's operation, which can be either mental (a thought operation) or interactive (e.g. looking at the screen, issuing a command). In basic cognitive psychology it denotes a thought act which changes the current state of knowledge. Within the computer system, "operation" refers to a primitive system operation (this connotation is not used here).

Physical level. The description of the physical characteristics of the user interface.

Procedural knowledge. Knowledge about procedures.

Production rule. An element in the procedural knowledge, consisting of an "IF <condition> THEN <act>" clause.

Production system. A set of production rules* used in a particular situation.

Program. A computer-readable set of instructions used to perform a particular task.

Problem solving. The process of searching a path from an initial situation to an intended goal. See also "Problem understanding"*.

Problem space. The set of knowledge states which can be derived from applying permissible operations to each knowledge state.

Problem understanding. The process of finding a problem space corresponding to the description of a problem. See also "Problem solving"*.

Representation. Something which stands for (represents) something else. In psychology the word is sometimes used to denote a conscious experience of a concept, an image or a word, and sometimes to refer to a theoretical construct. In computer science it is used to denote a formal description of data or "knowledge".

Schema. An interconnected set of knowledge items, which refers to a generic situation. A schema contains variables, which are instantiated by the particular situation. An example is the "schema" for narrative stories. Similar (but not exactly the same) concepts are captured by the words "scripts" or "frames". Schema seems to be the favoured term of psychological research (where it has a long history), whereas scripts and frames are preferred by artificial intelligence researchers.

Semantic network. A way of describing the relationship between concepts. In psychology it is used to describe the declarative knowledge in long-term memory.

Semantics. The conceptualization of objects and operations to be handled when working with a computer system (cf "conceptual level").

Sensory memory. The very short-term storing of sensory impressions, before the impressions have aquired any meaningful interpretation.

Short-term memory. Is here used to denote the result from an experimental paradigm, which consists in presenting a subject with some material (usually verbal or visual) and asking him to repeat it. Short-term memory is restricted in terms of the amount of material it can retain (see also "working memory") and the length of time it can retain it.

Syntactics. The rules governing the form of the communication between user and computer system (cf "communication level").

Transfer. The use of prior knowledge in a new situation. Transfer can be non-intentional, when similarities between the old and new situations evoke associations; or it can be intentional, when the learner searches for some prior knowledge which is applicable to the new situation.

User model. A conceptualization of the user of a system, stemming from outside or inside the system. If it stems from inside, the term "embedded user model" may be used.

User's model of task. A user's conceptualization of the task to be performed, with or without a system.

User's model of system. A user's (explicit or implicit) conceptualization of a computer system, which often contains a conceptualization of how to perform different tasks in the system.

Working memory. The conscious representation of the material currently in use. See also "short-term memory". Working memory is restricted in terms of the amount of material (number of "chunks") with which it can work.

Preface

WHY?

I once put down the telephone after talking for an hour to a systems designer, and decided that I had to write a book about the cognitive aspects of human–computer interaction. I did so, together with my husband, in Swedish.

Since then I have talked to innumerable people about cognition and human–computer interaction: system designers and psychologists, students and researchers, engineers and secretaries. My desire to learn more about this subject has been inspired as much by talking and teaching as by disappointment with the computer systems I have personally used. And I have learned as much by reading and attending conferences as by doing research of my own.

When Michael Coombs of John Wiley asked me if I would be prepared to write a book about something which was close to my heart, I could think of nothing more appropriate than writing about cognition in relation to human–computer interaction.

FOR WHOM?

For everybody, I would like to think. Everyone needs to know something about the role of cognition in using computer systems! But the book has been written more specifically with certain possible readers in mind.

I have written for computer science students, like those I have talked to about human–computer interaction; their interest has been a great source of encouragement. I have written for students of psychology, who have to learn about Cognitive Ergonomics. Those I have met have been enthusiastic, and some of them have furnished valuable data that could be used in the book. I have also remembered the many psychologists in schools and various other organizations, who stayed an extra hour to discuss with me how computers could be made less stressful for ordinary users.

I thought about the practical needs of people responsible for computers in industry, and fruitful discussions with them revealed more problems than I had ever thought of. Even among "ordinary" human-factors people a need to know more about this particular field has emerged: they have the methods for studying human-factors problems, I have some knowledge of human cognition; it makes for a good combination!

People possessing different kinds of previous knowledge will obviously be most interested in different parts of the book. I have given some indication of the contents of the book in Chapter 1, and have tried to keep the various sections relatively independent of one another.

YVONNE WÆRN
Stockholm

Acknowledgements

A great many people have been more or less directly involved in the writing of this book.

In particular, I want to thank the patient members of the Cognitive Seminar at the University of Stockholm, who have had the not always easy task of reading and discussing the first versions of my ideas and reading most of the chapters as they took shape. They deserve to be mentioned first (in alphabetical order): Bernard Devine, Bassam El-Khouri, Göran Hagert, Ann Hjalmarsson, Cecilia Katzeff, Ann Kjellberg, Lena Linde, Marit Olofsson, Lars Oestreicher, Lars Rabenius, Carl Rollenhagen, Kjell Scherlund, and Göran Stensson.

Outside this invaluable source of argument and support, I have badgered many other people with special talents in the areas covered in the book. Part I on human cognition has been the subject of many comments, which have led to much reworking of the material, making it both more correct and more readable. The following are responsible for providing many suggestions for improvements but they cannot be held responsible for the fact that the chapters could still be better: Nils-Erik Gustafsson (Linköping), Åke Hansson (Uppsala), Preston Ginsburg (Philadelphia), William F.G. Haselager (Amsterdam), Kristina Höök, (Uppsala), Lars Oestreicher (Uppsala), and Gerrit van der Veer (Amsterdam). The special chapter on Learning Computerized Tasks has also benefitted from comments outside the Cognitive Seminar, and I should like particularly to thank Thomas Greutman (Zürich).

For the analyses of the different applications, I have had expert help in the chapter "From Ideas to Text" from Kerstin Severinsson-Eklundh (Stockholm). The database experts in the Cognitive Seminar in Stockholm, Cecilia Katzeff and Lena Linde, have commented on the chapter "From Question to Answer". One of Sweden's foremost experts on expert systems, i.e. Sture Hägglund in Linköping, has taken a lot of trouble to explain to me that this area is by no means consistent. I hope the chapter "From Problem to Solution" reflects at least some of this diversity. The chapter on CAD has passed through the toothcombs of Håkan Helldén, Torsten Kjellberg, Gunnar Sohlenius, and the CAD expert closest to myself, my husband Karl-Gustaf. The experts are not of course responsible for the content of the chapters. Thanks to all you experts, and forgive me if any errors have slipped through!

Part IV has benefited greatly from my cooperation with Ulla Holmkvist at the Swedish Broadcasting Corporation. We arranged some interviews about computers, their nature and their possible effect on human thinking, and much of the material thus generated reappears in these chapters. Thank you, Ulla, for an exciting and inspiring time!

A patient and originally anonymous reviewer of the book also merits particular thanks. Unusually the reviewer, Ken Eason, revealed his identity and offered to help me with the final organization of the book. His support from the first tentative chapters to the completed book has been invaluable. Thank you, Ken!

This book is the result of an interdisciplinary approach. Two projects have been the main sources of inspiration.

The first is the cooperation with colleagues at the Royal Institute of Technology in Stockholm, mainly with Ann and Torsten Kjellberg, but with ample support from Gunnar Sohlenius. Thank you for educating me in mechanical engineering and CAD!

The mother source of inspiring interdisciplinary cooperation has been the working group Human Factors in Telematic Systems, in which Gerrit van der Veer acts as coordinator and Peter Innocent, Steve Guest, Eddy McDaid, Mikael Tauber, William F.G. Haselager and Lars Oestreicher are the most diligent of participants. Thank you all for our debates about goals, concepts, and methods.

Thanks are also due to the various funds which made it possible for me to employ the assistants who carried out the investigations reported here, as well as to go to conferences, and to buy necessary equipment. The following agencies have provided the research grants necessary: The Swedish Board for Research in the Humanities and Social Sciences, The Swedish Work Environmental Fund, The National Defence Research Institute, and The Swedish National Board for Technical Development. Finally, the Cooperation Scientifique et Technologique has made it possible for me to work with the interdisciplinary and international team mentioned above, where many of the ideas presented here first saw the light of day.

But what would ideas be without their linguistic dress? The job of tidying up my academic Swenglish was taken on by Nancy Adler, always enthusiastic and patient even during the summer and Christmas holidays. Thank you, Nancy, for your support!

I hesitate to thank a computer system for its support, but since this book is about computer aids I shall do so anyhow. The work started with very poor computer aid, passed on to some mediocre support and ended up with a useful system, without which the book would never have been written. Thanks, Oscar—even though you sometimes drove me mad!

Last but as usual not least I must thank my husband Karl-Gustaf for his patience when I was stressed and did nothing but sit in front of the word-processor. Parents (Nina, and Greta and Torbjörn) and children (Annika and Nina-Helene) were also neglected. Thank you for your patience! I shall soon be back to normal!

Västerhaninge, July 1988

To my parents, Nina and Torbjörn

Chapter 1

General Introduction

FROM HUMAN–COMPUTER INTERACTION TO COGNITIVE ERGONOMICS

The field of human–computer interaction is at present attracting many researchers. One important reason for its popularity is related to economics: it has been found that neglecting the human user in the design of computer systems is an expensive oversight, with the result that computer companies and other organizations which need to use computers have been forced to look at the human-factors side of computer systems. Another reason lies in the challenge of the problems themselves. Computers offer apparently unlimited facilities, if we only knew how to bend them to our advantage. Thus researchers in many different disciplines can envisage ways in which computers touch upon their own specialities. Some approach it with optimism, fascinated by the new opportunities. Others approach it with scepticism, analysing the drawbacks which may arise if we fail to consider the negative consequences in time.

In this book I analyse the field of human–computer interaction (HCI) from a psychological point of view. What kind of interest has psychology in this field? The word "human", the first in the term HCI naturally legitimizes the psychological interest, but we might still wonder whether we really need a special field for the "psychology of human–computer interaction". Some people have suggested ironically that we could just as well call for a "psychology of human–car interaction" or a "psychology of mathematics".

These suggestions are not in fact as far-fetched as they sound. There is for instance a "psychology of music" and even a field known as "traffic psychology". This reflects a recognition that application poses special problems which cannot be tackled by pure scientific theory; the gap between the basic scientific knowledge of the science and the demands of practical application is too great. The theoretical concepts cannot just be applied as they are. New concepts have to be developed, new methods, and new knowledge, all of which means that a bridge has to be built to span the gap.

The psychology of human–computer interaction is the bridge between psychology and human–computer interaction (HCI). Several other bridges can be envisaged, and there appears to be a computer science of human–computer interaction, for instance, as well as a philosophy of the same subject. Some researchers seem to be concerned with what we could call the anthropology of HCI, others with its sociology.

Since the bridges are built from different positions, they also touch the field of HCI at different spots. This means that the view of HCI may differ, depending on the particular scientific approach. But since the whole field of HCI is an interdisciplinary one, no single science can work on it in isolation. Rather, collaboration with other sciences implies a particular perspective, a particular bridge to be constructed. My own interdisciplinary partners have been computer scientists and mechanical engineers. Traces of the insights I have gained will, I hope, appear here and there.

The approach I have chosen in this book is to analyse the question of human–computer interaction with the help of certain psychological principles which seem to be relevant. These principles will be described, their implications for HCI will be analysed, and with their help certain special issues will be addressed. In this way you, the reader, will be given an opportunity to understand and evaluate the suggested principles in light of your own particular purposes and to apply them in contexts that are relevant and interesting to you.

Before choosing these principles, the field of human–computer interaction has to be described. First we can say that it is defined by its name: some interaction between a human and a computer is postulated. What does this mean? People interact with computers in several ways—in automatic cash dispensers, by telephone, by sitting at terminals. The definition suggested here allows only for those situations in which people interact with computers via terminals or personal computers.

Looking at such situations we find that computers are used as information-processing systems to support people's needs for this kind of processing. Further we can identify two different human needs in such situations: to perform the task and to handle the system. Both needs are concerned with the processing of information.

These needs suggest a particular subset of psychological principles as being relevant. Problems connected with the way people process information are handled within the field known as "cognitive psychology", which is concerned with principles of perception, learning, and problem-solving.

The cognitive approach to this field has already led to the definition of a further field, known as "cognitive ergonomics", which is well expressed by the following definition:

"COGNITIVE ERGONOMICS aims at developing knowledge about the interaction between human information processing capacities and limitations and technical information processing systems. This knowledge should support the design of these technical systems, as well as the design of education and other kinds of user support."

(From the Statutes of the European Association of Cognitive Ergonomics, EACE, 1987).

This quotation raises some questions which will be tackled by the present book, i.e.:

— what are the properties of the human information processing system?
— what types of interaction arise between human information processing and technical information processing systems?
— what are the particular requirements on the design of technical information processing systems, from a human point of view?
— what effects may technical information processing systems have on human thinking?

These questions can be regarded as approaching the problem of human–computer interaction from four different perspectives: the cognitive, the task, the human interface and the effects perspective. Thus, the book will present these different perspectives in turn, trying to answer the questions to some extent at least.

Part I presents the cognitive perspective and gives some first hints about how principles from cognitive psychology may be applied to human–computer interaction. If you are already familiar with cognitive psychology you can skip that part. But those who are not so familiar may find that kind of information inspiring, as I have been told by some system designers. In this part you will also find some new and more particular facts about learning computerized tasks. This is covered in chapter 5, which I hope will be rather new and useful for all readers.

In part II the task perspective will be taken by analysing the particular requirements of different tasks. Unfortunately, very little research has as yet been carried out with the perspective of analysing how a computer system fits into a particular task from the user's point of view. Much of what is said in part II relies on a common-sense analysis of what the task requires rather than on firm empirical data. The data that are available are of course presented, and my hope is that some researchers will be inspired to produce more data, confirming, rejecting, or (most probably) refining my analyses. I certainly hope that more research in the field of human–computer interaction will be devoted to the analysis of possible tasks to be performed with computer support. The progress of computer support will depend on how well we understand how tasks can be described, how computers can function as tools in the tasks and how these tools can be described to, learned and used by human users.

The user–interface perspective is presented in part III, covering a review of the literature within this rather well-researched topic within the field of cognitive ergonomics. Part III can thus be skipped by those who are already familiar with the research on designing command languages, menus, screens, and help messages. I hope others will find this review of the literature useful.

Finally, part IV presents the problem from the perspective of possible effects of computers. A cognitive approach to human–computer interaction cannot leave the problem without speculating somewhat about possible effects of computers in thinking. The effects envisaged in part IV deal with the possible transfer of knowledge from the computer world to everyday thinking. Also, the possible effects of computer concepts on the conceptualization of our own thinking are discussed. This part is by natural reasons more speculative than any other part. I hope it can inspire new thoughts, developing or critizing my own ideas.

Part I. The Cognitive Perspective

Introduction

THE THEORY CHOSEN

The theoretical background for the study of cognition as here presented is the so-called information-processing psychology. This theory differs from behaviouristic psychology by explicitly studying "mentalistic" concepts. We find such concepts in theories which try to describe how people are driven by "goals", make up "plans", "interpret" their surrounding world, and adjust their conceptions as a result of "feedback" from their actions.

The term "information-processing psychology" indicates that this theory has something in common with artificial information processing, such as it is performed in computers. The commonality lies in the assumption that thinking can be described as *operations* on *symbols*.

Thereby information-processing psychology differs from theories which regard thinking as emanating directly from the sensory impressions or from associations in a neural network. Information-processing psychology has generally no ambition to go down to the neural foundations of thinking. It works mainly on the functional side of this phenomenon, assuming that meaningful propositions about the functioning of thinking can be expressed without analysing the structure in which thinking is embedded to any greater detail. Thereby it also resembles computer science, in which the same program can be run on different computer hardware, and vice versa; thereby separating function from structure.

The similarity with computer science in these two respects should not lead to the mistaken conclusion that information processing psychology has taken computers as models for human thinking. There are many aspects of human cognition that are usually not covered by the artificial-intelligence approach to computer science—the varying expenditure of effort, the restriction of attention, and the fallibility of memory, only to mention some examples of that which will be covered below.

At the same time it has to be acknowledged that the theory has restricted its domain of application to that kind of thinking that can be handled as operations on symbols. This implies that it is rather far-fetched to treat emotions in this theory, since they are presumably as much related to immediate physiological reactions as to operations on symbols (although the latter representation has been attempted in some artificial-intelligence research). It is also difficult to

7

describe direct sensory and motor reactions in terms of operations on symbols (cf. Pylyshyn, 1984).

ONE BASIC PRINCIPLE

Psychology has been keen on finding general simple principles to describe human functioning. In the behaviouristic tradition, the S–R principle was used to describe all human behaviour. This principle is useful to describe that kind of people's behaviour which can be regarded as "responses" (the "R" part) to "stimuli" (the "S" part).

Another principle has to be used in order to capture people's goal-oriented behaviour. Here the "test–operate–test–exit" principle, also called the TOTE unit, is useful. This principle was introduced in 1960 by Miller, Galanter & Pribram (1960).

This principle is presented in Figure 1. The principle captures the essentials of human goal-directed behaviour, not only when thinking is concerned. The human actor starts by asking whether the goal has been reached or not (the TEST box). If the goal has not been attained, the "no" arrow leads to an action (the "OPERATE" box). The result of this action is tested against the goal (the arrow between the operate box and the test box). This circle of tests and operations continues until the goal is reached, and the loop can be exited (the "yes" arrow to the "EXIT" box).

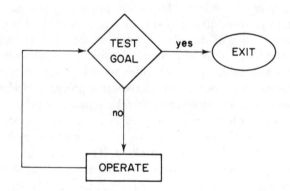

Figure 1 The test–operate–test principle.

TOTE units may be hierarchically organized, in which case one main task contains several subtasks in the "operations" box, just as chinese boxes. It is also possible for a human actor to be engaged more or less simultaneously in several TOTE units related to different goals.

Applied to human cognition the TOTE principle concerns goals concerned with learning, problem solving, etc. The operations envisaged in the TOTE unit then consist of mental operations such as attending, memorizing, drawing conclusions, the result will consist of the feedback derived from the action, and the test can rely on objective as well as subjective data.

Applied to human–computer interaction, the principle suggests that a good interaction ensues if people are given good opportunities to test whether they have reached their goal or not (which depends on the quality of the feedback derived from the computer) and if they are offered operations which they can easily perform. Here we could stop in principle, but there are so many more details which are interesting.

OVERVIEW OF PART I

Although information-processing psychology concentrates on cognition, it does not deny that there are factors outside of cognition which affect cognition. Such factors are discussed in chapter 2. The important concepts of arousal, selective attention and effort will be introduced and related both to cognition and to human–computer interaction. These concepts indicate that both the goal and the evaluation of the goal may undergo changes due to situational circumstances.

A very short review of the facts concerning human sensory–motor characteristics will also be presented in chapter 2. The size of the chapter should not deceive anybody into believing that this is not an important aspect of human–computer interaction. But this topic has been extensively covered by other authors, particularly as related to characteristics of the visual display unit.

Instead, the more complex information-processing activities will be focussed. Chapter 3 deals with human knowledge and its long- and short-term representation. The human problem-solving processes are presented in chapter 4. Finally, people vary, and the implications of these variations for human–computer interaction are discussed in chapter 5.

Chapter 2

Some Basics of Cognition

THE EVOLUTION OF COGNITION

Human cognition does not exist in a vaccuum. Instead it can be regarded as evolving from our interactions with our surroundings. We see and hear, we touch and manipulate our world. Not only does reality affect us; we also affect reality. By our actions in the real world we change that world. Reality tells us what we have achieved by providing us with feedback.

At the same time our internal systems are in constant interaction with one another. Our conscious system interacts with our physiological system in coping with fatigue or excitement, by handling our emotions and desires. Cognition depends not only on the "objective" nature of internal or external reality, but also on prior knowledge and on present goals and emotions. Thus cognition has to be described and explained as evolving from the functioning of an open information-processing system. No one factor can be held solely responsible for the effects as though it were independent of all the others. The system must be regarded as a single whole, although it may be possible to discern its various parts.

Since as human beings we are immersed in a total system involving our bodies in interaction with the environment, it is naturally impossible to separate and describe the cognitive part of "ourselves" on its own. Instead, in studying human cognition we have to address human behaviour (both internal and external) in connection with tasks, that require cognition.

The system from which cognition arises

Figure 2 can help us to see how cognition derives from the whole system of information interchange between internal and external reality. The external environment in a study of cognition consists of a task which can be defined as a situation in which there is a difference between the present situation and a goal situation. The subject is either given the task to accomplish the goal or imposes

10

this task upon himself. The existence of a goal excludes reflexes from the task concept. A task can consist of simply perceiving or interpreting a situation, it can imply learning some facts or skills, or it can require that a problem be solved.

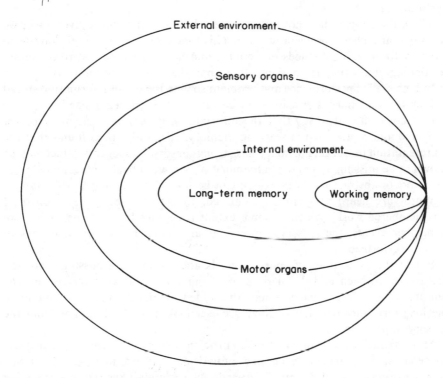

Figure 2 The system from which cognition arises.

The task impinges upon the person by way of the sensory organs. In the type of cognitive tasks most often studied the eyes and ears are the sensory organs generally involved.

The sensory organs may be directly related to the motor organs, in which case a reflex action ensues with no conscious representation intervening between sensation and action. We do not usually speak of cognition in this context.

If the sensory impression impinges on some element in long-term memory before an action results, the subject will be able both to perceive it and to interpret it. In this case we can speak of cognition. There is a conscious representation of the cognition in working memory. Working memory can be regarded as a part of long-term memory, i.e. the part which is being activated at the moment.

In order to carry out the task, the subject has to perform one or more actions, and these actions may be related more or less automatically to the perceived event. When a person performs an action without hesitating or making any mistake, and it is not a question of a reflex action, we usually speak of skilled performance.

When the subject does not know exactly how to carry out a given task, we can say that he has a problem to solve. This time he has to search his long-term memory for suitable methods or actions, and he then has to test these before continuing or starting again, depending upon the outcome of the tests.

In both skilled performance and problem solving the use of information stored in long-term memory is crucial. How can this use be conceptualized?

It is not sufficient to say that the information in long-term memory is just activated and represented in working memory. It has also been found that the representation in working memory has strong sensory components, which can be shown to be missing in long-term memory. When we actively remember things, we resort to abstract concepts, which can be formulated in words or images.

Words are heard or silently articulated. Images are seen. We reconstruct a remembered world, which to some extent resembles the real one. When we remember events, the sensory impressions are supplemented by memories of actions performed.

But at the same time, of course, details and outlines are missing, and new features have been added, all differing from the world as perceived by the sensory organs. The vagueness and the added details derive from content in the long-term memory. Let us have a closer look at such deviations from the sensory impressions.

Much skilled performance and much problem solving is dependent on abstract concepts, such as generic terms like animal, or relations, like "greater than", or propositions, like "if x then y". How do we remember abstract concepts like these, which in themselves have no sensory components? The solution seems to be that the abstract concepts can be denoted in words, and that they thus acquire the sensory components of sound or word image, or the motor component of articulation.

The meaning of abstract concepts may be conceptualized as a network of relations between concepts. Concepts that are already represented in working memory serve to introduce other related concepts into this memory as well.

This description of the way in which cognition arises can help us to identify the basic factors involved. Cognition is dependent on characteristics of the sensory organs. Problem solving is dependent on knowledge stored in long-term memory and on the possibility of keeping these in active use in working memory. Motor aspects are involved in handling problems which require motor performance, while their effects also serve as a feedback source. The cognitive performance as a whole is also dependent on the activation status of the internal environment, and it is this to which we will now turn.

COGNITIVE PERFORMANCE AND AROUSAL

It appears that that the degree of arousal in the internal environment affects all types of performance, including cognitive performance. The arousal in the internal environment may be low or high. A sleepy person will not perform as well as someone who is wide awake. Even minor shifts in arousal affect a person's ability to perform difficult tasks.

As long ago as 1908 this phenomenon found expression in the Yerkes–Dodson law, which is reproduced schematically in Figure 3. Although the law has been refined and discussed a great deal since 1908, the main idea remains: performance is optimal when the arousal is neither too low nor too high. Discussion of this curve turns chiefly on the possible existence of one or more "arousals", or one or more "performances", and on whether the curve has the same form regardless of the ease or difficulty of the task. However we define arousal and performance, we will find some (moderately difficult) task for which the curve described here holds for a particular person. The empirical problem consists in finding adequate variations and observations of arousal and adequate measurements of performance.

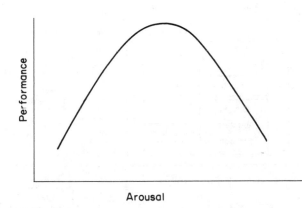

Figure 3 Yerkes–Dodson law.

The Yerkes–Dodson law has not only been the subject of much debate, it has also inspired a lot of research. Its form leads us to ask ourselves: how can we achieve an optimal arousal, and how might the arousal be influenced? It seems safe to assume that sleepiness, monotony and low motivation alone or together will lead to low arousal, whereas time pressure, noise and high performance requirements induce high arousal. If we assume that arousal will affect the amount of effort which a person may expend on a task, then we can say that performance outcome depends on the demands of the task. The effects of an arousal that is too low or too high will not be noticed in a very easy task, requiring little effort. In a difficult task, however, the effect of arousal will be more noticeable. But this prediction is complicated by the fact that in itself a difficult task increases arousal. Thus a moderately sleepy person may well be able to perform a difficult task but might fail at an easier one.

Also, of course, we are simplifying things for ourselves by talking about easy or difficult tasks. Who can decide what is easy or what is difficult? Only the person who is about to tackle the task. And his decision is based not only on various aspects of the task, but also on his judgment of his own capability and on his willingness to devote his energies to this particular task. A human actor can be regarded as regulating his efforts against the potential gains. In Figure 4 the self-regulative aspect of human activity is presented, together with its possible interaction with the cognitive aspect. The figure shows that two rather independent systems, the emotive and the cognitive, affect the goal posed by an actor. Starting from his perception of the task, the actor assesses the demands of the situation and his own capabilities in this context. These assessments are cognitive. At the same time, the present situation will affect both his present emotions and motivations. These two sets of factors will then determine the actor's choice of a processing goal. The goal in turn will determine the strategy for performing the task.

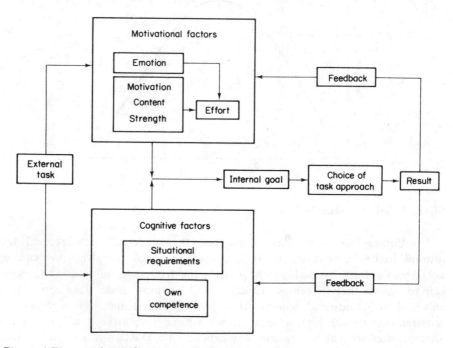

Figure 4 The emotive and cognitive feedback loops of human activity.

When the task has been performed, the feedback will be evaluated as indicated by the backward directed arrows. The cognitive feedback contains a characterization of the situation achieved. The emotive feedback contains a characterization of the emotional and motivational experiences at the final stage (whether the goal has been attained or not). These two types of feedback form the basis for learning (the cognitive feedback) and for deciding whether or not to continue working with the task if it has not been finished (the emotive feedback).

It has to be pointed out that the "choosing" of a goal and the "evaluation" of feedback is not necessarily conscious on the part of the actor. The goal may be implicit, and the subject may well be satisfied or dissatisfied with his own performance without being able to tell the reason why. For intentional learning, however, the cognitive content of the feedback should be processed in a conscious way.

To summarize, it is suggested that people perform some (more or less conscious) cost-benefit analysis of the situation. When they decide which strategy to choose, they "calculate" what benefits can be gained at as low a cost as possible. When they evaluate their results, they check whether or not their calculation was correct. This will then form a basis for the next cost-benefit calculation which will determine the goal posed and the strategy chosen for the next attempt with the same or a similar task.

Selective attention

Part of the strategy for processing the task is concerned with distributing resources among the various aspects of the undertaking. Human attention is subject to certain restrictions and it is not possible for all aspects of the task to be considered simultaneously. What are the restrictions on attention and how do people handle them?

Selective attention comes into play when two or more different stimuli are impinging simultaneously on our senses and we have to decide which of them to attend to. The question of selecting a particular stimulus is natural to our visual system, since the eye cannot focus on more than one spot at a time. It is equally natural to the motor system, which is unable to perform more than one single muscle action at the same time. The auditory system, on the other hand, allows for attention to two different stimuli simultaneously. We can therefore ask ourselves whether selective attention also applies to auditory stimuli. If this is so, then we should also consider other restrictions on attention apart from those related to sensory or motor capacities.

An answer to the general question of selective attention has been sought in the following experiment. A subject wearing earphones is presented with two different messages, one in each ear. He is then asked to "shadow" one of the messages, i.e. to articulate it as it is presented and as soon as he has perceived it. Afterwards the subject is asked to report on the nature and content of both messages. It has been found that subjects are able to say very little about the message which was not shadowed. They can say something about its physical characteristics (e.g. whether it consisted of noise or speech, or whether the voice was male or female), but little else. It seems that people "tune in" to the shadowed message, attending to it to the exlusion of the other. This is known as the "cocktail-party phenomenon". Like a cocktail-party guest concentraing on one person's words and ignoring all the other conversations going on around him, the subjects in the shadowing situation ignore the non-shadowed message.

There are, however, some notable exceptions to these regular findings. If something "interesting" occurs in the unattended message, people will often take note of it. For instance, they will catch their own name if it comes up in the disregarded message and will switch their attention to it. Subjects can also follow a meaningful message that is shifted from the activated to the non-activated ear (cf Treisman, 1960). Thus it is the meaning that catches the attention, rather than the physical location (Figure 5). These results suggest that both messages do reach the sensory memory. Actual selection then depends on the person's strategy. This strategy may mean following the instructions to attend to one ear only or it may mean trying to listen intermittently to one message or the other (time-sharing).

Figure 5 If something "interesting" occurs in the unattended message, people will often take note of it.

We can then conclude that selective attention is a phenomenon occurring during the short period of representation in sensory memory. It could be claimed that it is not the sensory organs *per se* that require selective attention, but the conscious representation requiring effort.

It should be noted that there are two somewhat different reasons for resorting to selective attention (cf. Kahneman, 1973). One is related to the difficulty of performing two similar tasks concurrently. When similar processing mechanisms have to be used, there will be interference. We can call this a "structural" limitation, leading to the selection of one task over the other. But there are also general processing limitations, i.e. limitations connected with the amount of effort available for processing in general.

The above examples concern how people divide their attention between different stimuli. But a single stimulus contains a number of cues, and selective attention may be relevant also in perceiving a single stimulus. It has for instance been suggested that people under stress (i.e. under increased arousal) will reduce the number of cues to which they attend in a situation (Easterbrook, 1959). This suggestion can explain some of the results that have been reported as supporting the Yerkes–Dodson law. If we assume that people are able to eliminate irrelevant cues, then this restriction on the cues utilized will raise the level of performance. It can also be hypothesized that at very high levels of arousal only relevant cues will remain, and that any further reduction in cue utilization after this point will lower the level of performance. Easterbrook's hypotheses have been confirmed in several studies.

Some exceptions have also been found, however, which suggest that the matter is not quite as simple as Easterbrook's argument implies. For instance, it has been found that people who are anxious find it difficult to concentrate on a task. This could indicate a wider rather than a narrower range of attention. But as anxiety is usually related to high arousal, we would thus expect a narrow range of attention under conditions of anxiety. A possible explanation is that a smaller proportion of attention capacity is available for task-relevant processing. Either the anxiety itself or the monitoring of the anxiety-inducing stimuli may be calling for processing work not directly related to the task. This would increase arousal as well as distracting attention.

Attention and effort

Common sense tells us that attention is selective. The relation between attention and effort is also fairly obvious; most people recognize that attention calls for some kind of effort. The limits on our processing capacities may well depend on the amount of attention which we can expend during the time necessary to perceive, conceive, or process a particular stimulus. In an intellectual task the effort expended (as measured by some objective measurement) is clearly related to the amount of information which has to be attended to (Kahneman,

1973). It has also been shown that subjective effort, i.e. the self-rating of effort, is related to the amount of information to be processed (Dornic, 1977) as well as to the time spent in processing this information (Wærn & Askwall, 1981).

It thus seems clear enough that effort is a limited resource which can be distributed according to the demands of the situation. The problem is the apparent lack of any adequate measure of the amount of effort available. In all studies using the concepts of attention and effort, the amount of effort has been inferred from the performance studied and the experimental variations performed. This can easily result in a circular line of reasoning; a low performance being explained by a low effort, which in turn "explains" the low performance. This circular line of reasoning can be applied to the Yerkes–Dodson law as well; the lower performance on the right hand side of the curve can be explained by the task demanding too much effort. As long as no independent measurements of performance and effort are made, the explanations are of little value.

The assessment of the amount of effort available is difficult because no method exists for measuring the difficulty of the task independent of the effort spent. It can, and has been, suggested that a task which can be performed automatically, i.e. without any conscious attention, will require less effort than a task which has to be consciously attended to. Higher levels of arousal would affect the performance of tasks requiring conscious attention (i.e. effortful processes) more than performance of tasks requiring no attention (i.e. automatic processing). Some evidence supporting this contention can be found in studies which have shown that organizational ability (presumably requiring attention) falls off at high levels of high arousal, as well as does the use of imagery. However, there is also evidence that people learning in a state of high arousal still use a rehearsal strategy, which must require attention. Further, it has been shown that high arousal may heighten the performance in automatic tasks, by narrowing attention exclusively to the relevant stimuli.

But the relation between effort and the difficulty of the task concerns more than just the type of the task. It also depends on the individual involved. Certain tasks are obviously difficult for some people and easy for others. Children cannot do things which we as adults find perfectly simple; novices have difficulty with tasks which experts can do automatically. It is thus impossible to say anything about the attentional requirements of a particular computer task, unless we know what knowledge the prospective user can bring to the situation.

IMPLICATIONS OF HUMAN SELF-REGULATION FOR HUMAN–COMPUTER INTERACTION

Because of the balancing of costs against benefits, it is difficult to predict what will happen when a novice user encounters a computer system. It is probable that the first impressions of the system will determine both the goal he sets for himself and the amount of effort he will spend on his first attempts. If it seems that much can be gained by little effort, the user will be willing to expend more effort in the hope of gaining yet more. This means that a system should allow the beginner to use processes which he feels capable of performing. The accustomed computer user is helped by prior experience, both in judging the requirements of the situation and in assessing his own capacities. It is therefore an easier task for these users to decide whether or not to make the effort needed to learn the system. It is also easier for them to derive an appropriate strategy for processing the task. Thus a system meant for experienced computer users should highlight similarities and differences with other computer systems (preferably those the user already knows about).

The various aspects of selective attention are very important when it comes to performing tasks with the aid of a computer system. A task supported by a computer may be seen as consisting of two subtasks: the main task to be performed and the subsidiary one of handling the computer system itself. If both these tasks require attention, performance in one or the other is likely to suffer, compared with the case in which only one of the tasks has to be given full attention. This will be particularly noticeable if the computer tasks have to be performed under stress (e.g. time pressure, noisy environments), or if those concerned are anxious while they are working with the computer (e.g. afraid of "destroying" something).

The analysis of effort suggests that a thorough analysis of the situation must be made before we can design systems for different people in different situations.

This analysis can start from the Yerkes–Dodson law, taking into account the possible effects at both ends of the arousal curve. At the lower end, we can envisage very simple systems or very monotonous work, with a consequently low level of arousal and a correspondingly low performance. The risk for these tasks consists in people finding it boring, losing their attention and thereby starting to make errors. In such situations a more challenging task might heighten both arousal and job satisfaction, while still being performed correctly. Some work situations have been found to have suffered from the computer system taking over interesting tasks and thus impoverishing the worker's job.

We can also ask ourselves whether the system itself can help a user who is tired or non-motivated. Since the performance at the lower end of effort is low, the system might help the user with reminders ("do you really want to delete this file?", for instance) or checks on details which might else be easily forgotten.

At the upper end of the continuum we can envisage complex systems and heavy demands on quick and correct performance. This would promote a high level of arousal. If the person concerned is unable to produce all the effort needed (either because there are other things to do or because the system itself requires too much effort), performance will probably deteriorate, either because the individual narrows the range of his attention too much so that crucial task-relevant cues are disregarded, or because he devotes his attention to non-task-relevant cues. The usual reason for a computer support for complex tasks is to relieve the problem solver from some demanding thought operations. As we shall see in the part on the task perspective (part II), this well meant aim is not always fulfilled in computer aids.

SENSORY–MOTOR CHARACTERISTICS

The characteristics of the sensory and motor organs can be regarded as representing "bioware" restrictions on the human system. Human cognitive performance cannot go beyond these restrictions. It is impossible for us to base any knowledge or problem solving on the sensory experience of infra-red light (although we may overcome this restriction by optical–electronical devices). Nor can we derive any knowledge, or base any decisions on ultra-high-frequency sounds. The same applies to our motor organs. Our cognition will be restricted by the speed with which we can perform different acts, as well as by the acts we can perform at all.

It is thus relatively easy to base recommendations for the design of human–computer interaction on these "bioware" characteristics. If a computer system does not allow for these at least, it will be of no use to human beings. Most computer systems naturally comply spontaneously with the restrictions imposed by human bioware. However, as we shall see, some technical restrictions conflict with human sensory requirements. In such cases human beings will have to work at the limits of their capacity, and we will have to expect both stress and errors.

Quantitative characteristics of vision and audition

Where the sensory organs are concerned, the following aspects have to be considered: the minimum duration for a stimulus to be detected, the duration of the sensory impression after the stimulation has ceased, and the amount of information that can be maintained in memory storage. I am indebted to Card, Moran & Newell (1983) for compiling the following figures from psychological investigations using different subjects and under different circumstances. Since the various studies have produced somewhat different results, the authors decided to give a range of figures rather than an average. I have followed their strategy.

Table 1 provides an overview of the three aspects for vision and audition respectively.

The figures in Table 1 can be used in a variety of contexts. For instance, the

Table 1. Characteristics of the sensory system

	Vision	Audition
Minimum time for detection	50–200 msec	ca 100 msec
Sensory memory—time for retention of 50% of the information	90–1000 msec	900–3500 msec
Information retained immediately after presentation (partial recall)	7–17 letters (written)	4–6 letters (spoken)

detection time for visual stimuli indicates that two stimuli presented successively within a period of time less than 50–200 msec will be perceived as one continuous stimulus. This has an application in the making of movies, where 20 frames per second is the usual presentation rate for a movement to be perceived. As we shall see in the chapter on physical aspects of communication (chapter 14), the sensory characteristics of the eye must also be considered in order to avoid the perception of flicker on a screen. The higher the light intensity and the greater the size of the screen, the more the limit is pushed down, which means that a quick refreshment rate will be required in order to get a flicker-free screen presentation.

The decay rate in sensory memory means that the intervals between various pieces of information that are to be integrated should be short enough to prevent the loss of the sensory trace of one piece before the next one arrives. This means, for instance, that interruptions in the presentation of visual information (such as screen changes during the reading of a text) may become detrimental as early as after 90 msec! The sensory information in auditory store lasts longer, which means that auditory messages survive interruptions better than visual messages. (Note that we are speaking of information which has not yet acquired a meaningful interpretation.)

The amount of information retained immediately after presentation tells us something about the interaction between rate-of-information-given and the demand for meaningfulness in the material presented. So long as the material cannot be interpreted (i.e. meaningfully related to material in long-term memory), sensory memory will provide the only way of retaining it. When too much meaningless material is presented and then removed, some parts of it will drop out of sensory storage, which naturally means that the person has even less chance of arriving at an interpretation of the information. An overload situation of this kind arises when a lot of information flashes past and the recipient has no chance of controlling the pace of it. Thus the tracking of several simultaneous and unpredictable processes must be regarded as a quite inhuman task.

In the case of meaningful material, it is difficult to distinguish between the contribution of the sensory organs and the contribution of the cognition system. And it is here that working memory comes into the picture (cf chapter 3).

It should be noted that the figures in Table 1 refer to the situation in which the subject's attention is focussed on the point where the information is appearing (in the case of vision). In a visual task, we also have to take into account the need to move the eyes. The eye cannot focus on an area covered by an angle of more than 2 degrees. As soon as a message appears outside this angle, the eyes have to move. With eye movements it is possible to embrace an angle of 30 degrees. Beyond that, the head must be moved.

Qualitative characteristics of vision

Human beings are astonishingly good at recognizing very complex visual patterns. The simulation of human capabilities by computer in these fields has proved unexpectedly difficult, partly because the human sensory organs include certain mechanisms which preprocess the stimuli. It is naturally impossible to test this explanation by directly experimenting on human sensory organs, but some evidence for the existence of special mechanisms for processing visual stimuli has been obtained from studying the physiology of the sensory organs of animals such as flies, frogs and cats.

It has been found that the retina itself contains special detectors enabling the animal to spot movements, edges and slits. Similar receptive fields have been found at the cortical level (Hubel & Wiesel, 1962). Hubel & Wiesel found simple cells in the primary visual area which are responsible for the detection of edges. At a higher cortical level, complex cells were found which react to edges or contours in specific orientations. These cells are also very responsive to movement, and even seem to have a "preferred" direction for movement (e.g. left-to-right rather than right-to-left). Still more complex, so called "hypercomplex cells" appear in the visual association area, and are sensitive to contours of various types. Here we find such specialized skills as the detection of an angle of 90 degrees.

The study of humans has naturally been restricted to observations in a variety of experimental situations, without any equivalent measurement of physiological excitation patterns. But these studies suggest the existence of "inbuilt" mechanisms for visual processing.

Feature detectors have been suggested as such inbuilt mechanisms. It has been shown, for instance, that the visual confusion of different letters can be explained by analysing their features. The nature of after-effects offers further evidence of the existence of feature detectors. An after-effect follows a certain kind of prolonged or strong stimulation, and always involves the perception of something opposite to the original stimulus. The prolonged inspection of a red stimulus leads to an after-effect in green. If we look for a long time at something moving in one direction, a waterfall, perhaps, we will perceive a movement in the opposite direction when we turn our eyes to another object—the water in this example will be seen flowing upwards.

Prolonged stimulation of a single receptor does not only lead to after-effects, in controlled experiments it has been found that all perception of a stimulus will disappear after a while. Thereby it can be shown that some connected parts of figures will disappear, and not only a single spot, which further supports the existence of feature detectors.

Other suggestions of complex mechanisms relate to the way in which we perceive complex and unfamiliar stimuli. Several studies in the tradition of Gestalt psychology have shown that the organization of complex stimuli follow the "laws of Gestalt". The most important of these are illustrated in Figures 6–9. The Gestalt laws also represent one important explanation of our ability to perceive our world in three dimensions. We even seem almost unable to perceive some two-dimensional renderings as they are drawn in two dimensions, as is shown in Figure 10, depicting an "impossible" object. We can see very well

Figure 6 The "proximity" law. Figures which are situated close to one another are perceived as forming a unit, a "Gestalt".

Figure 7 The similarity law. Figures which are similar to each other are perceived as one Gestalt.

Figure 8 The good continuity law. We tend to perceive a picture of an object as contiguous, even if part of it is hidden.

Figure 9 The law of closure. We fill in gaps in our perception to get a full Gestalt.

that this object is impossible, and still we cannot persuade ourselves to see the drawing in two dimensions. In fact, it is rather difficult to draw such an object without particular tricks—try it! Some artists have exploited this particular characteristic in creative pictures, see the Dutch artist Maurits Cornelis Escher and the Swedish artist Oscar Reutersvärd.

Another interesting effect of the Gestalt quality of our perception lies in the so-called Gestalt shifts, illustrated in Figure 11. If you look long enough at this figure, you should experience a "shift" in your perception of it. Sometimes you feel you are looking at the box from above, sometimes from below.

Many artists have exploited such gestalt shifts—among others Salvador Dali—a phenomenon that can be entertaining in some situations, but annoying in others.

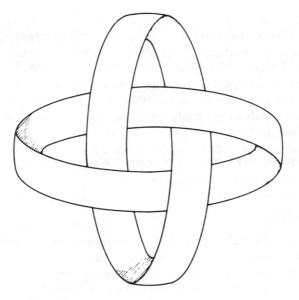

Figure 10 An impossible object.

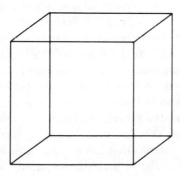

Figure 11 A glass box can give rise to gestalt shifts.

Qualitative attributes of audition

One of the most interesting aspects of human audition is the ability to perceive complex stimuli such as speech sounds. It has proved difficult to achieve speech perception by any artificial information-processing mechanism, chiefly because speech perception requires an enormous amount of knowledge before it can work as effortlessly as in human beings. But this difficulty also has another cause, namely the processing that precedes cognitive processing.

There is some evidence that our auditory apparatus is "programmed" to perceive speech sounds in a different way than non-speech sounds. It has been found, for instance, that newborn infants react differently to speech than to other sounds. Another evidence from adult perception is the following. It seems fairly natural for us to distinguish between the syllables "da" and "ba". However, a look at the pattern of frequencies produced by these two sounds, suggests a continual gradation from one to the other. And yet if people are exposed to a series of sounds, shifting gradually from "da" to "ba", they will make a sharp distinction between the two at some point, which does not correspond to any particular difference in the physical stimulus. Thus the perception of difference cannot be related to the physical stimulus; rather, it must be connected with some aspect of our auditory apparatus.

Motor characteristics

Hitherto, interaction between people and computers has generally occurred in screen output on the part of the computer and some kind of motor input on the part of the user. At present the most common inputs are via keyboard or mouse. In both cases the motor characteristics of arms, hands and fingers are important, and Card, Moran & Newell (1983) again provide some interesting data.

Every movement performed consists of a series of discrete micromovements, each requiring about 70 (30–100) msec. Performance checks cannot be made on every micromovement, since feedback from action to perception takes 200–500 msec. Rapid actions such as those involved in typing or speaking therefore have to take place in automated sequences of motor acts.

When a cursor is moved towards a target with help of a mouse, the time to reach the target depends on the time required for movement and for feedback. As the cursor approaches the target, feedback and corrections are needed in order to hit it. This means that feedback loops are needed, each one requiring about 230 msec. It can be shown that the average time needed to move a cursor to a target depends on the relative precision required, i.e. the ratio between the target's distance and its size. This time can be estimated with the help of Fitt's law, which is expressed in the following equation:

$$T_{pos} = (I_m \log_2 (2D/S) \qquad \text{Fitt's Law}$$

Here T_{pos} stands for the time to reach a certain position, D stands for the distance to be moved and S stands for the size of the target. I_m is based upon the following calculations involving the feedback time and a constant due to error:

$$I_m = - (\text{time}_{perc} + \text{time}_{cog} + \text{time}_{motor} / \log_2 \text{error}$$

I_m has been calculated as 63 msec/bit on an average, with a range between 27 and 122 msec (Card, Moran & Newell, p. 53).

IMPLICATIONS OF SENSORY–MOTOR CHARACTERISTICS FOR HUMAN–COMPUTER INTERACTION

The characteristics of the human perceptual apparatus and motor organs have been used more or less consciously by most designers of output and input media (see also chapter 14). So, for instance, recommendations of refreshment rate on the screen have been based on both the basic facts about human vision and tests with different visual display units.

Still some aspects of hardware seem to suffer from a neglect of the human needs. So, for instance, it has been found that reading from a screen is often less efficient than reading from paper, mainly due to the bad quality of the writing on the screen.

Software design has hitherto largely ignored consideration of the human bioware requirements. Here a few implications will be mentioned, with the hope that the software designer will see more problems and solutions than I can at the moment.

The restrictions of the visual apparatus imply that warnings and help messages outside the area of focus should last 230 msec (for eye movement) + 100 msec (for detection), if they are to be detectable by an average recipient in an average situation. In the slowest case they must last as long as 700 msec + 200 msec. If a message is long and difficult to comprehend it should stay even longer, if there is to be any chance of processing it in working memory.

When it comes to the presentation of text on a computer screen, two types of solution can be envisaged. Either the text is presented instantly one screen at a time, whereby the reader can read the text as in a book. Or the text is presented continuously and halted when the screen is full. In the first case, the presentation rate should generously exceed the reading rate. "Instantly" would mean within 50 msec (the shortest detection time). When the text is presented continuously, the presentation rate should not be slower than the reading rate of the reader, to ensure that he does not have to wait for the next bit of text to appear. If we allow for one eye movement (saccade) per word, the slowest reading rate would be 700 msec per word. The quickest reading rate would be 70 msecs per word. We could also envisage readers requiring less than one saccade per word, which would make their reading rate even quicker. We can compare this to a rather common transmission rate of 300 baud, which corresponds to a presentation rate of roughly 35 characters per second. With an average of five letters per word, this makes 7 words per second, or 143 msec per word, a rate which is far too slow for good readers.

Since graphic screens are getting increasingly popular, the particular characteristics of our visual perception have to be considered in graphic design.

However, the technical limitations of computers or visual displays sometimes make compromise necessary, and this complicates the cognitive task of the people using the equipment.

It is for instance all too easy to violate the laws of Gestalt in a computer aided design sysem. Consider for instance the case in which many help lines have to be used in order to construct a figure. On a drawing board, the help lines can be drawn softer so that the main lines are clearly distinguished. On a computer screen, different shades of lines are often not allowed. The user can then only keep the figure in mind among the help lines by expending continuous effort. A slight interruption may well result in the "cognitive disappearance" of the figure the user is working on. In order to avoid this calamity, the user has to get rid of the help lines. This is of course possible in any computer aided design system, however the time taken to redraw the figure varies. A good system should allow for a quick refreshing of the screen without help lines, or the user will lose track of his plans for the construction.

Another case concerns Gestalt shifts, which are most disturbing for CAD designers working on three-dimensional problems with a 2-D presentation including hidden lines. The figure on which they are working at the moment can suddenly shift perspective, appearing to turn inside-out. I have heard designers complaining that the "system contains a bug, so that the figure shifts perspective". The "bug" is in their own perceptual apparatus. The solution is not necessarily that the system should remove lines which would be hidden from the eye or paint the surface of the object to provide object-like pictures. A system which can build on some other Gestalt laws, such as a common movement (not shown here by natural reasons) could equally well overcome the problem of Gestalt shifts.

One of the forthcoming computer offerings consists in synthetic speech. With our knowledge about human speech perception, we can predict that it will be difficult to produce synthetic speech which is easily comprehended without further training. At present, people find it difficult to remember what has been said when a message has been produced by synthetic speech, probably because of difficulty in encoding this kind of speech (Waterworth & Thomas, 1985). If our auditory apparatus perceives the synthetic noises not as speech but as non-speech sounds, then greater processing capacity at a higher level may be required in order to compensate for the perception of pattern that would otherwise have taken place earlier at the sensory level.

The implications are that either users have to be trained or that the speech should be presented at a slower rate than natural speech (with longer pauses between words and sentences, not slower presentation of each word). At our present stage of technological development it may also be advisable to use synthetic speech for short messages only, and preferably only to complement other output (e.g. for warnings). It can even be suggested that synthetic speech should sound unnatural, at least in a situation when people cannot know if there is a "real" person speaking or not. This recommendation applies for instance to telephone services, where I have found myself asking the recorder to repeat the message when I did not hear it the first time.

As to implications of our motor restrictions, Fitt's law can be used to warn the system designer against placing several menu options too close to one another, since the time required for hitting the option with the cursor will grow as each option occupies less space. The relative rate of movement of the mouse and the cursor on the screen should also be attended to.

In the case of keystrokes needing no conscious feedback checking, we find that several keystrokes performed with the same hand can follow one another at an average interval of 140 msec (70 + 70 msec). If alternate hands can be used, the keystrokes can follow one another at intervals of only 70 msec. Thus a skilled typist (using a mixture of keystrokes with the same or alternate hand) would be able to type at a speed of about 100 msec per keystroke or 600 keystrokes per minute. This calculation is consistent with data derived from skilled typists. However, if the hand has to be moved to reach a mouse or function keys outside of the natural range for typing, the time taken will be much longer. My own experience as a rather skilled typist is that movements outside the range disturb the trained positioning of the fingers on the keyboard and may even lead to corresponding errors, like typing "weeoea" instead of "errors". Careful studies have to be performed of how to combine cursor movements by keys or mouse with ordinary typing for various tasks in order to avoid errors and optimize input speed.

SUMMARY

In this chapter we have discussed some essential aspects connected with human cognitive performance, with particular reference to those aspects which are important in the context of human–computer interaction.

Human cognition can be said to evolve from the individual's interaction with his internal and external environment when facing a cognitive task. A cognitive task is loosely defined as a task in which human knowledge is involved. It may refer to the intake, storage or use of knowledge.

Cognitive performance is embedded in a more or less conscious judgment process. A person who is given a cognitive task assesses the amount of effort that will be needed to perform that task and chooses a strategy for tackling it in light of the expected difficulty and his assessment of his own capacities.

A general constraint on cognitive performance is due to attentional limitations. The impossibility of performing more than one task simultaneously because the same sensory or motor organ is involved, implies a structural limitation. A general functional limitation is connected with the amount of effort available for a particular task, and this is something that varies according to the chosen processing strategy.

The sensory and motor organs impose some definitive limits on performance. These have to be considered if people are to perceive the information given and to react in a way which they themselves will find satisfactory. Also, some qualitative properties, in particular the tendency to form perceptual "Gestalts", are important in considering the design of the surface of the human–computer interface.

Chapter 3

Long-Term and Working Memory

LONG-TERM MEMORY

A task seems difficult to us if we do not know how to perform it. This proposition may seem trivial, but it conceals a very important truth, which will be explored below. First we must ask ourselves what knowledge is stored, and how, and for how long?

Memory has been the subject of more research than almost any other topic in the history of cognition. It is probably also the least understood. Our ability to retrieve simple facts from memory is sometimes amazingly good, and sometimes curiously poor. It is difficult to design a computer system able to handle the amount of information which an adult human being has available at any one moment. It is almost impossible to build a system which can retrieve knowledge from this multiplicity as quickly as we can do for ourselves.

The most amazing aspect of all is our ability to recognize things. Recognition lies at the heart of our ability to perceive and interpret the world around us. A single striking example can serve to demonstrate the range of our capacity for recognition. A group of subjects were shown 500–600 words, pictures or sentences (Shepard, 1967). After a while 60 of the stimuli were mixed with other stimuli of a similar kind. The subjects then had to recognize which stimuli they had seen in the first showing. The answers were correct in 88% of cases for the words, in 97% for the pictures and 89% for the sentences! Performance was still remarkable after a week: 87% of the pictures were correctly recognized.

And yet we often find that our ability actively to recall the name of a person, a novel, or a street is painfully inadequate. We may have the name on the "tip of the tongue", but we are still unable to get it out.

What do we know about human memory? First we know that knowledge stored more or less permanently differs from knowledge which is available at the present moment. Potentially we can remember much more than we can perceive at any one instant. It is as though we let our attention glide around in

31

our memory store like a torch in a dark room. This is why modern researchers speak of "long-term memory" rather than just "memory". Long-term memory refers to all the information that is potentially available. The portion of long-term memory that is attended to at any particular moment is called "working memory", and it will be discussed under a separate heading.

Here we will restrict ourselves to certain inferences to be drawn from various studies of learning and memory, as touching on the structure of knowledge in long-term memory.

When we start thinking about our knowledge, we find that we have to deal with at least two different types of knowledge. On the one hand we know what the world is like: we know what a certain tree is called, we know the name of the capital of Sweden, or what causes ice to melt. This "knowing what" is usually called "declarative knowledge".

On the other hand we know how to perform different kinds of action, both motor and conceptual. This knowledge concerns "knowing how" and is usually called "procedural knowledge".

Our everyday use of the word "knowledge" refers chiefly to the concept of "declarative" knowledge. This is the knowledge we usually acquire at school, the knowledge we can communicate to others. It is conscious and we often experience a conscious effort in seeking to retrieve it.

On the other hand we find it difficult to describe our procedural knowledge. It is easy enough to turn a somersault, but try explaining to a child how to do it without a demonstration! Or think about the simple act to tie a knot—a declarative version of this procedure would not be very comprehensible!

These differences can now be related to different ways of representing knowledge. It has been suggested that declarative knowledge is represented in the shape of abstract propositions, while procedural knowledge is represented in the shape of procedural rules.

Declarative knowledge

What, then, is an "abstract proposition"? One way of understanding this concept is to make it concrete, by envisaging a graph in which different components are related to one another. A single concept can then be described in terms of its relation to other concepts. See Figure 12, showing part of a graph which could be drawn up for the concept "an orange". This example indicates the complexity of even a very simple area of knowledge, and if we wanted we could add yet more nodes and links to our knowledge of "an orange". The graph also shows how other knowledge is evoked by our thoughts about the orange, and how we can easily learn about new fruits by using the same graph and simply changing some of the links.

More complex knowledge may be described in a similar way. Consider the following proposition: oranges are good for your health, because they contain

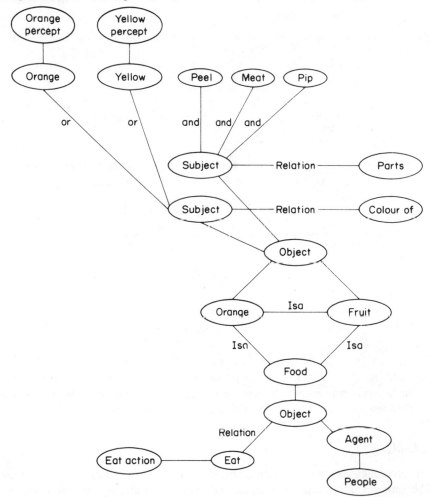

Figure 12 A network of concepts related to an orange.

Vitamin C. This could be expressed as in Figure 13. Or in the following set of propositions:

Oranges contain Vitamin C
Eating Vitamin C is good for your health
Thus eating oranges is good for your health.

Adding new nodes and new links makes the graph still more complex. Indeed, if our long-term memory were organized on a basis of nodes and links alone, we would need a very powerful mechanism for searching the network for any desired piece of information. A parallel search in all directions would

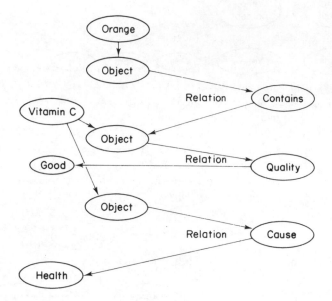

Figure 13 A proposition represented as a semantic network.

soon result in a combinational explosion and an unmanageable confusion of possibilities. Keen selectiveness in choosing search mechanisms and/or further organizational principles is necessary if we are to avoid this kind of overload, which does not seem typical for a human way of working.

"Chunking"

Our efficiency has usually been attributed to further organizational principles. The important concept here is related to the "chunking" of information in memory.

We may learn for instance that oranges are good for our health. We may then form a "chunk" consisting of oranges and lemons (since we aready know that lemons are similar to oranges). Thus we may easily infer that lemons are good for our health, without having to draw the conclusion from scratch. An even more efficient chunk would consist of inferring that all kinds of fruit are good for the health.

Another way of exploiting the idea of the "chunk" is to suggest that we economize on our long-term storage of information by not explicitly relating all possible information to every possible concept. Instead we could take one concept as "prototypical", storing the information related to this concept and then relating other concepts to the prototype. This idea has been suggested by researchers studying ways in which people categorize concepts (cf Rosch

& Lloyd, 1978). It was found that one item was more "typical" of a certain category than others. For example an apple is more typical of the category of fruit than a nut. A crow is more typical of the category of birds than an ostrich.

The "chunking" of information in long-term memory is one of the most useful explanations of our ability to process complex information. It can also explain what happens when people become experts in a particular field: they chunk the information in their field and thus do not have to bother about every detail each time they encounter a complex situation.

A striking illustration of the existence and usefulness of chunks appears in a study of chess masters (Chase and Simon, 1973). Some chess masters and some novices at chess were shown boards with different constellations of chessmen. Some of the constellations corresponded to positions actually reached during ordinary games of chess. Others were purely random. It turned out that the chess masters could recall the "real" constellations much better than the novices, but when it came to the random patterns they were no better. Their long-term memory contained chunks corresponding to "meaningful" constellations, but they had no particular chunks for random patterns and thus had to process them by considering each piece separately, just as the novices did.

Schemata, frames, scripts

Chess masters are naturally not the only ones who organize information to make it easily available. Everyday life offers plenty of opportunities for observing regularitites: we go to the store to shop, we go to the restaurant to eat. Let us examine a supermarket situation. Every supermarket situation has some aspects in common with all such situations: taking a trolley, looking for things to buy, putting them in the trolley, walking up and down the aisles, and ending up at the check-out counter. Variations may be due to the location of items and the makes provided, but the common features between supermarkets are sufficient for us not to have to attend to every detail.

The stored representation of common apsects between similar situations are called "schemata" by Rumelhart & Ortony (1977), "frames" by Minsky (1975) and "scripts" by Schank & Abelson (1977). It has been found that these higher-order schemata are essential to us not only in handling our everyday world, but also in understanding what other people tell us.

We become aware of our dependency on regularities when we visit other countries. When I find I cannot buy stamps at the place where I buy my post-cards, I feel quite lost. The first experimental demonstration of our reliance on familiar "schemata" in understanding the world around us was carried out by Bartlett (1932). He asked people to read a story, emanating from a "foreign" culture. Their recall showed regular distortions of the original story. For instance, the story told how a dead man returned from a battle, reported it, and then fell down dead. The subjects recalled the story as being about a man returning from war, severely wounded, reporting it, and then dying. Their version is of course more compatible with our "schema" of how a story should run.

Semantic networks of propositional knowledge, prototypes for conceptual knowledge and schemata for recurring regularities can be regarded as "prototypes" of the representation of declarative knowledge in long-term memory. Other organizational principles which have been suggested can be regarded as variations on these themes.

Procedural knowledge

Procedural knowledge differs from declarative knowledge in that it embraces actions rather than propositions. People are often unable to talk about their procedural knowledge, whereas they can easily speak of the declarative knowledge to which they are currently attending. The most commonly referred to procedural knowledge is the motor skill. Usually we cannot tell how we cycle, for instance. Skilled golf or tennis trainers may however transfer some of their procedural knowledge with the help of different metaphors.

When thinking is concerned, a common type of procedural knowledge is represented by our knowledge of our language. We do not use the rules of grammar consciously, but we usually follow them in our production of sentences. We can see that learning to read often starts with a declarative approach, spelling out each letter at a time (depending on the teaching method, that is) and only slowly transforms into a procedural skill, where even words can be skipped. A skilled programmer has probably proceduralized a lot of programming knowledge.

Even if the procedures are not conscious, researchers have expressed them in terms of rules as follows.

IF situation is X

THEN action Y.

This rule is called a "production rule". A whole procedure is performed by invoking different production rules in several "recognize–act" cycles. The current situation is inspected, and compared to the "IF" part of the currently relevant rules. When a rule is found, in which the "IF" part complies with the description of the current situation, then the action described in that rule is performed. This is usually referred to as the "firing" of a production rule. The set of productions which are relevant in a particular situation is called a "production system".

Social skills, whether adaptive or maladaptive belong to our procedural knowledge. A concrete example of the function of production rules in a particular behaviour may be taken from Gordon Bower's suggestion of how to model some maladaptive thinking (Bower, 1978).

Production rules associated with paranoid–aggressive thinking:

> IF someone pays me a compliment
> THEN he is manipulating me
> IF someone is manipulating me
>   and he is smaller than me
> THEN punch him.
> IF someone is manipulating me
>   and he is bigger than me
> THEN insult him.

If we remind ourselves that people cannot usually inspect or communicate procedural knowledge, we can easily understand that a paranoid–aggressive individual will be unable to say why he punched the small person who paid him a compliment.

This way of expressing a procedure calls for some idea of a mechanism for comparing the current situation with the "IF" clauses in the set of production rules in long-term memory. There may be several productions with the same IF clauses. If it is not possible to fire all these productions simultaneously, perhaps because of motor or general capacity restrictions, then the mechanism has to be able to select which production rule to apply. An important part of our cognitive apparatus thus consists of the rules used to solve the conflict (so-called conflict resolution rules) between competing production rules.

These conflict resolution rules should also be regarded to be autonomous, i.e. not requiring conscious reflection. Otherwise the whole procedure would be considerably hampered.

Some well-argued suggestions for solving conflicts between rules with the same "IF" clauses have been made by Anderson (1983). As a part of his ACT theory Anderson suggests five principles for conflict resolution: degree of match, production rule strength, data refractoriness, specificity, and goal-dominance.

Degree of match refers to the possibility that parts of the "IF" clause only can be matched against the current situation. As we have seen above, the "IF" clause may contain several "and" clauses. It might then be suggested that the production rule used should be the one in which most "and" clauses are satisfied. Various experiments have supported this hypothesis.

The important conflict resolution principle refers to the strength of the production rule. There is a long tradition in the psychology of learning that "memory traces" may be of different strengths. Even though we no longer talk about memory traces, the general idea of "strength" is useful. Anderson uses it to vary the applicability of production rules. He suggests that each production rule gains strength from being used. This means that production rules which are often used will be stronger than those which are used less often. A conflict resolution mechanism which favours stronger production rules would then lead to the selection of strong production rules over weak ones, provided the "IF" clauses are the same. This could lead to a loop in the use of production rule, if it were not for the existence of the next conflict resolution rule, namely the rule on data refractoriness.

Data refractoriness means that the same production rule cannot be used more than once for the same data. The rule is somewhat more general in the ACT theory, implying also that the same data cannot serve the same pattern simultaneously. This is one way of explaining the "Gestalt shifts" described above: since, given the same stimulation, two patterns are possible but only one of them can be seen, there will be a shift whereby first one pattern will be perceived and then the other.

The specificity principle implies that more specific production rules are chosen before more general ones, provided both apply to the same situation. This rule enables us to learn different reactions towards stimuli belonging to the same class. Without this rule we would never learn that the plural of "man" is "men" rather than "mans". The general rule for nouns says that the plural of a noun is formed by adding "s".

Finally, the principle of "goal-dominance" implies that a production rule that is consistent with the current goal will take precedence over all other potentially applicable production rules, even though these might be stronger or more specific.

It should perhaps be noted that procedural knowledge can be organized in two essentially different ways: one organizational principle is related to the productions system, in which production rules are organized in order to form a single procedure. Thus in long-term memory we find production systems corresponding to adding numbers, reading and writing, using a wordprocessor, and solving particular problems.

The second organizational principle stems from the declarative part of the production rule, i.e. the "IF" clause. Semantic associations, prototypes or schemata, all help to determine which production rule to start with, and thus which production system should be applied to a particular situation. The relationships between the concepts in declarative knowledge also affect the possibility of changing from one production system to another. This may happen if new associations lead to new descriptions of the situation, which complies with the "IF" clause in a production rule, not contained in the presently used production system. However, due to the principle of "goal–dominance", the new production system may have difficulty in making its way over the currently used one. This can explain the rigidity of some behaviour and the difficulty to change approach to a particular task.

WORKING MEMORY

Working memory cannot be regarded as a "memory" in the same manner as long-term memory. Rather the concept of working memory is derived from an interconnected set of observations indicating that information being attended to quickly decays and that the amount maintained for the brief period concerned is limited.

Working memory can (to some extent) be regarded as the currently active part of long-term memory. Working memory is therefore a convenient concept for denoting the information with which we are concerned at the present moment. Unlike the information in long-term memory, the information in working memory lasts for a short time only. A usual estimate of its duration is 20 seconds, with half the information being lost after about 5 seconds. For this reason the first designation for the suggested concept was "short-term memory". I prefer the designation "working memory" to stress the active aspect of this kind of memory compared with the dormant aspect of long-term memory.

The limit on capacity is another feature which suggests that a special memory concept is called for. Observations indicating that only a small amount of information can be simultaneously attended to at any one time, have helped to shape our concept of working memory. Perhaps selective attention is responsible for the phenomenon we call "working memory". Or perhaps there is some sort of temporary store which we can call "working memory" and which is responsible for our attentional limitations.

Some experimental paradigms

A well-known experimental paradigm provides a measure of what is called short-term memory capacity (not working memory). Subjects are presented with a number of items, sequentially in the case of auditive items but as often simultaneously in the case of visual items. The items are familiar but unrelated to each other. Immediately after presentation (lasting about one second per stimulus), the subject is asked to recall as many of the items as possible. It has generally been found that people can recall between five and nine of them, or as George Miller put it (Miller, 1956): "The magical number seven, plus or minus two."

However, it soon became obvious that estimating our attentional capacity was not quite as simple as this. If we remember five to nine items, what does it mean? Two crucial questions emerge: how much information is there in an item, and how much work is going into the remembering?

The first items used in this short-term memory paradigm consisted of letters, digits, or simple pictures of objects. However, when meaningful words were tried instead of letters, much the same figures were obtained, but now for words rather than letters. Capacity was about seven, but seven what? The solution lay in introducing the concept of "chunk", which we have already met above. Every item presented which could be regarded as a meaningful unit, was seen as a "chunk". The next question is then: how much can be contained in a chunk? This question was posed by Simon (1974), and it was pointed out that a familiar phrase (such as: "discretion is the better part of valour") obviously could not be regarded as a single chunk. In the short-term memory paradigm people were only able to recall about 3–4 such phrases. The result was the same for nonsense syllables. From a list including ZEF, XOD, and similar groups of three-letter syllables, only three to four could be recalled. ZEF is not of course a meaningful unit. But how much attentional capacity does it take?

Short-term memory experiments also showed that the items presented first and last were remembered better than items presented in the middle. This "serial position effect" had previously been found in studies of list learning. Now it was possible to relate its effect to the processes used by subjects during and after the presentation of items. The last items were remembered, because people could simply rely on sensory storage; it was not necessary to encode them in short-term memory at all. The first items were remembered, because subjects were making an active attempt to learn them. A strategy often reported consisted of rehearsing just these items.

Thus it appears that the measurement of attentional capacity using the short-term memory paradigm is inflated on two counts: first, it includes sensory memory as well as working memory, and second, it may be affected by different remembering strategies. Because of this weakness in the short-term memory paradigm another and supposedly "purer" way of measuring working memory capacity has been tried.

Subjects are presented with a continuous list of items (letters, figures, and the like). They are told to be ready to report as many items as possible, as soon as presentation ceases. Since the subjects do not know when presentation will cease, there is no point in starting to rehearse the items from the beginning. This arrangement yields a more modest estimate of working memory capacity of about three to four items. This estimate refers to the contents of sensory memory which can be reported, as well as any item that the person may have been able to rehearse immediately before the list came to an end.

Can working memory be separated from other types of memory?

So can we really say that working memory is different from sensory memory or activated long-term memory? Physiological data provides a hint. Sensory memory is related to the activity which persists in the sensory organs after the stimulus has ceased. Such sensory storage is much shorter than the intervals reported from working memory experiments. Further, if people are required to report a single, randomly chosen stimulus, the estimation of sensory storage is much higher than in the short-term memory paradigm. Thus short–term and working memory phenomena cannot refer to sensory storage only.

Observations of people suffering from particular kinds of brain damage such as senile dementia, suggest that working memory may genuinely be a thing apart from long-term memory. For instance, there are people who can tell us a lot of their childhood, but who find it very difficult to say what happened a few seconds ago. However, these effects could just as well be due to the patient's difficulty focussing their attention.

The phenomena which we include in our definition of working memory are related to active attention, and to active attempts to represent information from outside. Long-term memory, on the other hand, can exploit information already stored. Here the only effort required is to express the information as it passes by. The act of searching for specific information also calls for conscious effort.

We could now conclude that working memory belongs somewhere between long-term memory and sensory storage. The sensory mechanisms and sensory memories help to keep the information stored in attentional focus. This helping function of the sensory mechanisms has been identified by researchers studying the way information is stored in working memory. For instance what items are confused with one another: is it items that mean the same (like WEAK and SOFT) or those that sound similar (like WEAK and LEAK)? The answer is that similar sounding items are more often confused in working memory than items whose meanings are similar. Thus working memory has been seen as storing items in an "acoustic format".

These results hold for verbal items, where acoustic storage seems fairly probable. It also seems likely that items with visual components are stored in working memory in a pictorial format. This idea has been supported by a number of experiments. One of these required people to judge whether one figure was similar to another, although the two were being rotated through different angles. It turned out that it took longer to see the figures as similar, the greater the angle of rotation (Shepard & Metzler, 1971). In another experiment subjects were asked to learn a map and then to scan mentally from point to point on it. It took longer to scan between points, the greater the distance between them (Kosslyn, Ball & Reiser, 1978).

These results suggest that the processing of images in memory is similar to the processing of visual information in reality. This can be explained by assuming that working memory relies on perceptual storage.

IMPLICATIONS FOR HUMAN–COMPUTER INTERACTION

What are the implications for human–computer interaction of these findings about long-term and working memory?

First, the difference between declarative and procedural knowledge should be considered both in designing and in making instructions for computer systems. Declarative knowledge is needed in the teaching of new concepts, but it is a slow type of knowledge to use when action is required. Procedural knowledge can be applied quickly, since the actor need not attend to each single automated procedure.

Systems should thus be designed to facilitate the acquisition of procedural knowledge as far as pure systems handling is concerned. At the same time, optimal use of the system may require some declarative knowledge, which allows the user to compare different methods for different situations and to approach new tasks.

Working memory can be regarded as the "bottleneck" through which all information, from outside as well as from inside, has to pass as soon as conscious attention is required. Only automated procedures, reflexes, and free associations are exempt from the limitations posed by this narrow passage. As soon as we want to achieve a goal, as soon as we have to learn something new, and as soon as we have to attend to something in the outside world, working memory will impose a limit on our processing capacity.

But these limits are variable. Novices at a computer system will perceive their own working memory capacity as painfully small. They have to process each new item separately, because they have not yet formed any "chunks" in long-term memory related to the handling of the system. At first even the login procedure may exceed their working memory capacity, not to mention the command sequences required to search for and inspect a file.

One way of reducing the load on working memory is to lead the novices through the required procedure by letting them make successive choices through a sequence of menus. However, the advantage of menus is quickly lost, if the menu offers too many levels of successive alternatives. The novice then risks "losing track" of the path through the levels. Thereby the user will have difficulty remembering other alternatives, if he winds up with one he does not want. We shall see later that users of hierarchical information systems complain of "getting lost" in the complexity of possibilities.

The limitations of working memory is probably the most important factor to be considered in trying to achieve a "user-friendly" system. The strain on working memory for a total novice can be estimated by counting each goal and subgoal as a "chunk". To these chunks should then be added the methods for achieving the goals and subgoals. If the task to be performed by the user with the system can be described within the limits of working memory, the user will find the system easy to handle.

SUMMARY

Within the limits imposed by the effort expended and the sensory–motor capacities, the most important factor affecting cognitive performance is connected with the contents of long-term memory. Experts differ from novices in what they can say about facts in the world (declarative knowledge), and in what they can do in the world (procedural knowledge). Declarative knowledge requires attention, and it can be used flexibly in different situations by intentional transfer. Procedural knowledge can be applied automatically and is linked to a particular situation. An error in an automated procedure is difficult to spot, since the procedure is not generally accessible to inspection. Declarative knowledge can be transformed into procedural knowledge as a result of learning.

Working memory can be regarded as the activated part of long-term memory. It is restricted in the amount of information it can retain (7 $+/-$ 2 "chunks"), and in the retention of the information (half-life time about 7 seconds).

Long-term and working memory interact, because the size of the chunk depends on the content of long-term memory. "Meaningful" material is easier to keep in working memory, because it has only to be "activated" in long-term memory; "nonsense" material, on the other hand has to be rehearsed or elaborated with material from long-term memory in order to be remembered.

Working memory can be regarded as the "bottleneck" through which all information has to pass. The implication for human-computer interaction is that complex computer messages may be digested only if they relate to prior knowledge.

Chapter 4

Complex Information Processing

We will now turn to more complex information processing, including tasks which are considered "intellectual", i.e. problem solving, decision making, prediction and logic. Some necessary preconditions for such complex processing will also be examined, as well as the consequent cognitive skills.

PROBLEM SOLVING

Having looked at the way in which people allot their resources, select information, and store knowledge, we are now ready to examine how people use their knowledge in new situations—in other words, how they solve problems.

Problem solving occurs when there is a goal to be reached, when the method for reaching the goal is not yet known, and when attempts to reach the goal are being made. This definition distinguishes problem solving from routine performance (when the method is known), from free association (when there is no explicit goal) and from wishful thinking (which implies no concrete efforts to achieve a goal).

The goal may be well defined or more vaguely so. Let us examine a task whose goal is typically well-defined (whereas the situation is less well-defined, however.)

Problem 1.

Five missionaries and five cannibals are wandering about in the jungle. Unexpectedly they come upon a river too deep to wade across. Nor is there any bridge close by. But there is a boat on the shore which they can use. The boat can take only two people at a time. How are the missionaries and the cannibals to arrange their passage over the river? If the cannibals outnumber the missionaries on either side of the river at any one time, they will eat them. The task is to get both parties over safe and sound.

It is easy to envisage both missionaries and cannibals on the other side of the river. The method to get them there, however, is of course not clear. In that case it would be no problem!

Now let us turn to a task whose goal is less well-defined.

Problem 2.

The task is to construct a coat stand, using two boards and a cramp (Figure 14).

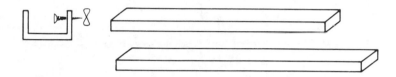

Figure 14 The material from which a coat stand should be constructed.

In everyday life problem solving concerns both well-defined and ill-defined goals. Well-defined goals can be found in puzzles and teasers published in the Sunday papers, or in the sort of questions that school-teachers ask. Much computerized work can be said to have well-defined goals. In wordprocessing we may need to correct a spelling mistake; in a CAD task the designer may be asked to change some dimensions in the design to a given size. Ill-defined goals can be found in constructive problem solving. Perhaps we have been asked to construct a ship or to design a house. Social and psychological problems generally have goals which are ill-defined.

We should not confuse the greater or lesser clarity of the goal with the difficulty involved in solving the problem. A problem with a well-defined goal is not always easy to solve; nor is a problem with an ill-defined goal necessarily difficult.

There are two main aspects to the thinking involved in trying to solve a problem (well-defined or ill-defined): 1) the problem has to be interpreted (represented), and 2) the different paths from start to goal have to be searched.

These aspects are reflected in the tasks themselves, in that the main difficulty may be either in representation or in search.

Tasks which are difficult to represent

Tasks, whose main difficulty is one of representation, have been studied in particular by members of the so called "Gestalt" psychology school. The coat stand problem is one of their classic problems. Here is another.

Problem 3.

A carpenter is about to build a staircase from the hall up to the first landing. The staircase is open on the hallside, where it is to be covered in tiles. Each tile is to be as high and as wide as the height and depth of each step (see Figure 15). If the staircase is to have 50 steps, how many tiles will be needed?

(Wertheimer, 1945)

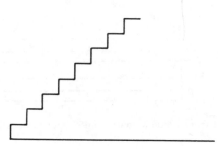

Figure 15 The staircase problem.

A suitable representation of this task renders it easy to solve. All you have to do is to extend the figure to form a rectangle. This is the same as taking a staircase of the same size as the original one and placing it upside down over it. The number of tiles needed is thus equal to half the size of the rectangle, or $50 \times 5\frac{1}{2}$.

This problem can be solved in other ways, but they are less efficient.

The following problem demonstrates the importance of representation even more vividly.

Problem 4.

A man wanted to extend a window in his attic to twice its size, but he did not want to alter its length or width. How could he do it? (Answer at the end of the chapter.)

What are the difficulties inherent in problems of this type? First, the formulation of the problem is often such that the representation most readily arrived at is not adequate to the problem. The representation of the staircase has to be transformed into a rectangle before the problem becomes easy to solve, and the representation of the window is dependent on the form of the window envisaged, as well as the interpretation of "length" and "width" in this context.

This characteristic of representational problems led the Gestalt psychologists to speak of "realizing structural features and structural requirements" (Wertheimer, 1945). In order to solve a problem, they meant, you have to "change the situation in the direction of structural improvements", which in modern information-processing terms means to represent it in a different (and more adequate) way from the one that first occurs to you.

We find similar difficulty with problems that are simply clumsily formulated, like this one:

Problem 5.

A dog weighs 10 pounds plus half his own weight. How much does the dog weigh?

(Answer at the end of the chapter.)

Some representational problems are difficult because of the "implicit restrictions" which people unnecessarily introduce. In the coat stand problem, for instance, people are reluctant to allow themselves to use the ceiling to help them construct their coat stand. Somehow, using the ceiling seems to them to be "forbidden". They usually fail to consider the ceiling at all, and when the experimenter suggests it to them, they often claim the solution as a "cheat". (The solution to the problem can be found at the end of the chapter).

In some cases the implicit restrictions are due to the Gestalt character of our perceptions, as in the following example.

Problem 6.

Try to connect all the points in Figure 16 using no more than four straight lines and without lifting pen from paper.

(Solution at the end of the chapter.)

Figure 16 The nine dot problem.

The Gestalt psychologists are not the only ones to have identified "restructuring" as a major principle in human problem solving. Anecdotal evidence from many great scientists attests to the existence of restructuring. "Suddenly I saw it in a new light" they often say, and we "ordinary" thinkers can recognize similar reactions in quite trivial situations. We should not become "fixated" on a particular line of thought but should strive to think "laterally" thus runs the message of Edward de Bono, who has concerned himself greatly with human thinking (de Bono, 1977). And more recently the need to restructure problems has resulted in yet another recommendation: "Use the right half of your brain!"

Thus problems of representation and restructuring appear to be important to certain types of tasks. But little is known about how we are to achieve this restructuring. It may be fun to attend courses in "right-brain use" or "lateral thinking", but the real usefulness of these lessons in new problem situations is open to question.

In human–computer interaction people certainly can become "fixated" on their first representations, finding it difficult to change them. In a later chapter on learning computerized tasks I shall discuss this problem more fully and shall examine possible ways of overcoming fixations of this kind.

Search problems

Search problems were introduced into psychological research by the information-processing theorists Allan Newell and Herbert Simon (1972).

The concept of "search" emanates from computer science. The missionaries and cannibals problem belongs to this type of problem, as does Problem 7.

The problem is usually presented with disks, placed on pegs as in Figure 17, and accompanied by this instruction:

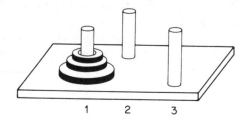

Figure 17 The initial configuration of the Tower of Hanoi problem.

Problem 7.

Move all disks, one at a time from peg 1 to peg 3. You may never put a larger disk on top on a smaller one.

The actions possible to perform are represented in Figure 18. This figure represents a "problem space" for this problem. A problem space represents the

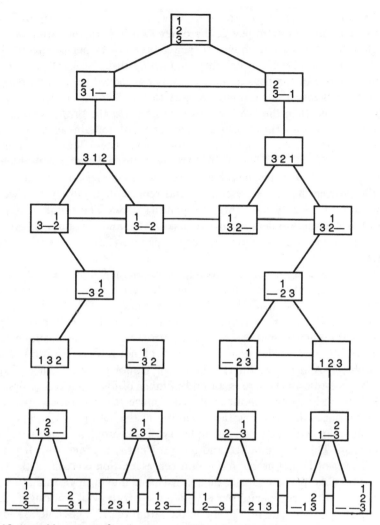

Figure 18 A problem space for the Tower of Hanoi task with three discs.

initial situation (at the top of the graph) and all other situations which can be derived from this using the permitted moves. Each situation can be regarded as a "knowledge state", i.e. a collection of all knowledge relevant to the problem at that particular stage. In this simple graph, the knowledge state corresponds to the state of the disks and the pegs in the real world. New knowledge states are derived by using "operations". In this problem the operation allowed is very simple: move small disk from top. In each new knowledge state, there are restrictions on how this operation can be applied. The restriction in the Tower of Hanoi problem lies in the size of the disk on the peg to which the small disk is to be moved. Thus, at the first step only disk "s" may be moved. There are two possible moves: one to peg 2, the other to peg 3. In the latter case, in the next step disk "m" can be moved to peg 2, but not to peg 3 since disk "s" is smaller. There is also the possibility of moving disk "s" back to peg 1 or of moving it to one of the pegs to which it was not moved in the first step.

Search problems become difficult when they call for an overview of several possibilities, i.e. when the problem space is large. In the graph we can see that the problem space for three disks is fairly small. It contains only 26 states and the shortest path from start to goal is only seven steps long. It is apparently quite easy for people to solve the problem with three disks. In a problem space of this size it is probably possible to review the states in working memory, once the problem has been understood and represented. However, if we extend the number of disks beyond three, difficulties arise. The number of steps required to solve the problem with four disks is 15, and this number far exceeds the usual estimates of working memory capacity. (For five disks 31 steps are required.)

What do people do when they encounter problems which overtax their working memory capacity? Allen Newell and Herbert Simon suggest that in such situations people use "heuristics" (Newell & Simon, 1972). Heuristics provide ways of searching among existing possibilities. With their help people can take short-cuts through the multitude of paths available. Heuristics can be regarded as "rules of thumb", which generally, although not always, lead to the solution of a problem. A heuristic for the Tower of Hanoi problem can be expressed in two simple rules: "If there is an odd number of disks, move the first disk to peg 3. If there is an even number of disks, move the first disk to peg 2". This heuristic reduces the search without leading to the solution.

Another way of reducing the complexity of the problem space is to redefine the problem. This may produce another problem space, one with fewer states. In the Tower of Hanoi problem a useful representation consists of the shape of "pyramids". The problem space then consists of moving pyramids rather than single disks. If this representation is linked to a strategy of working backwards, i.e. from the goal formulation to the initial situation, it is possible to reduce the problem difficulty considerably.

An even simpler representation is in the shape of a perceptual rule: whenever you have a choice, always move the disks clockwise (or anti-clockwise, depending on the number of disks).

The study of search problems has enriched our understanding of human problem solving in the following ways:

— The representation of a problem can be regarded as a definition of the initial problem situation, of the goal, and of the permitted operations. If either of these three components is wrongly conceived, the problem will not be solved.
— The difficulty of the problem increases with the size of the problem space

unless the problem solver has good heuristics for searching the problem space.
— Heuristics for searching the problem space can be learnt. They can be regarded as an important ingredient in the knowledge possessed by an expert in a particular problem solving area.

DECISIONS AND PREDICTIONS

Decision-making has been studied in situations in which people have to choose between alternatives with different outcomes. The outcome can be described as having a certain value, often a monetary value. The outcome may always occur, or only with a certain probability. The following is a typical example:

> Which of the following gambles would you prefer:
> A: you have a 1%   chance of winning 100
> B: you have a 10% chance of winning 10

The expected value of these two gambles (i.e. the value which results if the gamble is repeated an infinite number of times) can be calculated by multiplying the probability by the amount of the gain. In this example, the expected value of the gambles is exactly the same. Still it is found that some people will prefer one to the other.

In other cases it has been found that people prefer gambles with a lower expected value to those with a higher one. A classic example was demonstrated by Daniel Bernoulli as long ago as 1738 (see Bernoulli, 1954), and has become known as "the Petersburg paradox". It runs as follows:

> You throw a coin. The game is over as soon as tails comes up, when you will be paid 2 pennies.

The probability of the game ending after one throw is 1:2, after two throws 1:4, i.e. the probability of its ending after n throws is $(1/2)^2$. The expected value of this game is 1 penny for each throw. Since the number of throws is potentially infinite, the expected value is also infinite. Nonetheless, people probably prefer a game in which they have a 99% chance of winning 1 million.

The frequent observations of non-optimal behaviour in decision-making has inspired a good deal of research into the reasons for non-optimality. In the simple examples illustrated here, two factors may contribute to non-optimal behaviour: people's perception of value, and their perception of probabilities.

Subjective value

It was Bernoulli who first suggested that money has a subjective value which has no linear relation to objective value. If for instance the subjective value is logarithmically related to the objective value, then the Petersburg paradox is no longer a paradox. Later studies have confirmed that subjective value does indeed deviate from objective value. The function is not always logarithmic, but may take any form depending on how value is measured. We may even find asymmetric functions, for instance when the value of losses is compared with the value of gains—when, perhaps, the same amount of money seems to be worth more when you lose it than it does when you win it.

Subjective probability

Perceived probability also seems to diverge from objective probability. In various studies in which people are given the probabilities which are involved in a decision, it has been found that subjects tend to overestimate small probabilities and to underestimate high ones.

In other cases, people have been asked to estimate probabilities from certain observations. A task of this kind could be presented as follows:

> We have two urns, each of which contains both blue and red chips. In the first urn 0.7 of the chips are red and in the second 0.3. The task is to guess which urn a certain chip is taken from, and to estimate the probability of this urn having been chosen.

If we do not see the colour of the chip, there is no reason for us to assume anything other than a 50% probability for either urn. But the situation changes dramatically if we are allowed to see the colour of the chip. If the chip is red, we would probably guess that it came from the first urn. How probable is it that we are right?

This probability, which is based on our knowledge of the prior probabilities regarding the chips in the urns and on one observation, can be calculated according to Bayes' theorem:

$$p(H_i/E) = \frac{p(E/H_i)p(H_i)}{\Sigma p(E/H_j)p(H_j)}$$

where $p(H_i/E)$ represents the probability that hypothesis H_i holds, given observation E. This probability is also called the "a posteriori probability".

$P(E/H_i)$ represents the probability of finding an observation E under hypothesis H_i.

$P(H_i)$ stands for the priori probability of hypothesis H_i.

H_j stands for the alternative hypothesis(es).

In the present example we get the following equation:

$$p(H_i/E) = \frac{0.70 \times 0.50}{0.70 \times 0.50 + 0.30 \times 0.50} = 0.70$$

We can also calculate the odds in favour of hypothesis H_i by dividing its probability by the probability of hypothesis H_j. Before any observation has been made the odds are exactly 1, i.e. both hypotheses are equally probable. After the observation of the red chip, the a posteriori odds become 0.7/0.3 or 2.33.

It has usually been found that people judging probabilities in such cases are "conservative". In other words they usually assess the a posteriori probability much lower than *Bayes theorem* would suggest, and they estimate the change in odds to be much less.

Integration of information

In many decision-making tasks, people have to integrate a great deal of diverse information. The alternatives available vary in several dimensions, and outcomes have to be calculated by combining these in some way. Suppose that you want to buy a new car. You may have the following requirements: it should not be too expensive, and it must hold at least five people; its boot should be big enough to accommodate the baby cart and the skis, as well as the luggage for holidays; it should not use too much petrol, and it should be easy to get it repaired. For winter-use a front-wheel drive would be preferable, but you have no particular wishes as regards automatic or manual transmission. These requirements define the attributes which you want to consider in assessing the alternatives available. But how exactly should you proceed?

According to a normative model, the best procedure would be the following: Decide how important each attribute is to you. Then assess the value, as you see it, of each alternative car in each of these dimensions. Multiply each value by the importance you have assigned to that attribute and add the results together for each alternative. This gives you their subjective expected utilities and you can then choose the one with the highest utility.

But people do not behave like this when they have to make decisions. We know from our discussion of the limitations of working memory that such a procedure would be extremely difficult unless we had access to paper and pencil, or a calculator. So what do people do instead? A general conclusion seems to be that people try in all kinds of ways to reduce the complexity of the decision situation. One way is to choose a desirable attribute, and then to compare the alternatives in this one respect. Any alternatives lacking the chosen attribute are eliminated. Another attribute is then chosen and comparisons continue until only one alternative remains. This strategy is called "elimination by aspects" (Tversky, 1972). Other strategies have been suggested, for instance searching for one alternative which dominates all others (Montgomery, 1983).

Predictions

A predictive situation has much in common with the decision-making case. People are confronted by a variety of situations, which like alternatives in decision-making can be described by a set of values for different attributes. In decision-making, the contribution of each attribute to the total expected value depends on the person making the decision. In a prediction situation, however, these weights are unknown. The prediction situation can be schematized as in Figure 19.

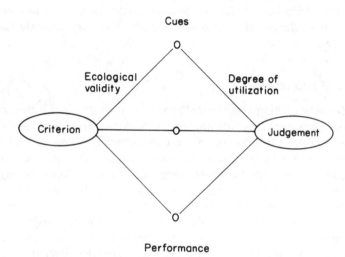

Figure 19 Prediction from given cues.

Prediction implies a judgment, which can be compared with a criterion. The criterion can be measured on a scale of some sort, as in the case with school grades. Or it may consist of nominal categories, as in medical diagnosis. The thing to be assessed (in these two examples a person) is described by a set of cues. For school grades the cues may consist of aptitude, motivation, sociability and parents' social status, and for a patient, perhaps the physician's observations and various results of laboratory tests. The cues may not all carry equal weight in predicting the criterion.

Psychological studies of predictive behaviour often proceed as follows. Subjects are given a set of cues and asked to assess their supposed combined effect. The cues are usually formulated in terms of an interval scale. The assessment also generally has to be given in quantitative terms.

In a pure laboratory situation the subject has no means of knowing how the cues are related to the criterion. The laboratory study of predictive behaviour has thus often been related to the study of learning in just such situations. The subjects are given the value of the criterion each time they have made a judgment. In this way it should be possible for them to learn about the importance of the cues in relation to the given criterion.

The normative model for finding the correct value of the criterion is similar to the model used in the decision-making case. The value of the criterion is equal to the weighted (by probabilities) sum of the values of the cues. How do people handle this task?

A spontaneous assumption might be that people would manage the task fairly well in "natural" situations. But various studies suggest that this is not so. Even people who have to perform tasks very similar to this one in their work often perform less well than we might expect. Meehl (1954) for example studied some psychologists who were asked to assess the ability of applicants, as described in a series of psychological tests. He found that experienced psychologists often assessed the applicants less correctly than the simple statistical combination of their test scores described above.

It has also been found that the greater the number of cues, the more uncertain the assessment gets (Hoffman & Blanchard, 1961). This accords well with what we know about the restricted capacity of working memory. Another interesting result suggests that although objective certainty declines after about five cues, subjective certainty increases (Magnusson & Heffler, 1969). This is also consistent with what was said above about the capacity of working memory.

In the less natural laboratory situation it has been found that people can learn to predict some outcomes fairly well. It is easier to learn cues that are linearly related to the criterion than cues that are related to one another in some other way. If the importance of cues changes during the experiment, laboratory subjects will come to recognize the change, but only slowly and inefficiently. If the cues are correlated with each other, subjects will not be able to use the intercorrelations very efficiently, even though their performance shows that they do make some use of them (cf Brehmer, 1979, 1980).

Thus it seems that people can make valid predictions only when the cues are few in number and linearly related to the criterion, and when the criterion is well defined. Real-life situations do not often fit these requirements. The relation between cues and criterion is usually unclear, as in medical diagnosis, for instance. The measurement of the criterion is also often unreliable; again diagnosis is a good example. Moreover it is often impossible to obtain any feedback on a prediction. If certain applicants are chosen for a university course, for example, there will not be any feedback on the further performance of the applicants who were turned down. Thus, the chances of making good predictions are vitiated not only by human weaknesses but also by drawbacks in life itself.

HUMAN LOGIC

Are people illogical?

The psychology of human cognition is full of examples of people tackling tasks in ways which do not conform to some normative rule. Logical reasoning is one such example. It is claimed that human beings do not reason logically. Why not? And what does this mean?

Claims that people do not reason logically are generally based on tasks whose content is logical. Categorical syllogisms provide a good example:

1.   All men are mortal
         Socrates is a man
         Therefore, Socrates is mortal

Most people find no difficulty in accepting this conclusion as true. But other syllogisms, apparently similar, may be more problematic:

2.   All A's are B's
         All C's are B's
         Therefore, all A's are C's

3.   Some A's are B's
         Some B's are C's
         Therefore, some A's are C's

The usual problem here is that people accept more conclusions as being true than pure logic would allow. The conclusions in both examples 2 and 3 are not necessarily either true or false. In categorical logic they would be called contingent. People not trained in logic tend to regard them as true.

However, there are also cases where many people fail to accept a valid argument:

4.   Some B's are A's
         No C's are B's
         Therefore, some A's are not C's

Anderson (1985) found that only 60% of a sample of undergraduate students agreed that this argument was valid.

There are also other cases in which people find it difficult to follow the rules of logic. Conditional syllogisms, for instance, can cause problems.

5.   If A, then B
         B
         Therefore A

6.   If A, then B
        not B
        Therefore not A

7.   If A, then B
        not A
        Therefore not B

In these three cases many people (the percentage varies) accept the conclusion in 5, do not accept it in 6 and accept it in 7. The conclusions in 5 and 7 are in fact contingent, i.e. not necessarily true or false. The conclusion in 6 is true.

A last, and slightly more complex example can close this demonstration of the difficulties involved in following the rules of logic. It is taken from Wason (cf Wason & Johnson-Laird, 1972).

Four cards are shown to the subjects as in Figure 20. Subjects were told that a letter appeared on one side of each card and a number on the other. The task was to judge the validity of the following rule, in the case of the four cards shown Figure 20.

If a card has a vowel on one side, it will have an even number on the other.

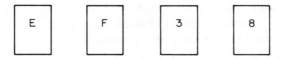

Figure 20 One example of the material for Wason's four-card problem.

The subjects were asked to say which card or cards they wanted to turn over to check whether the rule was valid or not. They were told to turn over as few cards as possible.

Many subjects (about 50% in several studies) chose to turn over card E and card 8. This choice does not help in determining whether or not the rule holds. In fact it is cards E and 3 which have to be chosen. In both cases a result failing to correspond to the rule would falsify it: if there is an odd number on the back of the E-card, then the rule is false. The same applies to the 3-card: if there is a vowel on the back of it, then the rule is false.

What is the explanation of these deviations from logical rules in human thinking? Several factors probably work together to produce a result which seems illogical. Following the problem solving tradition, let us examine explanations which attribute the difficulty to representation or to operation.

Representation of logical tasks

Several studies have confirmed that people find it easier to follow logical rules, if the relevant material has a meaningful content. Syllogisms, conditional sentences and four-card tasks have been given a real-life content, and in all cases people have become far more prone to reason "logically". These results can be explained in two ways.

The first explanation is that people do not reason logically at all; they simply apply their knowledge of the world to answering the questions. If they are told that all cats have tails and all dogs have tails, they will not conclude that all cats are dogs (cf example 2 above.) This explanation also applies to cases in which people judge conditional syllogisms containing plausible or implausible premises (Hagert, 1986). "If it rains you will get wet" is an example of a plausible premise. "If you talk Spanish then you are born in Spain." is an example of an implausible premise. Hagert found that people were more inclined to reason according to logical rules when they were judging conditional syllogisms containing plausible premises.

The second explanation of these results is that a real-life content is meaningful, and thus easier to retain in working memory. The amount of information that working memory can hold is, as we know, somewhat limited. But meaningful information is easier to "chunk" and thus easier to retain in larger quantities—a hypothesis that is supported by Hagert (1986). Subjects who were given an implausible and yet meaningful context in Wason's four-card task, chose the logically correct cards more often than subjects who were given the "nonsense" content. Thus a meaningful content helps people to process logical statements more logically.

The role of representation is further illustrated in the handling of logical quantifiers, which present some special problems of their own. Let us look at the following statement and the corresponding diagrams.

"Some G's are not H's"

Venn diagrams may be used to facilitate the representation of the different possible meanings of this proposition. The possibilites shown in Figure 21 emerge.

A Venn diagram is a powerful aid to thought. It helps us to visualize statements which are difficult to interpret verbally.

Thus people who have not learnt Venn diagrams may have more difficulty in interpreting and using logical quantifiers. I shall be returning to this later, when discussing database search in chapter 9.

In most studies of logical thinking, it has been found that negations are difficult to handle. This can be explained as a representational problem: how can we represent something which is NOT? Negations also pose operational problems, which will be discussed below.

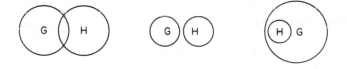

Figure 21 Venn diagrams can serve to illustrate the different meanings of the proposition "some G's are not H's".

A last difficulty in the representation of logical problems is connected with the interpretation of the logical connectives. The problems are formulated in ordinary language. But the interpretation of, for instance, "if...then" is far from unequivocal in our everyday language. Sometimes "if...then" implies that the antecedent is one of several possible causes of the consequent, as in the sentence "If it rains, I will get wet". Sometimes "if...then" implies that the antecedent is the only possible cause of the consequent, as in the sentence "If I push the button, the lamp will be lit". In yet other cases, "if...then" implies an equivalence: "If the liquid turns blue when I add BTB, then it is alkaline".

Formal logic only accepts the first interpretation. The hypothetical statement is strictly unidirectional. The others are compatible with an "if and only if" interpretation, where the order of the clauses can be changed without changing the meaning of the conditional. It has been argued that people often interpret "if..then" as "if and only if". In that case, the sentence can easily be turned round: "If the liquid is alkaline, then it turns blue when I add BTB". With this interpretation it could also be possible to say "If I am wet, it has rained". But we do not do it, because we know there are other reasons for getting wet.

Operations in logical tasks

What, then, are the possible operational difficulties in handling logic? Do people really think illogically? Several researchers have adopted this standpoint, among them Philip Johnson-Laird (1983) who argues that people have no need to think logically, because they understand statements by relating them to the real world. They construct models of reality and elaborate the relations in these models, rather than thinking in terms of logical operations based on abstract propositions.

Peter Wason (Wason & Johnson-Laird, 1972) suggests another operational explanation for various weaknesses in human logic: people do not seek to falsify hypotheses or propositions, they try to verify them. This could explain their tendency in Wason's four-card task to select the cards mentioned in the rule. By testing these particular cards, subjects can verify the rule but cannot falsify it.

An even more process-oriented explanation is suggested by Anderson (1985).

As we have seen, Anderson found that students tended to discard the conclusion in the following example:

> Some B's are A's
> No C's are B's
> Therefore some A's are not C's

He asked them to analyse the statements and the inferences to be drawn from them as follows:

	1 Some B's are A's
	2 No C's are B's
From 1 it follows that	3 Some A's are B's
From 2 it follows that	4 No B's are C's
From 3 and 4 it follows that	5 Some A's are not C's

When this stepwise approach was used, he found that 80% of the students (as against 60% originally) were able to accept the conclusion. There are several reasons why this conclusion is difficult to accept: it contains abstract rather than meaningful statements, it contains negations, and it contains quantifiers. It is thus difficult to retain the task in working memory for the time needed to process all the information, and a partition of the problem of the kind suggested by Anderson (with an external memory available) can help to overcome the practical problems of working memory.

METACOGNITION

In problem solving and learning, in decision-making and prediction it is vital that people check their own performance against the outcome obtained. They will be able to learn from their mistakes provided they can see a reason for their failure. They may be able to concentrate on their "weak spots" provided they recognize them. So what do people know about their own cognitive processes? This question introduces us to the concept of metacognition, or "cognition about cognition".

This is a fairly recent concept, going back to Flavell's discussion of "metamemory" (1970). But the idea that people possess a particular faculty allowing them to observe their own cognitive processes is not new.

Some examples can illustrate the usefulness of a special metacognition. Answer the following question as quickly as possible: "Do you know the telephone number of the King of Sweden?". You are not likely to hesitate long before answering "No". This answer cannot be reached by going through all the telephone numbers known to you and finding that the number requested is not among them. Rather, your prompt answer shows that you have some kind of knowledge about your own knowledge, you know that the King of Sweden does not belong to your social circle or your professional contacts, and so you do not have his telephone number.

Common remarks like "I'm so bad at maths", or "I can't spell", or "I'm sure I know his name, but I can't recall it just now" are examples of the same kind of thing.

Our assessment of our own capacity can thus be regarded as an example of metacognition. This assessment plays an important part in our initial approach to a problem situation. Our assessment of our own capacity determines the amount of effort spent on the task and our strategy for approaching it. If we perceive the task as too difficult, we may not embark on it at all. If we perceive it as very easy, we may not devote enough effort to solving it.

Does metacognition work accurately? The answer to this question, as in the case of all the other cognitive phenomena discussed above is "not always".

Flavell's early studies of metamemory were followed by many others (e.g. Brown, 1978, Flavell & Wellman, 1977) showing that children were not very good at judging their own memory capacity. They could not predict how much they would remember of a text they had just learnt. But the studies also revealed other important aspects of metacognition. For instance, older children approached the learning of lists of objects by trying to organize the lists according to classes of objects: fruits, toys, animals, etc., while younger children were incapable of exploiting organizational principles of this kind. In other words, younger children could not plan their learning according to the requirements of the task.

Further studies then suggested that young children did not understand that they did not understand. They were given instructions how to play a game, and told to play it with another child. But the instructions were deliberately formulated to be quite inadequate to enable the child to play. The instructed children were told to ask the experimenter as soon as they failed to understand what they should do. But they did not ask, and tried to convey the instructions to the child they were playing with, without knowing themselves what they were supposed to be doing.

These experiments on child performance attest to the importance of metacognition in learning and understanding.

Similar studies concerned with adults have not generally been conceived in terms of "metacognition". The concept used here is "confidence". It has been found that adults are notoriously bad at judging their own knowledge adequately. In particular, they most often tend to overestimate it. Some studies have been made, for instance, of the confidence people place in their own answers to simple factual questions like "What is the capital of Bolivia?" " When did Charles the VI live?" " Who is the Prime Minister in West Germany?" (Lichtenstein & Fischoff, 1977, Koriat, Lichtenstein & Fischoff, 1980). For each question they were asked to tell how confident they were that their answers to each of these questions were correct.

The overconfidence might be explained by the subjects' looking mainly at positive evidence for their being correct. When they were instructed to find negative evidence, their confidence ratings became more accurate.

Defective metacognition was also observed in studies of predictive behaviour, such as those described earlier. People were asked to judge an outcome from a set of cues (cf page 54). With the help of a special model of their judgments, it is possible to work out what weight should have been assigned to each cue in order to obtain the judgment produced. Subjects were also asked to report the weight they had assigned. It was frequently found that their own estimation of the weights they had assigned did not correspond to those calculated backwards from their judgments. This may mean that their metacognition was defective, but it could also indicate that they were not making assessments according to the linear approach suggested by the calculation model.

Why is our perception of our own performance sometimes defective? The most obvious reason is that the feedback we get from a situation is often quite inadequate. We have already mentioned the case of psychologists who assess applicants and who naturally get no feedback on the applicants whom they turn down. Physicians are in a similar situation: if they do not see the patient again, they cannot know whether it is because they have cured him, so he has no need to come back, or because they have failed to cure him, so he has gone to another doctor.

Another reason for defective metacognition may be that the feedback is difficult to process. When people are unable to utilize correlations between cues adequately, it may simply be because the implications of a correlation are difficult to understand, or that the job of having to integrate this information with all the other information involved is putting too great a load on working memory. An apparent inability to learn from experience (as noted by Brehmer, 1980) is mainly due to the deficiency of the feedback.

What role, then, does metacognition play in monitoring adult learning and problem solving? It has been found that people who believe themselves to be good at general problem solving will stick longer to a single line of approach to a complex problem and that they will tackle the problem more systematically than people with lower estimations of their own problem solving capacity (Dörner, Kreutzig, Reither & Stäudel, 1983). It has not been possible to establish in these studies whether the problem solving approach depends on the metacognition, or the other way round.

A study in which I have been personally involved (Wærn & Rabenius, 1985) indicates that metacognition during learning can lead to a change in learning strategy. Some psychology students were given difficult mathematical texts to learn. Their comments as they were reading showed that they started by trying to understand the text but that they soon found this to be impossible, since it contained concepts such as hyperboles, elliptics, etc. which were unfamiliar to them. They then switched to another learning strategy and just tried to memorize the text. This was also obvious from their comments and from their way of approaching the task. Instead of trying to envisage the figures described in the text and the relations involved, they now began to rehearse the text just as it was written.

SKILLED COGNITIVE PERFORMANCE

In our discussion of human problem solving, logic, decision-making and judgment we have mainly stressed the "weak" points in human cognition. The various studies reported have been concerned with tasks which are not "natural"; subjects have had to find their own ways of attacking them. Under the present heading we shall instead be looking at tasks with which people are familiar. These tasks may or may not be altogether "natural"; but at least the actors have already acquired a certain skill in performing them.

A skill can be defined in Welford's words (1968, p. 12): "a competent, expert, rapid and accurate performance" . Most research on skilled behaviour has been focussed on perceptual–motor skills. But, as Welford points out, all skilled behaviour involves a cognitive component:

> "Although a distinction is commonly drawn between sensory–motor and mental skills, it is very difficult to maintain completely. All skilled performance is mental in the sense that perception, decision, knowledge and judgment are required." (Welford, 1968, p. 21.)

Although all skills involve mental as well as sensory–motor components, cognitive skills may be distinguished from sensory–motor skills by the nature of the task. Our intuitive conception of what is "mental" and "cognitive" classifies all the tasks discussed hitherto as belonging primarily to the cognitive category. We would also be happy to call wordprocessing a cognitive task, whereas simple data entry would not satisfy our intuitive conception of what is "cognitive".

We also tend spontaneously to regard cognitive tasks as requiring more effort than simple sensory–motor tasks. However, this effort is only felt by people who do not yet know how to perform the task. Cognitive tasks can be performed effortlessly by someone who has acquired the relevant cognitive skill. Thus, problem solving can be regarded as one endpoint on a cognitive skill dimension, and cognitive skill as the other, as suggested by Card, Moran & Newell (1983).

If we regard cognitive skill as a special case of problem solving, we can adopt the same concepts as we used to describe problem solving above. We noted that difficulty in solving problems sprang primarily from two sources: the representation of the problem (i.e. the formulation of the problem space) and the search in the problem space. Anyone skilled in the performance of a particular cognitive task will already have acquired the ability to find the correct representation of the task swiftly and to direct an efficient search in the problem space.

Why are some people able to represent a problem without hesitation? It has often been found that experts in a particular field are also good at reproducing given information in their field. We have already seen how chess masters can reproduce the constellations of chessmen on a chessboard. Similar high recall performance has been found among programmers, who have been given programs to read and recall. The simple explanation of their extraordinary recall is that they recognize the information they are given. It is already stored in their long-term memory. A skilled cognitive performance thus relies on a large amount of declarative knowledge in the specific field.

The second area of cognitive skill concerns the control of search in the problem space. We might assume that highly skilled people have simply learnt a sequence of operators, contingent on the nature of the task. This suggestion seems consistent with the usual way in which computers are programmed. A more "human" explanation includes the idea of goals. Card, Moran & Newell (1983) suggest that a person's knowledge of a particular task consists of 1) a set of goals, 2) a set of operators, 3) a set of methods for achieving the goals, and 4) a set of selection rules for choosing among competing methods for achieving the goals (Card, Moran & Newell, 1983, p. 140). Their model is therefore called the GOMS model (Goal, Operation, Method, Selection).

From our discussion of problem solving the concepts of goals and operators should already be familiar. The new concepts introduced in the GOMS model concern the methods and selection rules. According to Card, Moran & Newell (1983, p. 145):

"A method describes a procedure for accomplishing a goal.... The description of a method is cast in a GOMS model as a conditional sequence of goals and operators, with conditional tests on the contents of the user's immediate memory and on the state of the task environment."

Thus the method reduces the search by suggesting a single path in the problem space. But several methods may be applicable to the achievement of a particular goal, and so the expert works out rules for selecting methods. These rules are contingent on the nature of the particular situation, and they tell the expert which method to choose in this case. A simple example could be a rule for choosing between using a pocket calculator or working it out in your head: if the calculation is simple (e.g. addition), and there are less than five numbers involved, then do it in your head.

The GOMS model is adequate for expert performances whithout any errors. But if the actor has to spend a lot of time coping with errors (either his own or those that appear to be beyond his control), the simple hierarchical GOMS control structure is inadequate. But in such cases we do not speak of skilled performance.

The GOMS model can be used to predict how long it takes a skilled person to carry out a particular task. Card, Moran & Newell report highly valid predictions for a text-editing task.

SUMMARY

Problem solving, decision-making and logical reasoning involve the use of knowledge in new situations. It has been found that human beings do not behave "optimally" in such contexts, if by "optimal" performance we mean one derived from calculations based solely on the nature of the stimulus. In solving problems or making decisions people use heuristics, which can shorten the solution path but do not guarantee that a solution (or a best option) will be found. In logical reasoning, the concrete meaning of the problem is more important than the abstract representation.

The individual's ability to judge his own capacities (metacognition) depends on the feedback he gets from his actions. Metacognition is involved both in evaluating the results arrived at and in deciding what process to adopt for a particular problem.

Skilled cognitive performance is no different from other types of skill. It is a question of choosing methods and operations appropriate to the achievement of a particular goal, and of performing the cognitive operations without error.

SOLUTIONS TO PROBLEMS

Problem 1: There are some different paths to follow. Figure 22 therefore gives the full problem space (given the assumption that the problem is solved by going by the boat as specified). The denotations are as follows: the slash indicates the river; the figures stand for the number of missionaries (to the left) and cannibals (to the right) on each side of the river; the dot indicates on which side of the river the boat is situated.

Problem 2: The coat stand is constructed with the help of the floor and the roof as indicated in Figure 23. The coat can be hung on the handle of the cramp.

Problem 4: The initial situation and the solution are shown in Figure 24. The original shape of the window is shown by the full lines, and the new shape is shown by the dotted lines.

Problem 5: The dog weighs 20 pounds (the dog's half weight is 10 pounds).

Problem 6: The nine-dot problem is solved as in Figure 25.

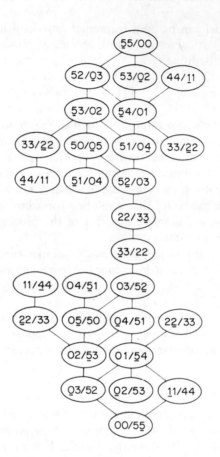

Figure 22 A problem space for the missionaries and cannibals problem.

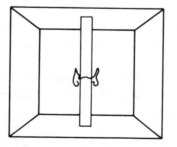

Figure 23 A solution of the coat stand problem.

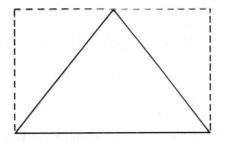

Figure 24 A solution of the window problem.

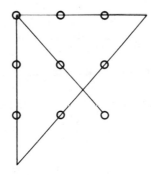

Figure 25 A solution of the nine-dot problem.

Chapter 5

Learning Computerized Tasks

GENERAL LEARNING PRINCIPLES

The transition from information to knowledge, or from working memory to long-term memory is usually referred to as learning. What we generally call "learning" is often also connected with some kind of positive change in the information stored in long-term memory.

Bottom-up learning

The earliest psychological studies of learning were based on material which was as meaningless as possible, namely nonsense syllables (Ebbinghaus, 1885). (Nonsense syllables consist of two consonants round a vowel, and they must not correspond to any known word. Examples are DAK, BOF, TUD.) Learning in such a case can be described as a bottom-up process. Small isolated bits of information are gradually piled on one another.

Ebbinghaus, without any notion of the concept of "working memory", found that a list of seven syllables could be learnt at a single reading. But a list of 36 syllables required 55 repetitions (on an average, and with Ebbinghaus himself as the only, highly experienced subject). This means that each repetition of the 36 syllables served to fix an average of a little more than a half of a nonsense syllable in long-term memory. The learning of meaningless material is slow even for an experienced subject like Ebbinghaus. Ebbinghaus found that the longer the list, the more repetitions were needed per syllable.

Other estimates made by Newell & Simon (1972) attest to the effort required to place new information in long-term memory. Newell & Simon estimate the time it takes to transfer one "chunk" of information from working memory to long-term memory at about 5–10 seconds. This accords well with Ebbinghaus's estimate of 10 seconds per syllable, if we accept that to him a nonsense syllable represented a chunk (he must after all have become quite familiar with them).

Much early work on human learning was based on material which was assumed to be nonsensical. It was soon found, however, that people discovered some "sense" even in nonsense syllables, and it became necessary to introduce some kind of "nonsense" calibration in order to control this factor. The value of this kind of research was seriously called in question when researchers found that nonsense learning had very little in common with meaningful learning.

Top-down learning

In most real-life situations people are able to relate the material to be learnt to something they already know. There are thus two essentially different aspects to meaningful learning: tracking down any appropriate prior knowledge, and learning the difference between the old and new situations.

What is involved in the finding of relevant prior knowledge? If a new situation is similar enough to another situation that is already familiar, people will be spontaneously reminded of the earlier case. They can then use any knowledge related to the old situation without further reflection. Here we can talk about "unintentional transfer". The crucial factor responsible for unintentional transfer is the similarity between the old and new situations.

Since similarity is defined by the subject, it is very difficult to predict what previous knowledge will be spontaneously evoked in a particular situation. Nor is it easy to tell what characteristics in the current situation will catch the attention of a particular subject. Unintentional transfer effects are thus difficult to control, either by the learner or the instructor. It is quite possible that some prior knowledge is evoked which is quite inappropriate to the present situation, and despite the fact that the instructor had no intention of suggesting such an association.

A safer instruction for an instructor would be to indicate the kind of prior knowledge that could be useful in the particular new situation. Learners will then be able to use the old situation as a basis for the intentional transfer of knowledge. They can of course engage in search for adequate knowledge on their own account, intentionally transferring old knowledge to the new situation. But the help of an instructor can make it easier to find old knowledge that really is relevant and useful to the new situation. I shall return to the concepts of intentional and unintentional transfer later, in discussing how people learn computerized tasks.

However, finding an appropriate prior old knowledge is only the first step in the top-down learning process. By definition, something new has to be learnt in a new situation. But the new aspects should not be regarded as nonsense material being added to old knowledge. It is necessary to relate them to the old knowledge in meaningful ways.

The two most common examples of meaningful relations will be described below.

The first example concerns the phenomenon of discrimination. We often see how children apply the same label to several different phenomena. As we passed a meadow full of cows in our car, our daughter exclaimed in great excitement: "Look, at all those bears!" Sooner or later children learn to discriminate between bears, horses and cows, and between birds and butterflies. One of the most important things to be learnt in using prior knowledge is discrimination. Discrimination can be seen as the adding of new relations to an existing concept. Our daughter's concept probably consisted of a notion of "big animals", and the only label she had was "bear". Taking the concept of "big animal" as one node, she then learnt that "bear" was characterized in a special way and "cow" in another. Some features were common to both such as size and four-leggedness, others diverged. Discrimination is also important in adult learning. Computer novices have to learn that a word processing system is "similar to" but also "different from" a typewriter.

Another meaningful relation to be learnt in a new situation concerns generalization. Generalization lies at the heart of much of our concept learning. When our prior knowledge includes knowledge of separate entities, the recognition of certain regularities or commonalities allowing us to treat the entities as to some extent similar will be of great value. Generalization, too, is a learning mechanism which is used spontaneously, as in children's language learning for instance. It is not uncommon to hear children saying "childs" instead of "children" or "mans" instead of "men". Why shouldn't the rule about forming the plural by adding an "s" apply here? Generalization is related to the capacity for "chunking" information, and it thus provides an important way of reducing the load on working memory. In a human–computer situation the users' opportunities for generalizing should be promoted as far as possible.

Thus meaningful learning has two distinct advantages over nonsense learning: it can exploit prior knowledge and it can make use of general learning mechanisms such as discrimination and generalization. Where some "nonsense" relations still have to be made, they will of course obey the same laws as in the "bottom-up" learning discussed above. Any complex learning process will consist of both types of learning. However, it seems likely that for better or for worse we always try to make use of notions that appear familiar.

Procedural learning

The learning processes described above refer to the learning of declarative material. Both nonsense syllables and normal texts belong to this category. But what about procedural learning? Does it differ from the learning of declarative material? Up to a point it does. The results of the learning of declarative material always have to be represented in a declarative format. That is to say, we have to transform them from the dormant state in long-term memory to an active state in working memory, in order to inspect them and express them in verbal form. This does not apply to the learning of a procedural skill. We do not have to be able to talk about it (this is one of the distinguishing features of procedural as opposed to declarative knowledge); we simply have to be able to perform the action. This applies both to motor skills, like riding a bike, or to cognitive, like mental arithmetic.

Three stages can be discerned in procedural learning (Anderson, 1982). In the first stage the procedure usually acquires a declarative description. We are often taught how to perform actions by being told how to do them. Take the case of the driving instructor telling you how to change gear. "First press on the clutch with your left foot, put in the gear you intend to use, press down the gas pedal slowly with your right foot while lifting your left foot upwards slowly. At the same time that you lift your left foot, you must press your right foot down a little harder so the engine doesn't stall." This illustrates a fairly involved sequence of instructions which has to be learnt together with the appropriate motor actions. Thus the declarative statements do not only have to be learnt by heart or understood, but they also have to be related to certain actions. We can call this first stage the "cognitive stage".

In the second stage we learn how to combine the various actions and build up a procedure from the separate declarative statements. At the declarative stage we may have to think for a long time about where to find the second gear; by the second stage, we can find it easily. The whole sequence of subactions is now congealing into a coherent procedure. We can call this second stage the "associative stage".

The third stage is responsible for the refinement of the procedure into a learned skill. This can be called the "autonomous stage". There is no clearcut borderline between the associative and the autonomous stages. In the course of transition from one stage to the next, parts of the procedure become "chunked" together. Perhaps we no longer have to consider our hands and feet as separate entities, but can see the action of pressing down the clutch and moving the gear as one single "chunk". Also, each action is now being performed more smoothly. Whereas we were uncertain at first exactly how to hold and move the gear lever, now our hand is slowly learning during the autonomous stage how to move, without requiring conscious feedback on each component in the movement.

Procedural learning can be described by an exponential function

$$T = aP^{-b}$$

where T is the time taken to perform a particular task, P the amount of practice, while and a and b are learning constants. This function gives us the curve illustrated in Figure 26.

The curve shows that people learn most at the beginning of the learning process, i.e. at the declarative stage. The pure procedural learning of the associative and autonomous stages is much slower. At the autonomous stage we ultimately reach the limits of performance times, as described above in our discussion of sensory and motor characteristics.

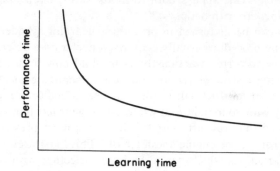

Figure 26 A typical learning curve for procedural learning.

Forgetting

According to a great many learners it is not the learning in itself that causes the problems; it is the forgetting. "Learning would be no problem, it only we didn't forget so much!" So, what is forgetting?

A radical view in current theory is that we do not in fact forget anything. Anything that has once been placed in long-term memory will remain there for ever. This view has been supported by neurophysiological evidence and by studies of people under hypnosis. Stimulation of certain parts of the brain will evoke memories not recognized by the subject. Under hypnosis it is possible to evoke childhood memories which were presumably forgotten.

So why do we believe that we forget? The first explanation of forgetting was that memory traces were formed during learning and that they "decayed" spontaneously from lack of use. This explanation was later challenged by experiments showing that we forget much less when we are asleep than when we are awake. These and other observations suggested that time as such was not responsible for forgetting; it was interference from new material. In particular it was found that if the new material was related to old material, then earlier relations to that same old material were forgotten.

The current view of forgetting claims that our forgetting problems are related to difficulty in retrieval. The material may still exist in long-term memory, but our chances of retrieving it are slight. Remembering is related to the number of cues in common to the present situation and the situation in which we learnt what has to be remembered. The fewer common cues, the more difficult it is to retrieve the material learnt.

The frequently observed superiority of recognition to recall can be explained by the number of common cues; in a recognition situation the relevant cues are generally more numerous and more relevant than in a recall situation.

This explanation of forgetting accords well with what we have discovered about the kind of learning that gives the best hope of remembering the material learnt. It is recommended that the material to be learnt should be elaborated, a process which generates many cues. It is also recommended that the material be organized, a process which encourages relation to higher-order concepts. It is even recommended that the material should be learnt in the same surroundings and in the same way as will apply at subsequent retrieval. This recommendation could be useful for students studying for exams: study in the room to be used for the exam, and try to imagine the questions to be asked.

PARTICULAR LEARNING PRINCIPLES RELATED TO A COMPUTER SITUATION

The reader may wonder what is so distinctive about the learning of computerized tasks to warrant separate consideration. I hope to make it clear here that learning computerized tasks does in fact differ from learning new languages, or mathematics or the capitals of the African countries.

There are two main reasons why the learning of computerized tasks represents something quite different from most school learning situations. First, the learners themselves are usually different from the learners in an ordinary school. Second, computer systems are developing extremely quickly at present.

What difference does it make that the learners are not school children? In schools we usually encounter children or young adults who expect to be taught. In the computer learning situation, we generally encounter adults who are experts at a particular task, who want to go on being experts at this task and who want to perform it as well as possible. They are not usually particularly interested in the computer system for any reason except that it may help to speed up their performance of the central task or to achieve a better result.

The most important difference between young pupils and adult experts lies in the learning strategies. In a new learning situation adult learners will most certainly try to rely as far as possible on prior knowledge. As soon as the new situation begins to resemble a situation with which the adult learner is familiar, we can assume that prior knowledge will be applied. Since computerized systems are generally introduced to support (or even replace) the performance of old tasks, this is only to be expected. In this situation the mechanism of transfer will thus be applicable.

One consequence of the present rapid development of computer systems which is relevant to the learning situation concerns the relation between documentation and actual systems performance. When systems are always changing, it is difficult for the relevant documentation to keep up. This means that the information provided in the manuals may not always be compatible with the latest version of the system. When the user has no time to sit down and wait to be taught, and cannot rely on the documentation, the only way to find a solution is to go direct to the system itself. This calls for a "learning-by-doing" strategy.

A further consequence of the quick development of computer systems is the welter of different hardware and software configurations that faces even fairly unsophisticated computer system users. To find their way through the jungle, computer users need powerful conceptual tools. They have to be able to see what is essential and what is not. They need to understand what "lies behind" different system designs and system decisions. They need to compare systems in order to get to grips with what will otherwise be a confusing situation. The suggested tool to help computer users from getting lost in the jungle is the "mental model". They may have been provided with a training model of the system by the system designers, or they may build a mental model themselves. But however they go about it, they will always try to find some order in the computerized chaos.

Thus, since adults try to capitalize on their prior knowledge, the problem of transferring prior knowledge to the computer situation has to be considered. Also, the disparity between systems actions and systems documentation raises the question of how people learn by doing. Finally, the plethora of existing computer systems and the multitude of possibilities available within a system, bring us to the question of how people build "mental models" of systems.

TRANSFER OF KNOWLEDGE

As I have pointed out, adult learners will use their prior knowledge in learning a new task. For many adults the use of prior knowledge is in fact an intentional strategy. They have discovered from their experience of learning about the world that it pays to make use of knowledge already acquired. As we have seen earlier, this kind of use constitutes an "intentional transfer". In addition, we all use prior knowledge unintentionally. This unintentional use occurs when learners introduce implicit assumptions into the situation which are not warranted by the situation itself, or when procedures are applied automatically. In such cases we can speak of unintentional transfer. Since adults have an abundance of available prior knowledge, the transfer effects will be more noticeable in adults learning than they are in the learning of children.

It is of course possible that adult learners try intentionally to avoid using prior knowledge. Even so, some prior knowledge is likely to be used unintentionally: it is in fact very difficult to exclude it, as we shall see in some of the following examples. Under the heading of "Transfer" I shall address problems connected with unintentional transfer. Intentional transfer will be discussed in the section on "The role of models in learning".

What prior knowledge is evoked?

In order to predict transfer effects, it is of course neither possible nor necessary to call upon all prior knowledge that a user has accumulated over a lifetime. In any particular situation only a small part of all prior knowledge will be evoked, and we must therefore consider what prior knowledge is evoked, and how.

The crucial point to evocation of prior knowledge lies in the similarity between the current situation and the user's earlier knowledge. When a new situation consists in a computerized version of a former task, we may assume that prior knowledge of the rules governing this task will be evoked.

However, the task as performed outside the system represents one source only of prior knowledge. The other source is connected with aspects of the situation which are not related to the task. The users may have certain ideas about what a "machine" can and cannot do. Superficial characteristics of the system and the system information may evoke particular associations and lead to unintended implicit assumptions. Nobody has yet attempted to account for this non-task-related evocation of prior knowledge. I shall quote one example below, which suggests that systems designers and document writers should consider this source of prior knowledge as well as the source stemming from the task itself.

Since transfer depends on similarities between present and past situations, we should consider how similarity can be specified. Similarity is of course a subjective term, and people may differ greatly in their perception of similarity between a computerized task and a non-computerized task. Some people may totally resist the idea of a computer system as resembling anything else, and this makes it difficult to base a system or systems instructions on similarities between the task outside the system and the task within it. At present we have no agreed means for specifying similarities between a computerized system and non-task-related knowledge, and this is why it is essential that new systems should be tested by users in practice. A systems designer cannot simply rely on his own intuition as to what chords of prior knowledge will be struck by the particular combination of system and documentation.

Describing prior knowledge

Prior knowledge has to be described so that it can be compared with the system to be learnt. Various ways of comparing prior knowledge and computer systems have been suggested.

Thomas Moran recommends that we analyse the external task (outside the system) and the internal task (in the system) in terms of the concepts involved and the operations performed on them. He calls this analysis the ETIT analysis, which is an acronym for External Task Internal Task (Moran, 1983).

In order to learn a new system, a user has to find the appropriate "mapping rules" between the external and internal tasks. The more mapping rules that are required, the more effort will be involved in learning the internal task.

David Kieras and Peter Polson analyse the system to be learnt and former knowledge related to the task in terms of the production rules required for performing the task (Polson & Kieras, 1985a, 1985b). (A reminder: a production rule has the form: IF <conditions> THEN <actions>.) The condition of the production rule contains goals and subgoals, as well as observations of the current situation. The difference between the goal hierarchies in the old and new tasks and the number of new productions which have to be learnt in order to perform the new task can then be used to predict ease of learning.

I have made a similar analysis (Wærn, 1985), in which prior knowledge is described in terms of the intended goals, the methods that can be used, and the conditions for using these methods that can be specified .

A formal analysis of the prior knowledge which might be evoked is not possible, but it is possible to make some educated guesses about the content of the rules of prior knowledge in the case of a similar task. The goals to be achieved and the conditions to be observed may then be compared with the computerized task. However, we have to accept that the quality of a prior-knowledge analysis based upon a task analysis will always depend on the analyst's intuition. Moreover, this kind of analysis does not allow for such non-task-related prior knowledge as may be evoked. Only careful consideration of the relevant situation, and of superficial characteristics such as the wording of commands or instructions, may suggest the nature of the prior knowledge evoked.

Transfer effects

The transfer of prior knowledge to the new situation may have quantitative as well as qualitative effects.

The qualitative effects are connected with the direction of the transfer, whether it is negative or positive—i.e. will prior knowledge hinder or facilitate new learning?

From previous transfer research, the following qualitative effects can be suggested.

1) If the old and the new tasks include production rules with the same (or very similar) conditions but different actions, then the transfer effect will be negative.

2) If the old and new tasks include production rules in which the same (or similar) conditions give rise to similar actions, then the transfer effect will be positive.

These suggestions make it possible to predict the direction of transfer effects in the case of single rules. But the total effect in the task as a whole will depend on the combination of rules and the quantitative effects, to which I will turn now.

The quantitative effects are connected with the strength of the transfer: to what extent will learning be facilitated or hindered? The following conditions suggest themselves from current research.

1) The more rules with similar conditions in prior knowledge and in the new task, the stronger the effect (positive or negative).
2) The stronger the relation between the condition and action with regard to prior knowledge rules, the stronger the effect (positive or negative).

Empirical data

To put some flesh to the bones, I will first make a detailed analysis of a single task, and suggest possible prior knowledge rules evoked and new rules relevant to this task. The task involves a change in a wordprocessing system such that:

"prohect" becomes "project"

(Wærn, 1985).

The rules in Table 2 can be specified for performing this task 1) on a typewriter and 2) in the relevant wordprocessing system.

Table 2. Comparisons of some production rules to be used in a typewriter and a wordprocessor. (Informal notation)

Typewriter	Wordprocessor
	Conditions and methods
IF old word and new word have the same length THEN use method: delete old type new	IF old word and new word have the same length THEN use method: type new word over old
	Methods and subgoals
IF method: delete THEN subgoal: move paper to delete position IF method: type over THEN subgoal: move typehead to word to change	IF method: type over THEN subgoal: move cursor to word to change
	Subgoals, conditions and operations
IF subgoal: move paper to delete position THEN operation: turn wheel IF subgoal: move typehead to word to change AND condition: word to the right THEN operation: press space bar	IF subgoal: move cursor to word to change AND condition: word to the right THEN operation: press right arrow key

It is assumed in the analysis that a person who is learning the wordprocessing system is already used to working with a typewriter. In the particular word-processing system studied the "normal" mode of operation was typing over. In order to delete and insert words, particular commands had to be used.

In a study of novices learning this wordprocessing system, the difficulties encountered by a subject who was accustomed to a typewriter are particularly interesting.

1. The subject always used the method of first deleting the word to be changed and then writing the new word. This procedure requires many more operations than simply typing over, the procedure which is contained in the rules for the wordprocessing system. However, the method of first deleting and then retyping is "natural" to anyone typing on a paper, as we can see from the rules for the typewriter.
2. The subject found it very difficult to move the cursor to the right. She repeatedly pushed the space bar, which in this particular wordprocessing system caused the existing text to be overwritten by blanks. This meant that the existing text disappeared and had to be rewritten. Since the subject used the usual tactics of a skilled typist, i.e. looking at the manuscript as much as possible rather than at the paper (here the screen), she destroyed a good many words before noticing what she had done.

Both effects could be predicted from the rule analysis. The inefficient method may not even have been spotted by the subject (a possibility which will be discussed below, in the section on "Learning by doing"). The method is natural to anyone using a typewriter when it does not lead to any errors. The second error, the habit of pushing the space bar to move to the right, was so automatic that it was very difficult to inhibit. This is a good example of negative transfer: the goal and conditions are similar in the prior knowledge rules and in the rules for the wordprocessing system, but the action required is quite different. Further, the relation between conditions and action in the old rule is probably strong in the case of a skilled typist, and this generates a strong transfer effect.

These observations serve to illustrate the theoretical analysis above. However, since data about a single subject may not seem enough to support the validity of the analysis, let us consider the data from some further studies. The first of these, reported by Polson & Kieras (1985a), is also concerned with wordprocessing. The authors predict the learning time (up to a certain criterion) from the number of new production rules which have to be learnt. Thus we can say that their theoretical analysis only allows for the positive transfer effects resulting from similar conditions in relation to similar actions. They found effects which agreed with their predictions: the more new rules to be learnt, the longer the learning time. These results have later been repeated in a study reported by Polson, Muncher & Engelbeck (1986).

A similar conclusion can be drawn from an investigation performed by Singley & Anderson (1985). These researchers studied transfer between different editors: two line editors and one screen editor (EMACS). They found almost complete transfer in the case of the two line editors and a substantial transfer between the line editors and the screen editor. In the last case, the amount of transfer (in terms of performance time saved) was only about half the amount of transfer between the line editors. The explanation of the difference lies in the degree of overlap between the production rules required for performing the different tasks. One of the line editors could be regarded as totally contained in the other. There the transfer was total. The screen editor had some rules in common with the line editors, but the subjects also had to learn some new rules. The authors report that a mathematical fit to the learning curve indicates that about 30% of the total production set for EMACS consisted in production rules which were specific to this editor.

It could be claimed that there is nothing very new about "discovering" that experience is helpful in new learning. (i.e. positive transfer). However, the merit of Kieras and Polson's and Singley and Anderson's work is that they formulate this insight more precisely and that they calculate quantitative effects.

Often in research, the validity of a model is questioned by new data. In a recent report by Vossen, Sitter and Ziegler (1987), it was found that there were great variations between tasks and subjects in learning times for the same number of productions.

No researcher has yet tried to calculate negative transfer effects in a similar way, even though this would be quite possible. It might be possible to establish which rules have similar conditions but different actions. And the more such rules there are of this kind, the greater the negative transfer effect is likely to be. At a deeper level, we might ask what happens in such a situation: Does the "old" rule still exist, when the new rule is learnt? If so, the old rule will have to be inhibited so that the new rule may be used. Or is the old connection between the condition and action sides broken and a new action replaces the old one? If this is the case, the old rule would not be easily restored, but would have to be relearnt.

Some findings suggest that the "old" action is not replaced, but is more or less consciously suppressed. This was particularly evident in a study concerning a very experienced programmer (Sääf, 1984, Wærn, 1985). Three persons learning Jackson's structured programming (JSP) technique were studied. Two had minimal experience of programming, and one had 20 years experience of programming in an ICL setting.

The task presented to the subjects was as follows:

"The computer operations department has given you a magnetic tape. They do not know what it contains. The tape is useful only if it contains a first record with some basic information (record type = G) and some

records of either type A or type B (record type = A or B). They want
you to find out if that is the case."

The subjects were asked to use the JSP method to structure the problem
before solving it.

This problem can be solved in the ways outlined in Figure 27. The two
subjects with little experience of programming solved this problem in about
three minutes. The experienced programmer took altogether an hour and a
half!

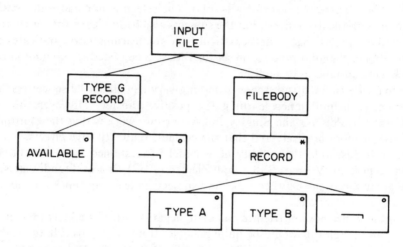

Figure 27 A solution in terms of JSP of the magnetic tape problem.

A closer examination of his approach to the problem (a think-aloud method
was used, i.e. he was asked to voice his thoughts and to record them on a
tape-recorder) shows that he started by trying to apply the knowledge he had
acquired from his previous experience of programming. Instead of obeying the
instruction to use the structured programming technique, he wanted to use a
program he remembered having written before. This was not allowed by the
experimenter, who told him to write a new program. Then the programmer
stumbled on the interpretation of "first record": should it be the first physical record or only the first record of an interesting sequence of records on the
tape? He asked the experimenter. At his next attempt he decided to write a
flow-chart solution, which took about 4 minutes. This solution was perfectly
correct, but the experimenter continued to ask for a JSP solution. Four days
later the programmer decided to approach the problem again, and to try to
achieve a JSP solution. His first attempt with JSP lasted about 18 minutes. He
obviously found difficulty in using the JSP method and said that he would prefer to use a decision table instead. He was not sure that he had understood the

functional specifications correctly. Again he complained about his difficulties in using the JSP method. At last he managed to produce a structure very similar to Figure 27. He was still not satisfied with his solution, and in his last attempt (which took 11 minutes and was again accompanied by complaints about the difficulty in using the JSP method) he finally produced a solution which included the idea of "backtracking", an idea that none of the other subjects had used.

From this example we see that it is no easy task to learn a new way of thinking. Old thinking strategies will interfere with the new approaches required. This particular subject apparently had to work through the old way of tackling the task (searching for existing programs, writing a flow-chart) before he could start thinking along the new lines required. And even then, he complained of considerable difficulty.

The last example can illustrate the effect of evoking knowledge which is not directly task-related. In the study in question, the subjects were learning to use a particular wordprocessing system (Wærn, 1984). In the course of the learning they were asked to perform various tasks. The task which is interesting here concerned the search for a particular word in a text. They were given the manual for the relevant wordprocessing system, but no other help. The word to be sought was not visible on the screen currently at hand. The manual contained the following instructions:

> command s<xxx> Search for word <xxx> on the screen
> command n<xxx> Search for next word <xxx> on the screen
> command r<xxx> Search for word <xxx> in the rest of the text
> command v<xxx> Search for next word <xxx> in the rest of the text

The subjects started their search by performing the first command in the manual, i.e. the "s" command. This did not produce any result. The system indicated that no such word was to be found. At this point the subjects began vain attempts at searching: they tried out the command repeatedly, some of them thought that the word wanted might have to be restricted to three letters, since the instruction contained three symbols. Others thought that the brackets < > were meant to be included in the command. After several such attempts the experimenter intervened and asked the subjects to look carefully at the manual. And most subjects—except one who was familiar with computers—said: "Well, it just says the same—I can't see any difference between the commands."

This failure to recognize the difference between the commands can be ascribed to certain elements of their prior knowledge: first they were accustomed to reading texts upwards and downwards, which is why they started by trying the first command. Second, they were accustomed to the fact that important differences in instructional texts are usually marked in some way. In the present case the difference was discretely concealed by very similar wording. The third factor in their prior knowledge which made the detection of the difference difficult, was connected with their knowledge of texts and pages of text: a text looking like a book may be regarded as providing continuous informative material. The pages in a book are simply a typographical convenience and have no relevance to the information as such. Why then should it be important to discriminate between the text on a screen page and "the rest of the text"?

While acknowledging that this explanation is totally *post hoc*, the fact remains: it was difficult for the novices to the system to find out what command to use, and there is nothing in the search task itself to suggest a reason for this difficulty. However, prior knowledge of reading and texts is related to this task. The evocation of that knowledge is not really surprising and the difficulty in reading the manual could have been predicted.

Conclusion

It seems that prior knowledge will be evoked, which is similar in some way to the situation to be learnt. This prior knowledge may or may not be task-related. Positive transfer effects arise when common elements exist between the old and new situations. Negative transfer effects occur when similar goals or conditions have to be related to new methods or actions. In the negative transfer case it appears that the prior knowledge evoked has to be suppressed in order to give the new actions a chance.

LEARNING BY DOING

I have earlier argued that in learning new computer systems people have to engage in "learning by doing". We can now examine this proposition a little more closely, to see what learning by doing requires, and how it proceeds in the case of computer systems.

Learning by doing is the equivalent of learning in a problem solving situation. Problem solving was described as a search in a problem space. This means that learning by doing involves learning the characteristics or nature of the problem space as well as learning how to search efficiently within it.

In a computer situation the system offers one or more problem spaces in the shape of the permitted operations and the concepts with which the system operates. The user constructs a problem space by selecting a subset of the operations and concepts which seem to be relevant for the task at hand. The search implies combining the chosen operations in some way so as to achieve the goal. A computer system is similar to most real-life tasks in that it allows the use of several methods for achieving the same goal. Thus the user has an opportunity of choosing which approach to employ. Learning thus involves choosing a "good" (if not necessarily the best) method.

Understanding the nature of the problem space

How can a user recognize the characteristics of the problem space of a particular computer system? One important aid is naturally the documentation relating to the system. Information about the functions which the system can perform and the methods to elicit these functions (commands, menu options, function keys, etc.) serves to define the operations in the problem space. Also, the objects in the problem space are stipulated by the manual. Thus the first-time user of a system knows as much about the problem space provided as he or she can remember and understand with the help of the manual. Experience of using the system may add to, or conflict with, the understanding acquired from reading the manual. (The manual may of course consist of an online manual or a more or less sophisticated help system. Here, for the sake of simplicity, I will refer to "manuals", without further specification.)

Some examples from a study of people learning to use a wordprocessing system can be used to illustrate learning by doing. In this investigation (Wærn & Rabenius, 1987) subjects were given minimal instructions about a wordprocessing system, consisting of six editing commands only, plus the possibility to type over words. By the editing commands the following functions were obtained: insertion of the typed text or an empty line, deletion of a single sign, a word or a line, and a displacement of a part of the line downwards. For moving the cursor the manual covered only the simplest arrow-key movements (moving the cursor one position at a time). The subjects were also told that they could undo a given command by giving a particular command.

The subjects were first given a set of simple editing tasks, where the commands included in the manual could be used just as they stood. Words had to be deleted, letters changed, and lines inserted. This meant that the problem space as presented in the manual corresponded to the given tasks . In the second part of the study, the subjects were given new tasks, in which "side-effects" of the commands could be used to advantage. An example of such a new task is shown in Table 3.

Table 3. An example of a task to be performed with a word-processor

Change the numbers so that they are arranged in neat columns:

	Grade 3	Grade 4	Grade 5
Question 1	2.07	1.53	1.37
Question 2	2.28	2.11	1.63
Question 3	3.13	2.96	2.59
Question 4	2.67	2.19	1.59

The numbers were always displaced to the right.

This task can easily be solved by placing the cursor far enough to the left of the first number on the row belonging to question 3, and deleting three empty spaces. This requires the following understanding of the problem space. 1) As regards operations: that a deletion at a particular position moves the symbols on the right of that position to the left. 2) As regards concepts: that an empty space is also a sign (a blank sign).

Before embarking on this task the subjects had learnt the particular wordprocessing system during two hours. This experience included deleting and inserting blanks, but only in full texts, not as here in a table of figures. The subjects had a manual available, which included all commands learnt (but of course not the particular method to be used in this situation).

The subjects were asked to think aloud while they were carrying out this task. Their comments indicate a variety of problems in learning to understand the problem space.

The following think-aloud comments were typical:

Subject 43

"The easiest way must be to take the numbers out and then write them back in again. But I can't delete the whole row, because then I won't remember what to write. So let me start at the 3, delete it, and write it there instead. And then I'll take the next."

Subject 15

"I'll just put in a 3 here and then take away the 3 which lies next to it, and then I can put in the next number. But then it is important that I remember, because now I don't know which numbers I've changed and which I haven't."

Subject 8

"So I take away this 3, and put it here instead, and I take away next, and put it here."

It should be noted that while deleting a figure, the figures to the right of it move one step to the left.

These comments represent the method used by most subjects: taking away the displaced numbers and retyping them in their correct positions. This method was probably derived from their prior training in changing words in a text. When this method for changing words is used in a text, neither the movement of the rest of the text, nor the blank signs, are "important". The text simply adjusts itself to the changes made. We could say that the critical characteristics of the problem space required for performing the present task are not included in the problem space used for deleting and inserting words in a continuous text.

Some subjects remarked that this method is very inefficient. In fact it requires two different commands for each number (24 commands altogether for correcting four groups of three-digit numbers, not including cursor movements) and it requires the users to remember the numbers deleted (or already corrected).

We may well wonder why most of the subjects continued to use an inefficient method, although many of them did not like it.

From the think-aloud comments we can discover various answers to this question. One appears from the following comment:

"Then I just type over like this: 3.13, and then I take away the rest with the space bar, and then continue to the next..."

This comment shows that the subject has adopted a method which allows no opportunity for any feedback about how to use the "side-effects" of the commands. When the subject types over and deletes with the spacebar, the numbers already written will remain in the same positions as before, which means that the required movement aspect will never appear.

However, although the movement occurs, some subjects will not detect it.

Subject 7

"The best way is to take away and write in again, I think. So I delete this one and this one, and then I go back to where I want the number to be. Then I write it there. Like this. And then the same here. And then I can try taking away the word at the position of the cursor. Yes. It was 3.13. Write 3.13. (This was accomplished by using the insert command) At the next position it should be 2.96. Take it away, write again: 2.96."

This comment is interesting in view of what happened when the subject used the commands to take away whole words at the position of the cursor. These commands take away a string of connected signs, and move the rest of the text lying to the right of these signs to "fill the gap" left by the deleted signs. This movement is necessary in a connected text, since otherwise there would be an empty space where the word stood before. In a connected text this movement may not be detected as a "side-effect" of the command to delete. The text would still look quite natural. In the present case, where the signs consisted of numbers, placed regularly in columns, it should have been much easier to detect the "side-effect". When the subject provided the "delete word" command, all the numbers to the right of the deleted numbers had moved five places to the left, a movement which should be very easy to detect. It is evident, however, that this subject did not detect it. Instead, she inserted the number in the right position (which moved the rest of the numbers four steps to the right again). As a result of this correction, the numbers to the right were displaced by two steps instead of three as they were to start with.

Fairly often the subjects failed to notice that the rest of the numbers moved when they altered the first number. The subjects seemed to be concentrating exclusively on the particular number to be changed.

Sometimes they detected the movement. The following comments illustrate this. (I have given them numbers in order to be able to refer to the comments later).

(Subject 4)

(After inserting three digits)

1. "Interesting that they move. Here they're very close, the columns, and then you find that they move to the right"

(In planning the next task):

2. "I can't help doing one digit at a time, I would like to change them all at once.

3. But then you have to tell the system where to start, since they jump back and forth, so you don't know. Obviously it's not enough, the cursor is misleading.

4. Now, let's see what happens, if I don't take this away first, if it will push the next aside.

5. In fact it's not so close, this column; or is it due to my manipulations?

6. Well, there you are.

7. I don't understand why they have to move so much! I have to move them back, one to the left.

8. Hmmm... is that why they move? That they push a whole row?

9. Well, I'll have to figure that out later..."

(The subject goes on to next task)

In comment number 1 the subject detects the movement caused by the insert action. In comment number 2 she indicates a desire to be able to perform the task in a more efficient way. In comment number 3 she imagines some kind of solution which lets the system take over the tedious work. She then is probably envisaging an automated version of her own method. In such a version, the movements will cause problems in placing the cursor. In comment number 4 she anticipates the effect of insertion. She observes and tries to interpret the current situation in comment number 5. Comment number 6 marks her action (insertion), and in comment number 7 she indicates both that she has observed the movement to the right and that she does not understand the reason why the rest of the row moved. In comment number 8 she is on the right track, but she abandons the idea (and the chance to learn by her detection) in favour of starting on the next task (and putting an end to the whole session).

When the session was finished, the same subject commented:

"There was something I really wondered about, and that was, why I couldn't write in a whole row without the whole thing moving"

Like many others in her situation, this subject had been unable to interpret the effects in such a way that she could make use of them, even though she was aware of them.

Some subjects were able to make use of some of the detected effects, but they still could not make any sense of them.

Subject 46

1. "You can move the text on a row to the left, but you can't move it to the right.

2. To move it to the left I push Esc and then the number of eehhh.. let us call them marks... which are needed to move the row to the left and then I push D, and then you give the command.

3. Then the whole text on the row is moved to the left—

4. I think.

5. Because it's not just the remaining text after the cursor which is moved.

6. But...

7. It pulls what is behind the cursor.

8. That's the way to take out superfluous letters in words.

(Experimenter: And that which is to the left of the cursor?)

9. That stays as it is.

(Experimenter: What did you learn today which you did not know yesterday?)

10. To-day I discovered that it was possible to move rows. Yesterday I used the command just to remove superfluous letters. And I never dreamt that you really could move all the columns in a row. It took a while before I found that out.

11. And it was a sheer chance that I did find it out.

12. I wanted to take away a digit, and suddenly I saw that the whole row moved.

(Experimenter: What would you like to do to move the whole row to the right?)

13. "I would like to have a command, like the one I used to move to the left, another Esc, but you don't use D. What can D mean?"

(Experimenter: Delete)

14. "If you imagine you have blocks, and then you take away some of them, and then you put in some new ones beside..."

15. Delete means take away, what's the word for add?

(Experimenter: Insert)

It is clear that this subject interprets the "d" command as performing BOTH the functions of deleting AND moving to the left (comments 3 and 8). This was because she detected the movement while deleting (comment 12). However, she was unable to use this information to create a new problem space which would have been more economical: the problem space of removing and inserting "blocks" of signs. She is on the right track, however, when she looks for a command corresponding to the "left-moving" command (comment 13). In her further attempts she does not succeed in using the insert command until the experimenter shows her how to do so.

The final grasp of the relationship between the task to be performed and the commands provided lies, as mentioned above, in a "building-block" model of the system. If deleting means taking away a block and moving the rest of the text to the left, inserting something (anything whatever) implies making room for a block and moving the rest of the text to the right. A building-block model gives us the smallest possible problem space for this particular task. What are the fundamental barriers to the creation of this model?

Some more comments suggest a few of these.

Subject 47

(The experimenter gives the command to delete three signs, when the cursor is positioned before the figures in the table, and the subject is asked to predict the result)

1. "You made the command to delete three signs, but you placed it before the signs!

2. Now you have removed three signs.

3. But I'm not so sure you've done that either.

4. In fact you've pressed on a spot where you don't have any signs.

5. So what will happen is that the 3 there won't disappear.

6. Instead it will move three steps to the left

(Performs the command, and observes the result)

7. Well, the 3 moved as well, but you didn't take it away.

8. Because you kind of pressed a little before it.

(Experimenter: How come it moved?)

9. Well, in a way you didn't delete anything. You just moved them. The same figures still stay there.

(Experimenter: But I took away three signs. What did I take away?)

10. Three squares on that screen.

(Experimenter: Yes, you could say that you take away three empty signs)

11. But that sounds so stupid: empty signs! People would think you were empty in the head!"

This and other similar comments show that the ultimate obstacle in the way of reaching the more efficient problem space is connected with the idea of "empty" or "blank" signs. The subjects cannot imagine that taking away or adding nothing (i.e. blank signs) can make any difference to the rest of the text. In a way this requires a new "insight", i.e. a new conception of the problem space of the system.

From these observations we can conclude the following. Four stages have to be passed through in order to create a new efficient problem space for a particular task.

1. The users have to perform activities which allow them to detect new aspects of the system's functioning. This means that users must allow themselves to "play around" with the system in order to investigate functions other than those immediately necessary. They must vary their actions in order to give the system a chance to show what else it can do.
2. The users have to attend to unexpected outcomes of their actions. By playing around with the system, new aspects may occur where they were not expected to turn up at all. Thus attention should be allowed to range widely over possible interesting outcomes.
3. The user must reflect upon the observations made. The discovery of new possibilities is not enough. Most of the users in this investigation were too impatient to allow themselves time to reflect (see for example subject 4 above). As a result of reflection, the new possibility detected can be related to the "old" problem space. In this way a richer problem space can be constructed, offering a greater variety of possible paths.
4. The user must create a model of the system which can be used for several tasks. This model may be regarded as a problem space containing more general operations than those which will be used in a particular task. From a model representing the underlying regularities of the system, the problem space required for a particular task can be constructed. This kind of model may therefore be referred to as a "generative" model.

Learning to search in a given problem space

Once the user has come to grips with the problem space, he has to learn how to choose an efficient way of solving each particular task. We can say that the users have to learn how to search in the problem space.

Search knowledge is a favourite conceptual topic of many researchers with an interest in learning and problem solving. One of the most important contributions of Newell & Simon (1972) consists in the development of the concept of "heuristics". Although though this concept was introduced in Chapter 4 above, I will recapitulate its main features here.

Heuristic methods represent a way of searching the problem space which does not guarantee that a correct solution will be found. This distinguishes a heuristic method from an algorithm: if you follow an algorithm correctly it results in the correct performance. A heuristic method is more of a "rule of thumb", but the search in the problem space will be much more efficient with the heuristic approach than it would have been without it.

If we have no heuristic knowledge at all we have one way only of finding a solution: trial and error. We can try one operation after the other to try a path in the problem space, discard that path and then go on to another. The efficiency of this search will depend on how systematic we are. If we set a gaggle of monkeys at the typewriter and let them type away at random, we may ultimately end up with the Encyclopaedia Britannica, but the search will certainly be very long, and tedious and full of redundancy. A more efficient search would take prior attempts into account and would try to avoid those that lead nowhere.

Heuristic knowledge can be acquired by doing. People who are experts in a certain field can be assumed to have acquired a lot of heuristic knowledge (apart from their declarative knowledge, which of course is also important).

Some of the heuristic knowledge acquired by experts is very closely related to a particular field of application. In such cases the experts know about what methods can be used in performing a particular task. They also know the conditions in which this relevant method is most efficient. This knowledge has been designated "method selection rules" (Card, Moran & Newell, 1983) (compare Chapter 4). These methods and method selection rules are what the designers of "expert systems" try to capture so that the system will operate as an expert would do faced with the same particular task.

Other heuristic knowledge is more general. We may learn how to perform a search in a problem space efficiently by using general rules. One such rule might state: If there are only a few paths which lead to the goal, start the search from the goal and work backwards. This is a good heuristic for coping with such problems as mazes. Another heuristic can be applied when only a few paths lead from the initial situation, or where the goal is ill-defined. A forward search would then be most efficient, as in many creative problems. If the searcher conceived a solution and moved back from it, he might stumble on necessary conditions which could not be fulfilled.

Another useful heuristic, used by most skilled programmers is to work from the top down. Here the problem is first defined on an abstract level, after which it can be broken down into lesser subproblems, until a level is reached where the actual coding can begin. Jackson's structured programming is an example of such a heuristic.

A good deal of the knowledge acquired in computerized situations probably consists of heuristic knowledge. Computer experts learn about available methods (though not necessarily by doing), and they learn to select the most efficient method for a particular task (this is probably learnt by doing).

But how do people go about acquiring such search knowledge? In order to learn to search efficiently they have to have some criterion of efficiency; they have to remember what they have done in order to avoid those actions which led to inefficiency or failure, and they have to discover what actions might be more fruitful.

In a study of learning by doing, Anzai and Simon analyse their data in more or less this way (Anzai & Simon 1979). The analysis is based on the problem of Tower of Hanoi, which was described in chapter 4 above. Their subject worked through the problem in four different episodes, which were analysed in great detail. In the first episode the subject adopted a selective method of search, by avoiding repeat moves. In the second episode the subject applied a fixed subgoal hierarchy, which is closely related to the structure of the Tower of Hanoi problem. In the two final episodes, the subject used recursive subgoals, a conceptualization that is still better suited to the problem.

The subject appeared to learn the strategies by using both conceptual and perceptual information. From the task instructions she derived task-dependent information of a conceptual kind. From perceptual observations in the task she derived information connected with the construction of subgoals. In the Tower of Hanoi problem it is easy for subjects to understand the concept of subgoals if they recognize that the pile of disks can be seen as a pyramid, which can be reduced by one disk at a time. Finally, Anzai and Simon's subject used prior information about classes of possible strategies to guide her search.

This result can be compared to those obtained in the investigation reported above, in which subjects were asked to change the position of numbers in a table. We received comments from several subjects indicating that they found the method inefficient. The subjects did not like having to follow the same sequence of commands over and over again, just in order to move a row of figures. The reported comment of subject 4 above is a good example of this.

At the same time as the subjects seemed unhappy about having to provide so many commands, they sought for alternatives, mainly by looking in the manual.

Subject 26

"I can't find anything else. Maybe I read carelessly."

Also, they seemed to feel that trying new alternatives was more of a bother than going on in the old safe but inefficient way.

Subject 45

"I'll do this the old way; I can't stand experimenting any more"

This comment raises the question of what criterion on efficiency users might adopt. The number of commands required by a particular approach hardly seems enough. Various other considerations must presumably be included in the efficiency calculus, concerning such things as the risk involved in trying new actions, the effort required in searching for new actions and to remember what actions have been performed.

Having to remember obviously presents a real problem, interfering with the performance, as the following comment shows.

Subject 33

"1. What did I do last time, when everything jumped so easily?

2. I took away a word, and everything moved one step to the left.

3. I'll move the cursor in any case.

4. What did I do?

5. I moved the whole row so easily.

(Makes a new attempt, moving the cursor backwards)

6. No, everything stays in the same place.

7. I can always try to move as usual."

Thus the subject remembers what she did before (comment 2), but forgets it immediately she's performed the preparatory action (comment 3).

It should also be pointed out, that not all subjects were dissatisfied with their actions. It was rather that they could not think of anything else to do. Their usual comments contained remarks like:

"Well, I just continue as before".

Sometimes they even remarked that the tasks were beginning to get boring, since "you have to do the same thing over and over again", but they did not consider any alternative action. Their conception of performing the task did not seem to include any idea of alternatives. They only thought about one action, which, once they had found it, was sufficient for their purpose. These subjects would not learn by doing unless they were forced to perform a task, in which the "old" action could no longer be used.

These examples and interpretations suggest that learning by doing in a word-processing task of this kind is rather different from learning by doing in the Tower of Hanoi task. The wordprocessing learners did not acquire much search knowledge even after 20 repeated tasks, whereas the learner in the Tower of Hanoi task had already found some new search strategies after only four attempts to solve the prescribed task.

Why is this so? A first explanation lies in the variety of the tasks concerned. The 20 tasks presented to the word-processing subjects included four repetitions of five different tasks. Even though the same general idea (the method to be learnt) could be used in 16 of the 20 tasks, there were still two different types of task to be learnt. The details of the task may have differed so much that the subjects were unable to benefit from general similarities. The Tower of Hanoi task on the other hand was presented on its own, without any variations. It could thus be claimed that search knowledge is learnt most easily by repeating exactly the same task over and over again.

The second explanation lies in the nature of the situation. In the Tower of Hanoi task the subject was in full control of the situation. The changes brought about by her actions could be fully predicted: if she moved a disk from one position to another, nothing else happened. In the wordprocessing task, subjects had to attend to new and unexpected developments in order to get information for increasing their search knowledge. But these happenings were either not observed (see above), or they distracted the subject's attention so that she forgot what she had just done (see comment of Subject 33).

Finally it should be noted that the distinction between the knowledge acquired with respect to formulating the problem space and the knowledge with respect to the search is mainly a didactical one. In real life, learning by doing means learning to understand the representation of the problem and learning to search simultaneously. This is obvious in the Tower of Hanoi case, where the idea of subgoaling is derived from the envisaging of the disks as a pyramid. It is also obvious in the wordprocessing case, where the most efficient method depends on understanding the representation of "blank signs".

This discussion of learning by doing suggests that several different factors lie behind the common observation that users fail to utilize the possibilites offered by computer systems. Users are not particularly interested in finding the quickest way to perform a task, since their efforts in trying to find it might detract their attention from the task itself to the detriment of their performance. "Efficiency" cannot be measured simply in terms of the number of commands used; it also has to be measured in perceived effort. Memory load and searching for alternatives both add to the sense of exertion.

Also, it should be noted that the user's chance of learning by doing may be fairly small, if the computer tasks vary a lot, or if the learning depends on observing "side-effects"—not to mention such an obvious condition of learning by doing as the "fool-proofness" of the system!

THE ROLE OF MENTAL MODELS OF COMPUTER SYSTEMS

In the field of human–computer interaction it has recently become very popular to talk about the users' "models of systems". This reflects the insight that a user's conception of a system may not correspond to the way the system actually works.

What is then meant by a model? The concept as currently used by researchers is prescientific. It is used to explain observations and to stir imagination, rather than to test hypotheses. There is no agreement on the definition of the model, on what it refers to or how it functions in the mental processes of the individual. We will therefore have to specify our conception of the definition, the usefulness and the content of a model before we can observe it and use it for making predictions.

In this section we will consider the definition and specification of the model concept and present some empirical data related to these questions.

Some characteristics of the "model" concept

First we should look at some of the different definitions of "model". However, for our purpose the dictionary does not give us much help with such definitions as:

— A person who poses
— A copy
— The original pattern according to which other items are made
— A miniature representation of a thing
    (selected examples from Webster's unabridged dictionary).

In psychology, the following definitions may be more useful, the first one suggested by Craik, (1943):

> "By a model we ... mean any physical or chemical system which has a similar relation-structure to that of the processes it imitates. By 'relation structure' I ...mean ... the fact that it is a physical working model which works in the same way as the processes it parallells, in the aspects under consideration at any moment...

> "My hypothesis then is that thought models, or parallells, reality—that its essential feature is not 'the mind', 'sense-data', nor propositions but symbolism, and that this symbolism is largely of the same kind as that which is familiar to us in mechanical devices which aid thought and calculation..."

The second is put forward by Chapanis, (1961):

"Models are analogies ... Scientific or engineering models are representations, or likenesses, of certain aspects of complex events, structures or
systems, made by using symbols or objects which in some way resemble
the thing being modeled".

Two points are essential in both definitions: the idea that a model represents
reality, i.e. is symbolic, and the idea that the model has a structure similar to
that of reality.

That a model should represent something which is to be modelled is unlikely
to cause much trouble (except if we believe in pure idealism). The similarity
aspect, however, is much more difficult to capture. What is similar between a
model and the thing modelled?

In a computer situation, when the reality to be modelled is dynamic, i.e. it
consists of goals to be reached and actions to be performed, there are at least
three aspects, in which we can envisage some similarity between model and reality, corresponding to the questions WHAT is performed, HOW is it performed,
and WHY does the thing modelled function as it does. In an individual's mental
model of a computer situation all these questions may be included.

The WHAT question refers to superficial performance: a music cassette gives
us music as does a grammophone record. The output is the same, although the
medium whereby the music is stored and retrieved in the two cases is quite
different. The test which Turing suggested for finding out whether computers
could behave like humans, consists of a WHAT question: let a computer and
a person both perform some action (answer questions, solve puzzles), and then
compare the performances. Most psychological work has been concerned with
modelling the *behaviour*, i.e. answering the WHAT question. Any model which
produces the same output as a human being has been regarded as a satisfactory
model of human performance. It should not be thought that it is easy to find
models which can generate the same output. If due attention is paid to the
conditions which must be fulfilled in order to comply with several behaviours,
the range of possible models may well be rather restricted. However, similarity
is judged exclusively in terms of the output. The rest is a "black box".

In a computer situation, a model based upon performance similarity contains
enough information to enable a user to understand the functional properties of
a system. When a wordprocessing system is compared to a typewriter, only superficial characteristics are considered. The keyboard is similar to a typewriter's
keyboard, the text on the screen is similar to a text on paper. This does not
mean that the typewriter is a sufficient model of all the functional properties
of a wordprocessing system, but it suffices to cover some of the functions. It
should be noted that this functional similarity does not include the processes by
which actions are performed, nor the underlying structure of the systems.

The next aspect of similarity concerns the HOW question, i.e. the processes
by which an action is performed. For any particular function it is much more

difficult to find a model which is similar to reality in its processes than to find one possessing functional similarity only.

We can take an example of human–computer interaction: The user of a wordprocessing system can find some processes which are similar in different systems. This applies only within the class of systems based on screen-editing or within the class of systems based on line-editing. Even here, the processes may differ greatly from system to system. For instance, in one system you always have to delete a text that you want to change as well as inserting the new text. Another system allows overwriting, whereby the unwanted text disappears at the same time as the overwriting action is performed. One system cannot be used as a model of the other where the process aspect is concerned. As regards the functional aspect, however, they may well be sufficiently similar to allow one to be modelled by the other.

Lastly, the WHY question concerns the underlying structure of the thing to be modelled. Only a model which is structurally similar to reality can answer the question WHY. This is an aspect of systems modelling, which few users have to bother with. It concerns the actual implementation of a system. The programming language, the methods for addressing memories, and allocating resources, as well as the particular hardware employed all answer the question WHY. We know that these details do not usually affect the functions a system can offer. They do not generally affect the processes either (from the point of view of the user). But they do matter a lot to those who have to get the systems to work. Even the users of small PCs must have at least some sort of fragmentary model of the apparatus they are using. They have to understand that disks may get full, that files may get overwritten and that it may not be possible to run some programs on their own particular computer. All these matters to some extent call for a model of structural aspects.

Users thus need and be able to use models which embrace functional and process similarities in relation to the reality being modelled.

What reality is covered by a system model?

The reality to be embraced by the user's mental model is the computer system. This reality is by no means well-defined, and we have to ask what is meant by the "computer system"? First it must be recognized that a computer system's reality differs from user to user; it can vary because of the way the computer is actually used. We can distinguish here between "outer tasks", which do not touch on the system itself, such as wordprocessing, book-keeping, database processing, and "inner tasks", concerned with handling the computer system itself. To a user engaged on an outer task, the computer reality is contained in the concepts and procedures required to perform the particular task. A user of a wordprocessing system will be primarily concerned with the reality of concepts such as words and lines, paragraphs and pages, and with corresponding activities such as typing, deleting, inserting, justifying, etc. This means that such a user hardly notes any difference between the "system" and the "task in the system".

The distinction between the "task in the system" and the "system" is likely to be more relevant for a computer programmer. His (or her) computer reality is very different from the reality encountered by an "ordinary" user. The outer task to be performed by a potential user involves just one of several possible functions which could be realized by the computer structure created by the system designer. Since he knows several systems, several programming languages, several operating systems, etc., he can make a choice about which reality to present to the users on a basis of this knowledge. The inner task will consist of getting the system to perform those functions.

Reality does not only differ in its content, but also in its scope. We should be very cautious in speaking of a "system model". Virtually no users will possess a model of the system as a whole (not even a systems programmer). Each user selects his own part of the task in the system reality for modelling. For instance, the user of a wordprocessing facility on a mainframe computer may need to use some parts only of the whole operating system, i.e. those that are for handling files and getting files printed. Nonetheless the user may have to handle a very involved reality in terms of wordprocessing. The system operator, on the other hand, may be more concerned with the operating system's reality and less concerned with the distinctions necessary in a wordprocessing task. Thus a system programmer may be familiar with many of the different inner tasks, but remain rather ignorant about the outer tasks.

This difference between the realities of system users engaged on different tasks, and even more between "end users" and system designers, gives rise to a corresponding disparity in their system models and their task models. These differences in individual models add to the problems of communication between these two groups of systems users.

We can thus conclude from the above that any consideration of users' "system models", must also take into account the reality to which the model refers.

The conceptual status of a mental model

When researchers and systems designers create models of systems or of users, the models are explicit. But what about users? Is the model an entity of which the users are aware? Or is it an implicit reality which represents unknown obstacles as well as invisible support?

Researchers and systems designers have used the concept of the mental model in different ways. But when it is claimed that users need system models in order to learn new systems (Halasz & Moran, 1983, Carroll & Thomas 1980), it is most probably explicit models that are meant.

Given that a model can resemble its modelled reality in different ways (in terms of functions, processes, or structures), one model can also enjoy varying conceptual status with respect to the different aspects. A model may be explicit in the functional dimension without being explicit as regards processes or structure. It may be explicit as regards processes but implicit as regards structure. It is also possible that people who can represent the structure of reality in a model, are nevertheless unaware of the consequences in terms of processes and functions.

In the following pages I will focus on mainly the effects of models as distinct conceptual entities. I thus look upon computer users as "creating" models, "understanding" models, and "comparing" models and observations. The explicit comparison may concern different aspects. At the same time I do not exclude the possibility that people simply act, without making any conscious represention of the relevant reality.

Functions of mental models

Models are not the same as reality. They are simply similar to reality in certain respects. Models can even be partly false, and still be useful. Which immediately evokes the question: Useful for what? What are models for? Why should anyone use a model? What needs does the model serve in our thought processes? Is a particular form of the model needed for a particular function?

Another quotation from Craik (1943) provides one answer.

> "If the organism carries a 'small-scale model' of external reality and of its own possible actions within its head, it is able to try out various alternatives, conclude which is the best of them, react to future situations before they arise, utilize the knowledge of past events in dealing with the present and future, and in every way to react in a much fuller, safer, and more competent manner to the emergencies which face it."

The functions suggested by Craik are related to the symbolic nature of the model. Without representation all we could do would be to act. We could never plan, decide, predict, or use prior knowledge. But Craik's description proposes no particular model requirements. And in fact any representation would serve for planning, decision-making, prediction and knowledge utilization. These functions can be fulfilled by a simple simulation of the superficial characteristics of reality just as well as by a sophisticated mathematical model generating the same superficial characteristics. But there are other functions that models can fulfill in our thought processes, in which the form of the model is important.

One example is problem solving, in which models can support the creation of problem spaces and the searching of such spaces. A model can suggest what operations are appropriate to the particular problem, and the conditions under which these operations can be performed. Some researchers have even suggested that the model can be regarded as the problem space, in which the problem solver operates (Halasz & Moran, 1983, Young, 1983). A major property of the model can be used to reduce the problem space: the model can simplify reality by leaving out irrelevant details, or by chunking concepts and procedures, thus reducing working memory load. The bigger the problem space, the more search is necessary, and the greater the risk of getting lost. The search in the problem space can be facilitated by models which serve as heuristics, or rules for searching. Thus models intended as an aid to problem solving should aim at reducing both the problem space and the search in that space.

In cases of skilled performance, models provide the user with efficient procedures. The user represents the conditions of efficient actions with the help of rules which specify what methods to use in order to achieve a particular goal in a particular situation (the GOMS rules presented in Chapter 4 above). It is possible that such rules may be automated to speed up performance. In such a case, the user is not aware of the model while performing the actions (awareness would slow down performance), but may still be able to talk about it before (in planning) or afterwards (in explaining to somebody else). These models enable users to "trigger" and "run" them automatically, but also allow users to develop the concepts in the model if necessary.

Another important function of models, for researchers as well as laymen, stems from the need for communication. People do not only work on problems or take actions, they also talk to each other about actions and problems. Communication represents one important way of getting to know about the world. If people are to understand one another, messages should be based on agreed and unequivocal concepts, and it should be possible for everyone engaged in the communication to handle the complexities of the problem.

A model which can perform these functions has to fulfill more severe requirements than one which is employed for personal purposes only. The model must be simple, yet expressive, it must be comprehensive, yet understandable, it must use conventional means of expression, yet cover the relevant aspects of the problem.

These characteristics of models are usually covered by natural language. In most ordinary life circumstances we can convey what we mean by natural language, even though natural language is vague and rather informal. This is due to the fact that we in an ordinary human conversation can always change our ways of expressing things when we find that our partner does not understand. If we want to be sure in advance that our message does not get misinterpreted, we have to be much more careful. We do not only have to choose our words carefully, we should also use consistent rules to combine them and for drawing conclusions, so that different people will make the same inferences. This requirement induces formality. By careful definition of concepts and careful choice of inference rules we can arrive at conclusions which we need not discuss, because they will always be valid. If we insist upon models being valid, we also have to formalize our definitions of concepts and rules. Thus the need to agree upon conclusions leads to the need for formalization.

Computers need formalization to a greater extent than people, because it is difficult or even impossible to supply a computer system with the same world knowledge as people posess. This poses problems for computer-naive people who are communicating on the subject of computer systems: they are simply unaccustomed to the formal way of expressing matters, which to them seems restricted and awkward. Even if the system designer can help by smoothing the interactions, their own indoctrination in formalization will make it difficult for them to explain formal models informally.

The last function of models to be discussed here is that of providing a spur to creative thinking. An important impulse to creative thinking is the perception of conceptual "gaps" or conflicts. How can models function in this way? We must remember that models are similar to, but not the same as reality. Some disparity will always remain between the model and the reality modelled. The difference may be less serious as regards some parts of reality and more serious as regards other. One model may be entirely appropriate to certain tasks, and quite unapplicable to others.

Since people often try to simplify things by using the same model in different situations, models are sometimes applied to parts of reality for which they were not originally intended. If a model does not fit a particular section of reality, the person will perceive a conflict. Conceptual conflict of this kind triggers conceptual activity. Different ways of resolving the conflict will be tested, both mentally and in practice. This is one of the chief ways in which science proceeds. But even our everyday thinking depends on this sort of conceptual activity. We have to question the range of application of models as well as the models themselves, and this in turn may mean that the range of reality represented and thus the models used will have to be changed.

The present-day computer user is quite likely to encounter conflict between the model he employs to understand the system and the output of the computer system. This may be due to inconsistencies in the system itself or inconsistencies between the system and its documentation, or to unwarranted assumptions on part of the user. Whatever its cause, this kind of conflict can start the user off on a creative train of thought about the system. He may ask himself: What if... and: Why not? Conflict may trigger exploratory activity, as well as attempts at creating new and better models. This may be one reason why many people become so fascinated by the idea of exploring the system rather than using it for any particular task, once they have overcome their first exaggerated respect for it.

Form of models

The different functions of models may need different forms, as I already hinted above. What kinds of forms can be suggested?

One dimension we have already encountered is degree of formality. On one end of that dimension we can suggest models which are vague in terms of how they relate to the reality modelled, and which also are vague in terms of which conclusions we may draw from them. Metaphors are examples of such vague models. On the other end of the formality dimension we find models with strictly defined concepts and explicit inference rules. Mathematical and logical models are examples of formal models. In the middle we have analogies, which may be regarded to be somewhat more formal than metaphors, if they are defined as structural isomorphs, as suggested by Gentner & Stevens (1983). Further towards formality we find models where the concepts have been defined but not the inference rules.

As already suggested above, formal models are needed for the purposes of drawing adequate inferences and for checking the validity of conclusions. On the other hand, informal and vague models may be better suited for educational purposes (to relieve working memory load) and for creative purposes. In some cases, reality might not in itself permit very formal models. There exist aspects of reality which are vague and which we might want to keep vague. The attempts to build formal but weaker models to cope with these aspects (fuzzy logics and non-modal logics for instance) attest to the need for both some degree of vagueness and some inconsistency.

The form of models may also differ in the presentation dimension. Models may be presented by pictures, sounds, verbal means, actions, and mathematical or logical functions. This dimension of models is particularly pertinent to the communicative and educational function. We find that different people prefer to conceive of different concepts in different forms. Some understand a conceptual argument in abstract terms, others have to construct it in very concrete terms before comprehending it. Many aspects of computer systems, such as conditional actions and procedures, iteration and recursion, have few concrete correspondents. Intermediary models have been suggested such as flow diagrams, structured graphs, etc. Since such models also are unfamiliar to computer-naive people, they do not facilitate the communication or education very much. The question of how to present computer concepts to computer-naive people has simply not yet been solved. People learn, for sure, but we do not know very much about how they learn in these particular situations.

The last dimension of form to be discussed here concerns the level of the model with respect to the reality covered. Models might differ by being more or less distant from the activity to be performed. In the same way as the request: "Open the window" does not quite specify HOW the window should be opened and might be difficult to follow for a man from Mars, the information in terms of a model like: "a wordprocessor is like a typewriter" is rather distant from that which you actually have to do in order to handle a wordprocessor. Clear procedural instructions like: "move the cursor to the word you want to delete and press the following keys: ctrl + O" are more informative for a beginning user. We might hesitate to name such explicit procedural instructions models. However, it is certainly possible that both novice and expert users themselves form local, procedural rules in order to cope with their tasks. The GOMS model (presented in Chapter 4 above) is one example of a procedural model, the contents of which has no claims for generality over tasks. Another example of a lower level model, yet which is useful, is Andrea diSessas "distributed model" (diSessa, 1986). These models are made up of multiple, partial explanations, which do not form a single, consistent conceptual model.

When people talk about "models" they often seem to imagine a more or less comprehensive model for a particular task. There are several situations, however, when there simply does not exist a single model to cover a task, particularly not in a computerized situation. It can then be asked what combination of general, not very well fitting models and specific, very explicit models, would serve users best. Research has just started towards understanding this aspect of models.

THE ROLE OF MODELS IN LEARNING COMPUTER SYSTEMS

It has often been suggested that the best way to introduce a new computer system is to draw an analogy between the computer and some similar situation that is familiar to the user. This is an example of how a conscious model may be used. It has also been found that even when they have been given no explicit model, users will try to find some analogy for themselves. A typical example of this is the wordprocessing system, which is often spontaneously compared to a typewriter.

The success of a particular model in a learning situation depends on the relation between the model and the thing to be learnt. First, we can ask ourselves how far the model is valid, i.e. leads to correct performance. Second, we can ask how complete the model is: does it cover all the necessary details ?

Validity of model

The question of validity seems fairly easy to answer: of course the given model must be valid. However, we have to remember that a model can never quite correspond to the computer system to be learnt. It is in the very nature of a computer system that it should present new opportunities, and so the analogy with something outside the computer situation will always be more or less misleading.

The analogy between typewriters and wordprocessing systems provides an illustration. With a wordprocessing system you can of course perform many more tasks than you can with a typewriter: you can type over what you have written, you can align paragraphs, and you can insert without having to worry about the length of the lines or the page.

What should we say about a model that is not altogether valid? Will it be helpful or harmful? Halasz & Moran (1983) suggest that several models may be needed in order to explain a computer system to a novice user, for instance, a filing cabinet model for modelling the management of files, and a guard analogy for modelling the use of passwords. At the same time they point out the possible danger of using models which are badly integrated with each other. Moreover, in any detailed consideration of computer systems analogical models might be dangerous by reason of their indeterminacy: the user may not know which characteristics in the analogy he can utilize in the new situation, and which are not relevant.

A study of models of varying task validity

I shall describe below a study which to some extent illustrates this point (Wærn & Rabenius, 1985). The aim was to discover which metaphor was more useful for learning a wordprocessing system, the typewriter metaphor or a building-block metaphor. Figure 28 illustrates the typewriter metaphor.

The typewriter metaphor included comparisons with a typewriter: "A wordprocessing system is like a typewriter. You can type a text by tapping the keys. If you want to correct something, you can delete and type over at a single stroke".

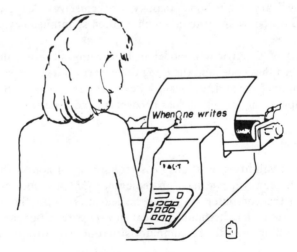

Figure 28 A typewriter metaphor of a wordprocessing system.

The building-block metaphor included comparisons with the production of a text using letters written on building blocks (Figure 29). "You can insert new text by putting in blocks with new letters, and you can delete text by taking blocks away. Changing a letter is the equivalent of exchanging one block for another." Figure 29 illustrates this metaphor.

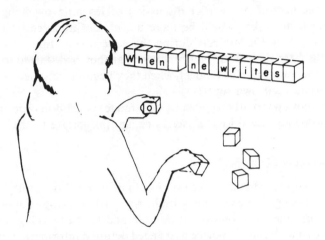

Figure 29 A building-block metaphor of a wordprocessing system.

It can now be claimed that the typewriter metaphor is more valid than the building-block metaphor when the required tasks are comparable with those performed on a typewriter. There is greater similarity between the wordprocessor's keyboard and the typewriter than between building blocks and a keyboard, and the output is more like lines on paper than rows of building blocks. Such tasks would include any in which words or letters are altered within a line.

The building-block metaphor would be more applicable to tasks requiring the spatial rearrangement of lines or parts of lines. The insertion of a new building block means pushing other blocks in the direction of an empty space, i.e., in a text, to a space where nothing has yet been written.

Two groups of subjects were each presented with one of these metaphors and with different tasks that were closer to one or the other of the metaphors. The results showed no difference in performance times between the groups, neither in the case of tasks seeming closer to the typewriter metaphor nor for others closer to the building-block metaphor. However, the typewriter metaphor led to shorter manual reading times during the first two of four blocks consisting of tasks requiring text changes with no particular spatial component. This result suggests that the typewriter metaphor was easier to use to start with and when tasks resembling typewriter tasks were being performed.

The result also shows that subjects fairly soon detected the differences between the model and the actions required. Their post-experimental comments demonstrate that some of them began to form models of their own, in which the proposed metaphor was supplemented with further low-level details.

In the spatial tasks, which were similar to the alignment of figures in a table, presented on page 83, many subjects failed to notice the feedback from the system altogether (cf our earlier discussion of learning by doing). Here the building-block metaphor would be more useful, but apparently its usefulness was not noticed by the subjects during the experiment. Interestingly enough, some months later several subjects reported that they had started to employ and appreciate the building-block model, when they began using the wordprocessing system to write their own reports.

Thus it is not apparently sufficient that a model is valid in order to be useful. It must also be perceived by the user as being appropriate to the task at hand.

The completeness of the model

It might be expected that a novice user would be worried by a full description of a system at his very first encounter with it. After all, working memory is limited, and models are meant to reduce rather than add to the working memory load. At the same time, however, novice users need detailed information of the system if they are to get it to function at all. It is thus important to consider what level of detail will be most useful to novice users.

The study we have just been discussing included an experimental variation intended to illustrate this question. Groups of subjects were given manuals containing varying amounts of detail. One manual was restricted to information about possible commands and their effects. This manual (which we can describe as functional) used phrases on the lines of: "Push .... and you will get ...." The other manual included certain explicit procedures for performing specific tasks. This manual (which we can describe as procedural) used phrases such as: "If you want to .... and the situation is .... then do as follows ..."

In the first part of the study, the subjects were given tasks which in principle could be solved by using the procedures described in the procedural manual. It was expected that novices receiving the procedural manual would solve the editing problems more quickly than subjects who had to combine the given commands themselves before they could perform the tasks. In the event, however, there was no difference in the time used to solve the tasks compatible with the procedural manual but there was a significant difference in the time used to read the manuals and this difference was in the direction opposite to that expected: subjects receiving the procedural manual took more time to read it than subjects receiving the functional manual.

This result may be explained by the fact that the procedural manual contained more information than the functional manual. Describing a whole procedure takes longer than describing the effects of single commands. However, at the same time, it must have taken the subjects longer to find the correct command in the functional manual than in the procedural manual, and we must therefore conclude that detailed procedures may not provide users with more help than would functional information sufficient for solving the tasks, given that the user engages in a certain amount of problem solving of his own. It may even take users longer to process the detailed information.

In the case of tasks which were not compatible with the procedural manual, it was expected that subjects would take longer to read this manual. They would need more time both to find the relevant information and to read the instructions provided. The results agreed with the hypothesis.

We concluded from this experiment that users do not need complete models of the tasks they are to perform. Rather, they should have models furnishing enough information to solve a range of tasks which they might encounter. Thus it seems that it may be more helpful to prepare a system and a systems documentation to support the user's problem solving activities rather than trying to provide complete instructions covering every possible detail.

How users think about their models

The model with which the user is provided does not necessarily correspond to the one the user creates while working with the system. It can therefore be interesting to consider the models that users actually have. One way of investigating these models is to ask users to describe the system. This naturally requires not only that the users have a model, but also that they are able to communicate it.

In an investigation reported by van der Veer (1985), users of a new accounting system were asked to describe the system to some other people. It appeared from these accounts of the system that users employed models associated with different levels, roughly the equivalent of the levels suggested in Moran's command language grammar (1981), to be described in Chapter 7. The model of the system was sometimes described in terms of the task to be performed (task level), or according to the objects and procedures which could be used (semantic level), or according to the commands to be used (syntax level), or according to the input made and feedbacks obtained from the system (interaction level).

In another study from our laboratory, using the same wordprocessing system already described, users were asked afterwards to describe their experience of the system in terms of advice to a novice user. This time the users were presented with a typewriter metaphor at the start and a manual, restricted to descriptions of commands and their effects (i.e. a functional manual). The task was to correct a table of digits, in which one row was out of alignment with the others (cf page 83).

Some examples from this study may serve to illustrate the contents of the

systems models which users consciously employ and their ability to communicate these models to other people.

First some comments indicating a task and semantic level, modelled as a
metaphor:

Subject 45

"It is important to remember, that it really works like a typewriter".

Subject 46

"You can look at the system like this: imagine you have some blocks lying
here, and then you take away one block and push in another."

It is interesting to note that subject 46 produced a building-block model, although she had been told that the wordprocessing system resembled a typewriter. We found in interpreting her learning by doing protocols that this insight
was gained by her attempts to solve the spatial alignment tasks.

It is also worth noticing that the insight gained by subject 45 (see think-aloud
comment below) was that it was possible to type over in order to correct single
signs and words. Therefore, her model got more similar to a typewriter model.

The following comments reveal an understanding that the wordprocessing
system deviates from the typewriter metaphor when it comes to functional details:

Subject 47

"It's different from a typewriter because you can't just type over on a
typewriter; you have to rub out first. And you can move lines sideways,
and you can make empty lines and move lines downwards, and all kinds
of splendid things you can't do on a typewriter. And it goes much faster,
because you can rub out whole words directly, and whole rows you can
rub out just by pushing some keys."

Subject 44

"You can take away something and it will still be there. That's not possible on a typewriter."

(Experimenter: what do you mean by "it's still there?")

"I mean, you can move things, and they'll still be there. That's not possible
on a typewriter. On a typewriter you have to delete things first."

And here is a comment which indicates that the model of the typewriter is sometimes changed as well:

Subject 44

"And here in the wordprocessing system you can regard a space as a letter or a sign. It's not the same on a typewriter. Or maybe you can look at it in the same way there, too".

And here are some comments which indicate the importance of understanding the relation between functions and procedures:

Subject 44

"It says in the manual that a sign may be a letter, a figure or a blank. But then the problem is, what is the blank? I realized that I should put in a blank, but I did'nt not know which key to press."

Subject 45

"It says in the manual that you can change single signs just by typing over them . It took me a very long time before I could do that. I was concentrating so hard on using the commands instead."

It is also obvious that users try to create models which provide principles applicable to different situations:

Subject 46

"If I want to push a line to the right, then I need some more blocks. Delete means take away. What's the corresponding command for "add"?

(Experimenter: insert)

"Insert. (The subject tries by giving the command: Insert)

"Nothing happened!"

"Perhaps I have to know how much to add, like in delete" (Tries the command: Insert 3)

"It moved!"

"It's stupid that you have to know how many you've got to move, instead
of having some sort of form, so you could see. . ."

Note: Subject 46's comments show that this user's model allows her to use the
blocks both for the delete and the insert command. She has not yet detected,
however, that the principle does not hold in all its details. In the delete command
you can tell how many spaces or signs to delete by giving a figure. The command
"delete 3" will delete three signs. In the insert command, however, you have
to tell exactly WHAT to insert (not how much). This subject's block model
induces her to think in terms of "moving", which also makes her discover that
the figures have moved. At the same time it is interesting to note that she did
not discover that the figure "3" was inserted where she had the cursor.

These comments suggest that novice users create systems models at several
different levels. They may try to formulate a new metaphor model, even though
they have been presented with a different one (cf the subject formulating the
building-block model). They may also discover differences between the model
that has been given and the actual system, as regards both functions and procedures. And, finally, they are dependent on models which are directly related to
the procedures to be performed and to the effects of these procedures. "Changing words" and "moving" are functions for which they have to find the best
procedures.

It is interesting to note in this context that some subjects had problems with
very simple procedures, here the "typing over" procedure. As Subject 45 expressed it: "I was concentrating so hard on using the commands". This comment
indicates that the user had a model of the wordprocessing system which was
related to a model of a computer: you have to use commands, it cannot be as
simple as just typing over!

We can also see that the subjects' model of the system depends on tasks
they have performed before. They have worked on problems requiring them to
"move" digits on the screen, and this is reflected in the way they talk about the
system in terms of "moves".

It should also be pointed out that the subjects found it rather difficult to
describe their idea of the system. When asked to suggest some guidelines for
novice users, they could only think of advice like: "just try as many different
alternatives as you can think of!" or "work slowly and systematically". And
even these comments came after considerable prodding on the part of the experimenter. These difficulties suggest either that the model was not conscious
enough to be communicable, or that it is difficult to communicate a model of
the system without describing a particular task.

It seems probable that, to start with, a user's systems model is not formulated
as a distinct entity of which the user herself is aware. Instead, the model may
simply consist of certain implicit assumptions. One such assumption was sug-

gested above: a wordprocessing system must be much more complicated than an ordinary typewriter. These implicit assumptions may then prevent the novice users from utilizing all the possibilities of a given system. Once a model has been explicitly formulated (to yourself or to others), it is much easier to check it against data, and to change it if inconsistencies are detected.

SUMMARY

General learning principles

In this chapter we started by looking at some general principles of learning. A distinction was made between declarative and procedural learning. We found that learning facts by a "bottom-up" method is slow, taking about 5–10 seconds per "chunk". If learning can take advantage of prior knowledge using a top-down method, much can be gained by transferring familiar knowledge and principles to the new situation. However, there is a risk that conflicting or inappropriate knowledge may interfere with the new material to be learnt.

Procedural learning passes through three stages, a declarative stage in which the steps of a procedure are learnt one by one, an associative stage in which the sequence of subactions are combined into a coherent procedure, and an autonomous stage in which the procedure is refined into a learned skill.

Forgetting can be regarded as related to difficulty in retrieval. The number of cues common to the retrieval situation and the learning situation is crucial to the amount of material that can be retrieved.

To a great extent the particular nature of learning computerized tasks requires "learning by doing", in which the principles of transfer from prior knowledge, problem solving and mental model formation will be of vital importance.

Transfer of prior knowledge

In the course of learning, prior knowledge that resembles the situation at hand will be evoked, intentionally or unintentionally. The present task will evoke similar task knowledge, while non-task-related features of the current situation may also evoke prior knowledge provided these traits are sufficiently similar to concepts or actions familiar to the user.

Prior knowledge can be described in terms of rules about the actions required in order to achieve a specific goal under specific conditions.

The transfer of prior knowledge to a new situation will facilitate learning, provided that the actions to be performed as well as the prevailing goal and conditions are similar to those in the earlier situation. But transfer will delay learning when goals and conditions are similar but the required actions are different.

Learning by problem solving

When users learn a computer system by experimenting with it, they learn to understand the nature of the problem space as well as learning to search in it.

In order to grasp the nature of the problem space, learners must vary their actions, observe unexpected results, and interpret these results.

In order to learn to search in the problem space, learners must evaluate the outcomes of actions, remember actions performed, and recognize that other paths apart from the accustomed ones are also possible.

Mental model formation

The definition of a model can be summarized under two points: 1) a model represents some part of reality, and 2) in some respects it resembles that part of reality.

There are three respects in which the model may resemble reality: 1) as regards function, in which case only the output of the system process is modelled; 2) as regards process, in which the steps in the processes are mapped; and 3) as regards structure, in which case the structure generating the process is mapped into the model.

The user of a computer system needs models for planning, problem solving, communicating and learning. A model is particularly useful in problem solving if the problem space can be simplified and the search facilitated. Other model functions are connected with communicating ideas and stimulating creative thinking.

The form of the model varies in several dimensions. We may distinguish between formal and informal models, between concrete and abstract models and between models on different levels. Different particular forms may be needed for different purposes and persons.

When novices are learning new computer systems, the teaching model not only has to be valid with respect to the required task, it also has to be familiar in some way in order to be understood.

Finally, novice users apparently create models of systems on several different levels. They experiment with small-scale attempts at using and understanding the system, and they try to fit these attempts into some kind of familiar metaphor which may encompass many of the details.

Chapter 6

Individual Differences

In the previous chapters human cognition has been described in general terms. However we have already noted that people differ in their cognitive performance. Their sensorimotor characteristics can vary as well as their knowledge. People differ both in problem-solving capacity, strategies, and cognitive skills. The time has now come to ask ourselves which of these individual differences must be considered in designing systems. Is it possible to make any recommendations about adapting system design to individual characteristics?

STABILITY OF HUMAN DIFFERENCES

To be able to adapt system design to user differences, we have to find variables which have a certain degree of stability as between different tasks and different situations. Table 4 lists a suggested dimension of stability (van Muylwijk, van der Veer & Wærn, 1983).

Table 4.   A dimension of stability, from most to least stable

Stable, resistant to change	
Personality factors	Intelligence Extroversion/introversion Fear of failure Creativity(?)
Cognitive style	Field (in)dependence Visual/verbal Impulsive/reflective
Learning style	Heuristic/systematic Operation/ comprehension learning
Personal knowledge	Schemata Semantic network Production rules
Changeable by influence from the outside world	

113

This table suggests some attributes which may be changeable to a greater or lesser extent. The closer to the top it lies, the more stable and less changeable the attribute. These ideas are based on attempts to educate people in certain attributes (van der Veer, 1983). It is very difficult to change intelligence, for instance, at least so long as the knowledge content, which is easily changeable, is controlled. It is difficult to change fear of failure, and extroversion/introversion are considered by some researchers to be fairly stable traits (cf Eysenck, 1967).

Cognitive styles appear to determine ease of learning to some extent, and may thus be considered responsible for the interactions between treatments and aptitudes which are sometimes found in educational research. Learning strategies are more easily changed, and personal knowledge naturally changes with learning.

SYSTEM-RELATED INDIVIDUAL DIFFERENCES

Let us now consider how we might use our knowledge about individual differences for predicting a particular user's need in a particular system. Here we know very little about how individual attributes are related to different characteristics of the system, but it seems likely that personal knowledge of computer systems and the tasks to be performed in the systems are related most closely to acceptance, learning, and performance in new computer systems.

Let us therefore start with some general comments on how users' prior knowledge may affect their approach to a computer system.

Users' prior knowledge

Different kinds of knowledge will be used in a computer system: knowledge about the task to be performed, knowledge about the system as such and knowledge about the system as a tool for the task. To simplify matters somewhat, we can say that programmers usually have a good deal of knowledge about the system as such, but little knowledge about the task—or the system as a tool for the task. Task experts on the other hand may know how to perform the task as such, but not how to use the system to support task performance. As they gain experience with a particular system, they learn to use it as a tool for their task, which does not mean that they learn very much about the system as such. The closer the system is to application, the less its user will learn from it about the pure computer aspects of the system.

This means that different computer systems will require different prior knowledge in order to be used efficiently. We can say that the critical aspect concerns the match between the system's requirements and the prior knowledge of the user. It is thus far too simplistic to talk about "expert" or "novice" users of a system.

Let us then consider what kinds of prior knowledge might help or hinder the learning and use of a computer system. First, those parts of prior knowledge which can be relevant in using the system can be regarded as being "transferred" to the new situation, thus facilitating the learning of it. This positive transfer effect has been demonstrated in several studies (cf chapter 5). Second, those parts of prior knowledge that come into conflict with the new system to be learnt will also be invoked, and will thus hinder the learning. The negative transfer effect may concern higher-order concepts, methods, or very simple automated habits, which were discussed in chapter 5.

It is impossible to say at present what prospective users of computer systems need to know in order to be prepared for using the systems in an optimal way. About ten years ago it was much easier—the recommendation of learning programming was a good one. Nowadays, when so many good application systems exist, it is difficult to envisage any general advice for "computer education". Rather, systems should perhaps be designed to allow for different types of prior knowledge. How this could be solved will be discussed below, after we have looked at some other possibly interesting individual aspects of variability.

Users' cognitive and learning styles

Another aspect which may not seem to have as much direct bearing on the actual use of a computer system, concerns cognitive and learning styles. But since all users have to start by learning the computer system, individual differences on these counts may have some bearing on designing systems which are "easy to learn" by different types of people.

The learning styles known as "systematic" and "heuristic" problem-solving refer to the way people learn by doing. Systematic people use abstract logical models or schemata, whereas heuristic learners use past experience and intuition (Bariff & Lusk, 1977). But it should also be remembered that the tasks may differ: some are well-structured and best handled by a systematic approach, others are unstructured and difficult to analyse. Simple programming tasks are well-structured and may well profit from a systematic approach. Decision-making tasks in an uncertain environment are ill-structured and may profit from a more heuristic approach.

An example of the effect of different approaches is given in one study where it was found that students on a computer course used more systematic approaches to mathematical and logical problems than students on psychology courses (Wærn, El-Khouri, Olofsson & Scherlund, 1986). Psychology is certainly a subject which encourages intuitive approaches based upon experience rather than on systematic search. So long as computer systems are built mainly with a view to handling well-structured problems in systematic ways, people of a more intuititive or heuristic bent may be at a disadvantage in handling computer systems. But people can learn, and this particular learning style is amenable to change, as has been shown by de Leeuw (1983).

Another cognitive style is referred to by the concepts of "operation" versus "comprehension" learning, which derive from work on Gordon Pask's conversation theory (1976), and have been adapted for use in human–computer interaction by van der Veer and Beishuizen (1987). These researchers found that individual differences in structuring and storing information proved to be relevant to tasks which were concerned with handling the computer itself (such as programming or system design). Perhaps students in computer science should thus be trained in a learning mode known as "versatile", preparing them to choose between operation learning or comprehension learning depending on the particular situation and the nature of the learning material.

Field (in)dependence has also been suggested as an important factor of individual difference relevant to all sorts of situations, and one having both cognitive and social effects (Witkin, Dijk, Faterson, Goodenough & Karp, 1962). Field independence tests have been used in the selection of air pilots, for instance. This factor refers to people's susceptibility to contextual clues, or their ability to see a figure separately from its background. Field-dependent people tend to be influenced by context, while the field-independent are relatively unaffected by this tendency. However, van der Veer and van der Wolde (1982) have shown that if general intelligence is controlled, the difference disappears. Nor has the possible relevance of this factor to computer situations been investigated.

The possible importance of a preference for a visual or a verbal representation, on the other hand, has been the subject of much debate since the advent of the "direct manipulation systems" (cf Chapter 12). Are there perhaps certain people (visualizers) who prefer direct manipulation with icons, while other kinds of people (verbalizers) prefer to approach systems by using verbal commands? The representational difference has been held responsible for differences in behaviour in cases where information could be handled in either way (Paivio, 1971). However, there is very little evidence as yet of its importance in human–computer interaction (Preece, 1982, Gerstendörfer & Rohr, 1987).

A tendency towards reflective or impulsive behaviour may well have implications for programming and for approaches to learning in computer situations. A reflective individual will reflect upon the problem more and will evaluate more alternatives than an impulsive person. Thus reflective people may cause less trouble to the system and make fewer errors, but they will also take longer to solve simple problems. Impulsiveness may be a hindrance to some computer tasks, at least to such tasks as require the consideration of several alternatives before action can be initiated. The tendency to react too quickly can be overcome, however, as research on impulsiveness in children has shown (Zelniker and Oppenheimer, 1973).

Stable personality characteristics

One characteristic that is fairly stable, regardless of the task, is general intelligence. General intelligence naturally changes as children develop, a fact to which due allowance has been made by the designers of computer-aided instruction. But only recently has the problem been tackled of building an interface to suit younger children for other purposes, for instance in learning to program. One might suppose that programming requires a higher level of intelligence, corresponding to Piaget's "formal reasoning" stage. However, Papert's development of the easy programming language "LOGO" (Papert, 1980), and other evidence from teaching children to tackle programming problems (Lawler, du Boulay, Hughes, & Macleod, 1986), indicate that programming can be simplified by paying due attention to the kind of people who will be using the programming language.

Introversion and extroversion constitute a well-known personality dimension (Eysenck 1967, 1977), which can be further divided into sociability and stress-tolerance. Extroverted people are more sociable and have a higher tolerance of stress. It might be expected that such people would find it easier to accept a computer system with threatening error messages, such as: "Fatal error in pass zero". Other people, less able to tolerate stress, would probably stop using such a system unless they had to. It could of course be claimed that no computer system should scare any user off, so it is not necessary to consider this dimension in terms of individual differences.

A related personality characteristic is the fear of failure, whereby the negative fear of failure can cause certain individuals to under-achieve. People who fear failure are afraid of competition. If the competition aspect is removed, their work will improve. In the classroom use of computers, the competition aspect may be more prominent than it is in solo use. It has been found that people with a high negative fear of failure can be helped if the situation is structured for them. These people will also need more help facilities than other people. They also benefit from learning algorithms rather than heuristics (de Leeuw & Welmers, 1978). These recommendations also seem applicable to the designing of an appropriate computer interface.

Lastly, creativity has been regarded as a stable attribute. In computer use, creativity is useful in designing systems and solving problems. However, in performing ordinary tasks such as editing or calculating, creativity is neither a hindrance nor a virtue. Present-day computer systems may be too restrictive to cope with the needs of creative users in situations which encourage or require creativity. Such users may also be impatient of accepting the fact that different systems have different operating systems, command languages, and interaction rules. It would be a pity to exlude creative people from the pool of potential users!

IMPLICATIONS FOR HUMAN–COMPUTER INTERACTION

From the above review of diverse individual variations and their possible importance in human–computer interaction, we can discern the following implications.

The least stable characteristic, i.e. user experience, is the one which is most useful in making recommendations about the design of systems. When it comes to the other individual differences, however interesting they may be, we know too little as yet about their relevance to the computer situation. However, research on these questions is under way, and new knowledge will probably be acquired. This means that user experience should be allowed for in designing user interfaces to computer systems. But how can this be done?

Several different ways have been suggested.

One way is to let the user define his interface himself, so that he could use the kind of commands, symbols or interactions he is used to. This approach calls for a user who understands what he wants to do, and only needs to change the names of the known functions. However, this would be impractical when several users collaborate in learning a particular system. The communication between users will be hindered if every user has a set of symbols of his own (the Tower of Babel syndrome).

An apparently attractive research idea just now involves adapting the system according to the user more or less automatically. This approach is more difficult than the one we have just described. It not only requires some parapsychological powers on the part of the system designer, who has to predict what the user might need, but also requires the system to detect the important attributes of the user to which the system is supposed to adapt. But diagnosing the user is no simple task, at least not if the diagnosis relies solely on evidence from the user's interactions with the system (cf Desmarais, Larochelle, & Giroux, 1987, Desmarais & Pavel, 1987). Also, of course, the adaptation of the system should not take place in a way that surprises the user, who is struggling to learn about the computer system.

A better idea might therefore be to adapt not the system itself but its meta-communication according to the level of knowledge of the user. It might be easier to build an "explanatory shell" to take care of differences, than to build a totally new system. Many systems incorporate a facility by which the user can decide how much help information he wants about system use. This help information is mainly concerned with handling the interface, and very little help can be obtained about the tool aspect of the system (cf chapter 15). Much more can be done in this respect if knowledge of the task (and not solely of the system) is taken into consideration and if we want to adapt variations to the cognitive and personality style of the users. Field-dependent people might require some characteristic marking of the help and error messages, for instance, so as not to confuse them with the communications about performing the task. Impulsive people might need to be reminded to check their acts before doing them (the warning: "Do you really want to delete all your files?" may not be enough).

SUMMARY

This chapter addresses the issue of how individual differences matter to human–computer interaction. Do different kinds of users require different kinds of computer interfaces?

It first asks, what are the human differences that are most stable, and it is suggested that general intelligence, extroversion/introversion, fear of failure and eventually creativity are the most stable personal traits, whereas personal knowledge is the least stable characteristic. Cognitive and learning style lie in the middle.

Starting with personal knowledge, the most relevant for the use of computers are experience with computers, computer interfaces and computer languages. Although these are easy to change, they will matter a lot for how easy to learn and how easy to use a particular system will appear to a particular user.

The cognitive and learning style differences may matter to the learning of computers, in that they influence how different users will approach the task of learning the system.

The adaptation of systems to individual differences may take place in different ways: through customization by the users themselves, through automatic adaptation of the system to the users, and through adaptation of the metacommunication of the system to the users.

Part II. The Task Perspective

Chapter 7

A General Frame of Reference

In this part I shall analyse human–computer interaction in a task perspective. In other words, the focus will be on situations in which a task expert interacts with a computer system in order to perform a particular task. For the purpose of the analysis it is assumed that the subject is in control of the situation, that he is responsible for the input data, and that he interacts frequently with the computer.

The following concepts will be introduced:

— Task
— Division of labour between task expert and computer system
— The task expert's model of the task versus the system designer's
— Communication and metacommunication between user and computer system
— Models of the communication partner.

The first chapter, the general frame of reference, will form a basis for concepts and ideas to be exemplified and analysed further in later chapters, where I shall analyse some various tasks which have already received computer support, i.e. producing and editing text, information retrieval, transferring knowledge and designing mechanical objects.

(Note: for the sake of brevity I shall refer below to "system" when I mean the total system of hardware, application software and interface with which a user interacts when using a computer. From the user's point of view, the "system" is equivalent to "what can be done in the system" and what is accessible through the system interface. From the system designer's point of view, the "system" comprises the programs for handling the task in the system as well as the interface.)

A GENERAL OVERVIEW

Figure 30 provides an overview of the concepts which are central to an analysis

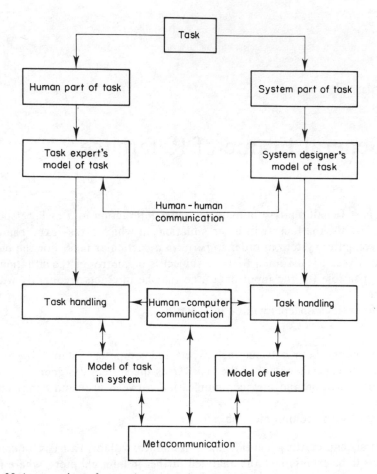

Figure 30 An overview of central concepts in human–computer interactions.

of human–computer interaction. I shall first present the concepts rather broadly, following this with a deeper analysis.

It is suggested that human–computer interaction should be analysed with reference to a task. The task is therefore located at the top of the figure. Some part of the task at least has to contain an information-processing component (otherwise a computer system would not be involved).

The next level of boxes refers to the division of labour between task expert and system. Some parts of the total tasks are performed by the task expert, others by the system.

The task may be conceived differently by the system designer and the task expert. Therefore the next two boxes represent the task expert's versus the system designer's model of the task. In order to sort out eventual discrepancies, task experts and system designers should communicate with each other—captured by the link denoted "human–human communication".

In order to be able to collaborate on the task, the subject and the system have to communicate with each other. This is captured by linking "human–computer communication" to the human task handling and the system's task handling.

The next level incorporates the recognition that users will entertain certain ideas about the computer as a tool in the task and that system designers will entertain certain ideas about the intended users and their needs. The mutual models are necessary if each side is to know what to expect of the other and if they are both to understand each other's actions.

Finally, at the bottom of the figure is a box called "metacommunication" with an arrow running between user and system and another pointing to the communication box. This concept refers to "communication about communication". The term metacommunication refers to all explicit information about a system: manuals, instructions, help messages and error messages.

Let us now examine in turn each part of the figure in greater detail.

THE TASK

A task has been defined as: "The achievement of a set of goals while maintaining a set of constraints" (Filkes, 1982). In a computer situation, the task expert evaluates the situation and decides which goals to achieve. He is responsible for initiating work on the task, choosing methods and tools for working on the task, and for evaluating the results of the work performed. The computer system is one of the tools used.

In some cases the task expert knows exactly what to do and when and how to evaluate the results. In such cases we can say that the task is routine. In other cases the expert may be uncertain about the operations to choose in any particular instance, and these cases can be designated as problem-solving situations. Finally, there may be cases in which the goal is not altogether well-defined and one of the most important contributions of the task expert is to create and identify a satisfactory result. These situations can be described as creative.

Obviously not all task experts will be helped by using a computer system. The task must naturally include an information-processing component which is complex enough to warrant the investment of time and money required to install and learn a computer system. Further, the problem involved in the information-processing component should be possible to solve with familiar methods.

If we look at current applications of interactive computing, we find a plethora of tasks which have been "computerized". From the start, computers were used (in batch mode) for calculations and data handling, applications which can nowadays be treated in an interactive way. New tasks amenable to computerization have been found since the advent of interactive computing. Wordprocessing and office automation represent the entry of computers onto the office stage. CAD systems have introduced interactive computing to engineers, some of whom may already have been accustomed to computers as calculating machines. Information retrieval from big databases is one of the standard methods used by business managers as well as researchers. Finally, we should not forget that the handling of a computer system may in itself represent a task in which another computer system may be used. Programming, system designing and system maintenance are tasks in which the experts are not only concerned with computers; they are using computer systems as tools—be it a question of new programming languages or new system development methods.

It is now time to ask ourselves whether the introduction of a computer into a particular task does not alter the task itself. The computer may introduce new goals and new operations. This is the case for instance when a wordprocessing system makes it possible to produce a text with straight right margins. Database systems in business may tempt managers to store more data than should really be necessary, then a new goal, i.e. trying to reduce the information overload produced by the system, is introduced. The system may change a routine task into a problem-solving one, as happens when an advanced wordprocessing system is used for simple letter-writing. It may change a problem-solving task into a routine one, as happens when a difficult diagnosis is performed by a computer system, working with expert rules. For a task expert, it may be desirable that the task itself should remain as similar to the "old" task as possible, and that the computer be regarded as just another tool for performing one of the operations in the task. This tool may be more efficient than others, but should not change the character of the task.

It has to be recognized that many task experts work on this (unconscious) assumption, i.e. that a computer system is no more than another tool to apply to their ordinary task. The consequences of this view are several.

First, the expert will continue to divide the labour between himself and the computer in the same sort of way that he has done in the case of other tools, such as electronic calculators or typewriters or other colleagues such as secretaries or assistants. This may mean that after the introduction of a computer the task expert has more "spare time" (i.e. the computer is more efficient than the old tools) that has to be filled in some way. This is almost certain to change his overall task.

Secondly, the task expert will define the use of the computer in relation to the task. However, the system designer may define the task in terms of what the computer can easily accomplish. This means that there may be a difference between the task model of the user and that of the system designer.

Thirdly, when the expert defines the task domain in terms of the characteristics of the "old" task, he may miss the opportunity for exploiting the new capabilities provided by the computer system. A CAD system, for example offers many more opportunities than those offered by an ordinary drawing board.

Thus, it can be seen that it is no easy matter to define the "task" when a computer system is introduced. On the one hand, there is one or possibly more than one task in which the computer can be used as a tool. On the other hand, once a computer system has been introduced it may be used for other tasks, which had not been thought of before the advent of the system. For the sake of simplicity I shall limit myself in this chapter to the existing task, leaving the new opportunities that arise to a later examination.

DIVISION OF LABOUR

Let us now turn to the division of labour between human and computer (Figure 31). What parts do we want the computer to perform? And who should decide what to do in a particular instance?

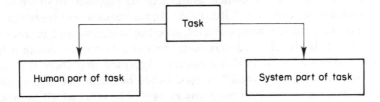

Figure 31 The division of labour part of Figure 29.

The answers to this question can vary. Do different solutions have different effects on the efficiency of the human–computer system as a whole? How do different solutions affect user satisfaction with the computer systems?

We can see the division of labour as a continuum of alternative allocations of function, from complete automation to solely administrative support from the system (Eason et al., 1987). In Eason's scheme, the functions are divided according to a tradition in ergonomics (cf Singleton, 1974), into those concerned with specifying need, developing and checking. At the totally automated end, the user only specifies the need, whereas the system develops a solution to serve the need and checks the results. In the middle, both the user and the system may develop the solution, whereas the user specifies the need and checks the results. At the end of administrative support, the system supports the user by listing and printing results, storing data, etc., whereas the user performs most of the functions.

We can now ask how different tasks could be placed along this continuum. In Table 5 some different aspects of tasks are listed. The aspects to the left are those in which a human being would prefer to perform most work. The aspects to the right are those where the computer could preferably take over most of the work.

Table 5. Different aspects which may affect division of labour

People prefer or are good at	Computer good at
Creative tasks	Repetitive tasks
Intuitive problem solving	Algorithmic problem solving
Low need for precision	High need for precision
Advanced check	Routine check

To my knowledge little research has been done which can help us to decide how responsibility and labour may be satisfactorily divided between human and computer. Some general recommendations can be proposed in order to guard against probable accidents (cf Price, 1985). In the cases where there is a choice it is claimed that human beings should take the initiative and be responsible for the result. It is also claimed that computers should relieve human beings of routine or tedious work. It is also commonly accepted that there is a case for computerization when a "manual" method would be inefficient (e.g. would take too long to perform or result in too many errors). The tasks which human users want to keep for themselves are the "interesting" ones that require creativity or intuition.

As is often the case with human desires, we soon find that this one too comes into conflict with reality. For instance there may be a conflict between the environmental need for accurate performance and the human need for stimulation. Let us analyse such a possibility.

Sometimes the "human factor" may lead to errors which must be avoided. In such cases, complex equipment may replace the fallible human being. In big jet aeroplanes, for instance, autopilots have taken over the routine flying. The complex automated process control adopted in nuclear power plants or highly automated factories is another example. The problem here is that there are some situations which the automated equipment cannot handle. Something—or somebody—is then needed to supervise the equipment. This responsibility has been placed on the shoulders of human beings who are called in to supervise the dials and to detect, diagnose and remedy any failures (see Figure 32). It is not difficult to understand that such work is bound to be both boring and stressful, as indeed various investigations have found (cf Johansson & Sandén, 1982).

We can see that the solution to the problem of the division of labour does not lie in allotting the main part of the task to the computer. If the human part of the task is reduced to merely producing input (into the computer) and watching output (from the computer), the human interest in the problem will be very low. We know very little about the general principles that may govern

Figure 32 Supervising process control can be both boring and stressful.

people's acceptance of computer aid. The few scattered examples suggest that the more the computer helps, the less the human satisfaction.

But this is an oversimplification. There are other examples suggesting that when computers are used as tools in complex tasks, people become more involved in their original task and feel more satisfied with their achievements. In such cases the computer may more or less take over certain subtasks which had previously been very demanding and which inhibited the efficient performance of the total task. The subtasks of design and planning in mechanical engineering can be used as one example. The designing of mechanical parts involves taking into consideration a lot of facts and making a number of involved calculations. Here the computer may be used as a tool for making the calculations and storing and retrieving the facts required for making different decisions. Using a computer system in this way, the human engineer is relieved of boring computational details and still has a lot of stimulating thinking to do.

Thus the division of labour between man and computer is a very delicate question. Generally speaking we can say that if people believe their performance of a task can be improved while they are also able to keep the "interesting" parts of it for themselves, they will be content to accept computer support. However, it may be difficult to predict exactly which parts of a given task will appear "interesting" to a given person. Some people may enjoy the challenge of making a text or a drawing as good (and personal) as possible. They may not agree that they have anything to gain from a wordprocessing or drawing system, even though they may perform their task more quickly with its help.

TASK MODELS

Our next question will concern task models, a term which will be used to cover the conception of the task that obtains when it is actually being performed.

A "task model" is a theoretical construction, containing a set of assumptions and principles which can be used to interpret (or explain) a person's behaviour in a particular situation (compare the system model which we met in chapter 5). A task model may or may not represent something of which the person to whom we attribute the model is consciously aware.

A task model can be conceived in the following way. If a person has to perform a particular task, this situation resembles any other case of problem-solving situation: both the initial situation and the goal has to be represented. The problem solver has to find operations or methods which can be performed in different states during the problem-solving process. He has to search for an appropriate operation in each state, and he has to evaluate the result achieved until he reaches the goal. The representations, the operations, the search, and the evaluation criteria are all ingredients of the task model.

Given this general background it seems probable that the task model of the users of a system and that of the system designer will not be the same (Figure 33). First, the task expert has probably adopted a particular way of representing the task (including the definition of the initial situation, the goal and the possible operations). Secondly, the task expert can be expected to have developed an efficient way of coping with the task, for instance in terms of what operations and methods to use in which situations. These representations and methods may be so integrated with the task that the task expert cannot communicate them to the system designer.

People attempting to analyse the information-processing element of a partic-

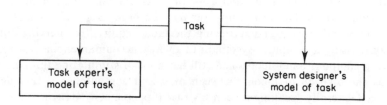

Figure 33 Tasks may be represented differently by task experts and system designers.

ular task in order to computerize it, often find that those engaged in the task have difficulty in describing what they are doing in words. For the purposes of the computer system, of course, the objects, relations and operations involved in the task must be made explicit. But people who have developed a pattern of habitual behaviour may not find it easy to raise the details of these habits to a level of conscious awareness. Also, the task expert may not need to know absolutely everything. A person may be quite capable of coping with a task, even though there are some gaps in his knowledge. It is almost always possible to correct any misconceptions or non-conceptions while actually doing the work.

Do task experts need a particular system task model?

There are tasks in which the explicitness required by the computer system is quite unacceptable to the task experts. It has been reported, for instance, that business managers are often unwilling to use decision support systems. Some managers have complained that the decision support systems are too demanding. While they simply want to get the overall feel of a situation, the system requires them instead to analyse details, such as the attributes involved and the attribute values that characterize different alternatives.

This, according to many managers, is an unnatural way of tackling decision problems. Their reaction is important—it will keep them from using the system. Which does not mean, of course, that they are right. They could well be more efficient and maybe even more accurate with a decision support system than without it.

It can be assumed that people devise task models which allow them to exploit their own particular assets. Thus three-dimensional visualization, pattern recognition and the detection of regularities might thus be tried in performing different kinds of task. A good systems design should be able to allow the user to employ such human skills as well as benefitting from the particular strengths of the computer such as rapid computation and information storage capacity.

Do system designers need particular task models?

Turning now to the task models which the system designers might produce, we find that their ignorance of the task to be performed is not the only problem. The choice of possible models may also be restricted or affected by the particular system or system-development method used by the designers. To my knowledge there has been very little research done on the effects of different system characteristics on the task models that are developed. It is almost always suggested that a particular system can be designed to do whatever the user wants it to. This is true in principle, but not in practice. In practice, time and economic restrictions will combine to produce a task model which might be more suited to the particular properties of the computer system used (perhaps the size of its memory or its language facilities) than to the task it is supposed to solve. It is said that no system designer deliberately designs a "bad" system. But there may well be circumstances beyond his control which may lead to just that result.

COMMUNICATION BETWEEN USERS AND SYSTEM DESIGNERS

The problem of making an implicit task model explicit may be solved by co-operation between system designers and task experts (Figure 34). Ideally, for instance, prospective users should be involved together with system designers in the development of the system in order to see that their own needs are satisfied. In the same way the system designers may want to point out the opportunities offered by a computer system to its prospective users.

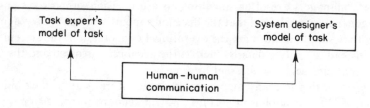

Figure 34 In order to understand each other's task models, task experts and system designers have to communicate with each other.

Most people agree that such cooperation is difficult to realize. Not only do users and systems designers employ different terminologies, but they also possess different knowledge to which apparently similar terms are applied. Several approaches to the cooperation problem have been suggested.

One involves the use of more or less formal methods for analysing and describing user activities (Bubenko, 1981, Bubenko and Lindencrona, 1984). This is a promising approach, but one requiring that users learn the formal methods employed. These in turn require users to have a pretty good idea about their own activities, which they do not always have. And in any case we know that the introduction of a computer system may change the users' ideas on this subject. In particular the very power of the computer system will tempt them to try to "computerize" more than is really necessary. Thus, the conceptual modelling of the task as performed without a computer system may not provide an adequate basis.

Another approach involves what is known as "experimental system development" or "rapid prototyping". A first, rough prototype is designed on the basis of a preliminary analysis of user needs. The users are asked to try out the prototype, and to suggest what could be done better or differently. Of course there are difficulties here too. First, the prototype must be designed with some care, so that prospective users do not produce a lot of complaints which are irrelevant from the designer's point of view. Secondly, the users must already have had some computer experience, if they are not to get bogged down in details about terminal use or computer jargon, etc. Thirdly, user opinions alone may not provide a good basis for diagnosing problems, since the users are often unaware of the implicit assumptions they make when they use computers. To counteract this problem various observational methods, such as think-aloud commentary or the logging of interactions with the computer have sometimes been used to supplement the opinions expressed. Finally, the prototyping method should ideally be allowed some iterative turns, and this may require more time than is usually devoted to the adaptation of a computer system to user needs.

As an alternative to working with prototypes some researchers have attempted simulations of prospective systems (the so called Wizard of Oz technique, where a person "simulates" the system). The success of this technique depends on the ability of the human simulator to capture the complexity of the planned system. In an experiment with a "listening typewriter", simulated by a person typing down the speech of the user, the users were rather unsatisfied with the slowness of the output and the need to speak slowly and carefully (Gould, Conti & Hovanyecz, 1983).

Another way of making prospective users familiar with a planned system is to make videofilms of interactions with a simple prototype system and having the users discuss possible advantages and disadvantages on the basis of the films. This technique has been reported to be able to elicit useful reactions and comments from the prospective users (Poulson, Johnson & Moulding, 1987). Again, iterations are necessary.

It can be concluded that all methods to involve the prospective users in the development of a computer system are costly. There seem to be no short-cuts to this problem, if the design aims at both efficiency in a certain context and user acceptance.

HUMAN–COMPUTER COMMUNICATION

Like so many other terms in computer contexts the term "communication" is used anthropomorphologically. We do not communicate with our car when we are driving it. Similarly, if we regard the computer as a vehicle of information processing, we may not think in terms of "communicating" with it either. We shall be seeing examples of this in our discussion of "direct manipulation systems" to be presented in chapter 12. However, if we regard the computer as the user's assistant, it seems appropriate to speak of communication. The user then has to instruct the system and the system must respond to his instructions (Figure 35).

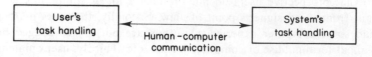

Figure 35 In order to use a computer system for any task, the user has to "communicate" with it.

It is obvious that a computer system differs radically from a human assistant in terms of its "intelligence". No matter how "intelligent" a computer system may be, its comprehension capacity will remain for the foreseeable future far behind the capacity of a human being. This means that the content and form of the communication must be adapted to the system's capacity. Even though system designers are busy tackling the problem of "natural language", the dialogue between men and computers will remain "unnatural" for a long time to come. At the same time, however, there are enough opportunities within the given limits to cater for at least some of the needs that a human user brings to human–computer interaction.

Any brief consideration of the way in which we try to instruct human assistants in particular tasks will reveal several features which may be difficult to carry over into a human–computer situation. We talk about plans and goals, and about ways of achieving these plans. We talk about particular steps to be taken, but we do not generally have to say anything about the particular sensori-motor acts that the assistant has to perform in order to do such things as writing a letter or filing a paper. Nor do we generally have to think about *how* we talk. Our language is "natural", both in terms of medium (speech) and vocabulary or syntax. Our instructions can contain a lot of implicit assumptions. When we say "write" we assume that our assistant will fetch paper and pencil and that we do not have to tell him or her to do so.

When we use a computer as an assistant, few of these conditions can be expected to apply (Figure 36). Instead we have to learn the rules of communication applying to the particular computer system. It is almost as difficult as talking to a visitor from outer space: we do not know what he may already know about our world, nor do we know what language he uses or by what means he absorbs or expresses messages.

The problems of knowledge, language and medium all have to be solved in designing a computer system. And the user of the system then has to learn the particular solutions chosen.

In order to simplify the task of the designer as well as the user, an important suggestion was made by Moran (1981) in his "command language grammar". Moran suggested that a system should be specified on different hierarchical levels. Each higher level should comprise all lower levels. Each lower level should contain a further specification of the definitions of the higher level.

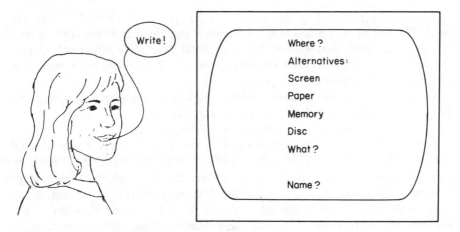

Figure 36 We have to tell the computer system where to write what, and under what name.

Three major components are described (Table 6):

"The conceptual component contains the abstract concepts around which the system is organized, the communication component contains the command language and the conversational dialog, and the physical component contains the physical devices that the user sees and comes in contact with."

(Moran, 1981, p. 5–6)

Table 6. An overview of the components and levels of the command language grammar

Conceptual component	Task level
	Semantics
Communication component	Syntax level
	Interaction
Physical component	Physical input
	Screen layout
	Acoustic output

The conceptual component contains the highest levels: the task level, which "describes the task domain addressed by the system", and the semantic level, which "describes the concepts represented by the system". We can say that these levels correspond to the system's model of the task. Our earlier discussion under the heading of "task models" is relevant to these levels.

Moran suggests that the conceptual component of the system can be separated from its command language. We can therefore go further down the hierarchy and look at the communication component.

The communication component contains the syntax level and the interaction level. The syntax level refers to the elements of the command language: its commands, arguments, context, and state variables. The interaction level refers to the actual interaction between user and system: the key presses to be performed, and the feedback used by the system.

The physical component is not included in Moran's exposition. It is described as covering the spatial layout level and the device level.

Let me here consider the communication component.

The syntax level relates (informally) to the system's task model through the commands and the arguments associated with the commands. Each operation in the task as defined by the system can be performed by a single command or a sequence of commands. Also each object in the task as defined by the system can be defined by one or several arguments associated with the commands. In order to handle the communication, the system (and the user) must consider more than just the task. Both have to know when a certain command may be issued (the command context). They have to keep track of some information about what has been said, received and done, and about what remains to be said, received and done (state variables). Further, the system designer must decide what information to make available to the user and when.

Each of these elements (commands, arguments, etc.) may now be defined in a way that is more or less "natural" to a user. We will say more on the psychological effects of different solutions to the syntactical problems later, in chapter 13.

At the interaction level it has to be decided which are to be the primitive actions to be performed by the system and the user. The primitive actions are the signals between user and system. Primitive system actions consist of the output of the system to the user, usually in the form of display actions or audio signals. Primitive user actions are associated with the various input devices (keyboard, tablet pen, speech, etc.) The primitive actions, as we can see, are related to the physical level through the output and input devices. The interaction level is also concerned with the timing of the different actions.

Different solutions are possible on the interaction level. Several studies have been made of the effects of different interaction characteristics on user performance. Some of these studies will be presented in chapter 13.

Thus it can be seen that the communication aspect is a very central issue in human–computer interaction. To a great extent it will determine the ease with which a novice user can learn a new system. All aspects that are unfamiliar to the user will add to his effort in learning to solve his task in the system. Also, an expert will prefer a system that allows him to perform his task with as little "extra" communication as possible. The ratio of communicating with the system versus performing the task must always be kept small.

METACOMMUNICATION

The communication about the task has in some cases to be supplemented by "metacommunication" (Figure 37). By metacommunication is meant communication between user and system about the communication requirements of the system.

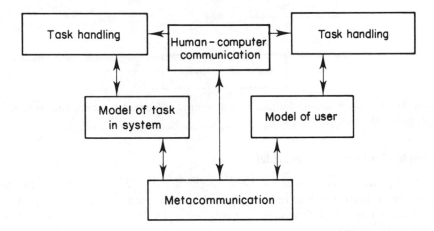

Figure 37 Metacommunication serves to facilitate the communication between human and computer.

Metacommunication is used to inform the user about such aspects of the communication which are not self-explanatory. A new user must be informed of how to start the system and how to stop it, and every user can then and when need information about the system's facilities and the appropriate ways to invoke these.

Manuals, system training and informed people provide metacommunication outside the system, help and error messages and on line tutorials provide metacommunication inside the system. A lot of work is presently going on regarding the problems of designing metacommunication, some of which will be covered later (chapter 15).

USER'S MODEL OF TASK IN SYSTEM

As we have seen in Chapter 5, users have to learn the system's model of the task before they can cope adequately with the task in the system (Figure 38). We can look at another example which will serve to throw further light on the concept of the user's mental model of the task in the system (referred to below as the "user's system model").

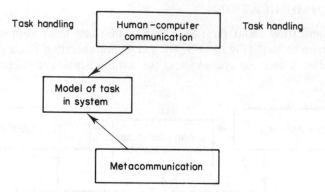
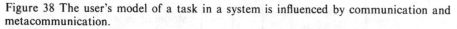

Figure 38 The user's model of a task in a system is influenced by communication and metacommunication.

Example of a user's system model

A rather primitive version of UNIX mail can serve as our example, as this is one of the systems which have been studied in a European collaborative project on "Human Factors in Telematic Systems" (van der Veer et al., 1987a, 1987b, Wærn et al., 1988).

Let us suppose that a user of this system has just received and read a letter. He thinks the letter would interest one of his colleagues and he wants to send it on. The help menu offers the following option: "m <user>", with the following explanation: "Forward current letter to colleague under his user name". In order to be able to use this option correctly, the user has to know (at least) the following:

— what is the "current letter"?
— what is the colleague called, as <user>?
— what happens to the letter in the user's own mailbox?
— what happens after the command has been issued?

A novice user of a mail system might only ask the first two questions. He will be concerned solely with sending the intended letter to the intended recipient. Somewhere in his manual he may find the information that the letter he has just read is the "current letter" which means that this piece of information becomes integrated in his system model. It may be more difficult to find the "user name" of the intended recipient of the letter. The user's system model may thus contain a problem to be solved before any letters can be forwarded: namely to discover the user names of possible intended recipients. The concept of "user name" does not come naturally to the novice computer user, and it may cause him some difficulty. A more experienced user will acknowledge the fact that user names and ordinary names usually differ, and will try to discover the relevant designation.

The user's system model can then be identified by way of the problems he encounters. If he is allowed to ask questions and to receive answers, we—the researchers—should be able to infer what concepts he is considering. If the user asks questions similar to the first two mentioned above, we would learn that his mental model contains the conceptual objects "letter" and "recipient", but not the system characteristics of these objects, which in this system are related to "currentness" (for letters) and "user identity" (for recipients). The occurrence of such questions, together with the absence of questions about the status of the letter sent or the consequence of forwarding a letter, indicates that the user has not yet acquired the concept of "existence of letters in mailbox" and the related concept of "a sequence of letters in a mailbox".

Of course, it is difficult to interpret the absence of questions. In this example I wanted to show that the relation between "naive" and "sophisticated" questions can be used to infer the limits of the user's knowledge.

At a later point in time, the user will come to an end of his "mail session", and will then be faced with the problem of choosing between "quitting" the system, and thereby changing his mailbox, or "exiting" from the system, without changing the mailbox. The distinction between "changing" and "not changing" a mailbox thus has to be incorporated in the user's model of the task. This distinction is probably not at all clear to start with for at least two reasons. First, the concept of "mailbox" is not clear. And, further, the concept of "change" is vague. What does it mean? Is it a question of changing the logic of the mailbox or its content? A careful user might be reluctant to change his mailbox. What would it actually mean? That something happens to the mailbox in the future? That letters disappear, before he has had a chance to see them? Let us suppose that he chooses the "exit" option, simply to keep things as they were to start with, and thus plays safe by not changing anything.

The next time he enters the system, the user who has chosen to play safe will find that the letter he forwarded is still there. This may induce him to form a system model of having forwarded a copy of his letter. Such a system model is quite compatible with the situation. A more difficult interpretation problem faces the user who has chosen to delete a letter in the previous session with the system, and has exited from the system without changing his mailbox. He will find to his astonishment that the deleted letters are still there! What model can be built on this experience? It is very likely that the user comes up with a model which says: "Delete does not work in this system". At this point, our user has built a model of his task in the system, which can be described in words as follows:

Letters are added to the mailbox, which soon contains a huge pile of letters, since the user can not delete any of them. Copies of letters are forwarded, only if he knows the recipients' user identities.

The "true" model (which Norman (1986) has called the "design model") of this part of the system can be described in words like this:

Letters are only deleted when the user exits from the system by updating his mailbox. Letters which are forwarded to other users are deleted if he updates his mailbox. The recipients' user identities have to be known before letters can be forwarded.

There is thus an obvious difference between the user's system model and the design model. This can be bridged if the user is instructed about the distinctions introduced and these may in turn be easier to capture if they are made clear in the user's interaction with the system. For instance, the commands chosen can indicate that "delete" only works as a preparatory command, and that "mail to another person" both forwards the read letter and prepares it for deletion from the mailbox.

Thus the user's system model is dependent both on his own preconceptions of the task and on the "system image", i.e. the information he is given about the system, his communication with the system, and the feedback he gets from interaction with the system. It therefore seems very important that the system designer should consider how best to promote an adequate system model in the user, and in order to do this, he needs a model of the user. Let us therefore examine this problem below.

SYSTEM'S MODEL OF USER

Every system designer needs to consider the user (Figure 39). The extent to which the user is considered varies from system to system.

At the most primitive level, consideration of the user simply means choosing a model of the task and considering only the information that the user requires in order to perform it. Systems which guide the user strictly through a sequential procedure, leaving him no scope for his own initiative, exemplify this level.

As soon as the user himself is allowed to decide which procedure to use, the model has to be a little more sophisticated. For a fixed system, which is the same independent of user, the system designer has to know something at least about the intentions of the "typical" user and the concepts with which he works. The commands and the feedback provided should then comply with these intentions and concepts.

A somewhat more sophisticated model of the user is required by system designers engaged in building flexible systems. The simplest type of a flexible system gives the user some different options as to communication or metacom-

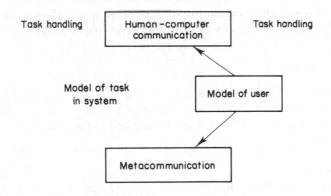

Figure 39 In order to design adequate communication and metacommunication, system designers have to consider a model of the user.

munication. "Do you want some information?" is a question, giving the user of an adventure-type system the option of skipping already known information. Similar options have been implemented in several systems. In order to offer relevant options, the user model has to consider various ways in which users may differ.

Still more sophisticated user models are required in order to design so-called adaptive systems. Such systems aim at adapting their communication and meta-communication to the current needs of the users. For instance, in tutorial systems, the relevant information has to be adapted to the user's current mental model of the task to be learnt.

This requires that the system builds some kind of model of the user (sometimes called "embedded user model", cf Murray, 1987). One of the most difficult problems in designing such user models lies in diagnosing the user's knowledge. If this diagnosis takes place solely within the system, the designer has either to resort to letting the system infer the users' knowledge from his input (keystrokes, commands, menu options chosen) (cf Desmarais & Pavel, 1987, Hecking, 1987), or to engage in some kind of diagnostic interview with the user. The latter can certainly annoy a user who wants the task to be performed as quickly as possible!

Another dimension of flexibility concerns systems tuned to the learning and cognitive styles of the users, or even to their personalities (see chapter 6). Very little has been done so far to describe the type of user model which would be needed to cope with other types of differences than differences in the users' knowledge of the topic.

When talking about adapting systems to different user characteristics, the problem of privacy should not be neglected (Pratt, 1987). There is certainly some private information that users would not want to include in a "personal profile" to be used by a computer system. Careful analysis of what information that really is useful and what information the user would allow to be used must precede all design of systems which include individual user models.

Embedded user models

Let us now look at the case of a systems designer who wants to produce an image of the system which will help the "typical" user to understand it. What must then be included in a description of the user's system model? The following elements are essential:

— the mental objects
— the properties of these objects
— the mental operations
— the conditions for using the operations
— the effects of the operations.

In our mailbox example, the mental objects are represented above by letters, recipients, and mailbox. These objects have certain properties. The properties indicate distinctions which have to be made in order to understand the effects of operations performed. The example illustrates the properties of "existence" (necessary in order to understand deletion), "space" (necessary in order to understand where the letter is) and "time", (particularly as far as the effect of deletion is concerned). These aspects of the user's system model have been further elaborated by Mikael Tauber, (Tauber, 1986, in press).

The mental operations to be performed include both actual operations in the system and "thought operations" outside the system. Inside the system, for instance, the user has to understand what it means to read letters in the mailbox, to mark them for deletion, and to forward them. Outside the system the user has to understand that he is not obliged to read all letters, even if they are shown on the screen. The user also has to decide which letters to keep where and which letters to delete without moving them elsewhere.

Where the conditions for the operations are concerned, they are often linked to the "mode" of the system. In the system exemplified here, only operations which can be performed in "read mode" are listed in the help list. The conditions for writing and sending a letter are different and must be looked up in the manual.

Finally, the effects of the operations must be considered in the user's system model. I have already mentioned that a user may not understand the distinction between "marking for deletion" and "actual deletion". This is due to an implicit assumption in his system model that the effects of operations are immediate. If, as in the exemplified system the effects are delayed and contingent upon some other operation (in this case on choosing "quit" instead of "exit"), the system designer should try to find a way of conveying this information that will promote the formation of an appropriate mental model.

Another factor to be considered in this last connection is related to the "default" actions which are performed by the system. How can a novice user of the system in our example know that a letter which is forwarded to another recipient is also marked for deletion in his own mailbox? What if the novice user also wants to keep the letter for himself? He would only be able to carry out the necessary operation (i.e. saving it in a file or in his personal mailbox) if he knows that the letter is marked for deletion. But, since marking is a default action, not mentioned in the manual, nor in the help list, nor anywhere else, he will have no chance of detecting the deletion until it is too late.

We can see that some reflection on the elements included in the user's possible system model will make it easier for the system designer to consider this model in his design. Further insight can be gained by observing users actually working with the system.

SUMMARY

In this chapter I have introduced a frame of reference which will be used for the analysis of human–computer interaction in the following chapters.

The starting point for this frame of reference is the user's task, rather than the possibilities of an abstract machine.

The computer can be regarded as a powerful tool to use in performing a task. This raises certain questions. The first concerns the division of labour, since a powerful tool is presumably used to facilitate the work of a human being. This division of labour is often obvious when the task requires some sort of physical action that is beyond human capacity, but it becomes more problematic whenever information-processing is involved. Should the human being be relieved of all intellectual activity? And, if not, what should be left to him?

The next question concerns the conception or model of the task. The prospective user of a computer system does not always seem to conceive his task in the same way as the designer. The computer system has its own conceptions—but does it really need them? Have the system designers perhaps fallen into a certain traditional form of computer thinking, which they are imposing on the rest of us?

To get the system to carry out the allotted task, the user has to "communicate" it. This communication consists of the input from the user to the system and the output and feedback from the system to the user.

Metacommunication supplements this with information about how to handle the communication. Metacommunication is provided by manuals, instructions or advisers, or it is presented in help lists and error messages.

As he works with the system, the user will arrive at some kind of understanding of how the system conceives the task. We refer to this understanding as "the user's mental model of the task in the system". This mental model may not coincide with the model intended by the system designer; and in any case it will continue to evolve as the subject uses the system. In order to convey to the user as clear an image of the system as possible, the system designer should take the user's mental model into account, which he can do by formulating it explicitly, either outside or inside the system. If the system stores a model of the user's system model, it will be more likely to provide adequate information at relevant times.

Chapter 8

From Ideas to Text

THE WRITING PROCESS

Now let us apply the foregoing general frame of reference to some different tasks, and start with the production of text. Here this subject will be defined as the title to the chapter indicates: from ideas to text, i.e. a certain topic has to be written about and it is a particular person's task to do it. This is an important activity which has been considered in many computer support systems.

From a series of experiments in which people were asked to produce a text on a given topic, the following main activities were derived (cf Flower & Hayes, 1980):

1. Retrieval of ideas
2. Analysis of ideas
3. Organization of ideas
4. Planning the sequencing of ideas
5. Translation of ideas into text
6. Writing the text
7. Checking the written text

Retrieval of ideas

Writing tasks carried out in accordance with given instructions, like much school-work or like the task set in the work by Flower & Hayes, generally start with the retrieval of ideas. The writer has to think through the ideas which might be relevant to the particular topic. At school or in a laboratory situation the information generally can only be retrieved from the knowledge already possessed by the writer. In a real-world situation, the information can be retrieved in other ways: by looking for books, by asking other people, or by searching a database. The task of retrieving relevant information is no minor one, and it will persist to a greater or lesser extent throughout the whole process of progressing from ideas to text.

Analysis of ideas

This activity cannot of course start until some ideas have been retrieved. During this activity ideas are scrutinized for their relevance to the topic and the planned readership, and questions are asked about whether the ideas are on the right level in relation to current knowledge and the intended readers. During this stage new ideas will also probably emerge.

Organization of ideas

This activity is closely related to the analysis of ideas. Some ideas develop naturally from others, some need further explanation before the connections become clear. The writer must ask himself, for instance, which ideas can be used to explain others and which can be regarded as a precondition of others. Loose associations as well as close logical relationships may both be valuable, depending on the goal of the text (to stimulate thought or to develop an argument) and on the intended readership.

Sequencing of ideas

A major stumbling block for most writers comes with the sequencing of ideas, in order to present them in a readable form. A text is a sequential medium, whereas the ideas themselves may be related to one another in several different ways: hierarchical, lattice, tabular, or simply just tangled together. In sequencing the ideas the writer is forced to consider how the reader should best be led through the web of associations. Where would it be best to start? What should follow? Maybe no topic has one natural sequence in which its ideas should be presented. Should the most important idea come first, to stir the imagination? Or should the less important be allowed to precede the others, leading on to an impressive finale? The sequence of ideas may be altered several times before the writer is satisfied with the text.

Translation of ideas into text

We know very little about the form that ideas may assume in a writer's head. The only thing we can be certain about is that they do not take the shape of a readable text. Some writers may have visual ideas, which then have to be "translated" into a verbal medium. Others may nurse ideas in verbal form, but the phrases used to express the ideas are not continuous; rather they consist of abstract words to which the idea can be hooked in a way that only the writer is likely to understand. One important activity is thus to try to express these ideas so that others may understand them as well. And the writer's efforts in this direction may well cause him to see the ideas in a new light, to find new ideas, or to organize the old ones differently.

Writing the text

Now it is time to start writing the text proper. This means not only finding words to express the desired concepts, but also finding the grammatical form for shaping the text. Here, too, questions of punctuation and spelling must be considered. It may be difficult to separate this activity from translating the ideas to text. If we want to draw a line between the two, we could say that writing the text is the more concrete activity, in which all the details in the text have to be considered.

Order and content of activities

The studies show that writers do not perform these activities in a simple sequence. Rather, the subprocesses of the writing are recursive, i.e. they can appear both as themselves and as part of other subprocesses.

It can also be seen that the content of the processes swings between the more abstract and the more concrete. To begin with, ideas about the content of the text may be rather vague, and this naturally affects the retrieval of ideas. When an author does not yet quite know what he is going to write about, there is little to guide the search for ideas. This means that either too many or too few ideas will be retrieved. If the author is retrieving ideas from his own memory, he may get stuck in one line of argument; if the ideas are retrieved in some other way, like searching for books, talking to people, or utilizing computer-based information retrieval, the risk at the earliest stage is that he gets too much information rather than too little.

When the writer starts analysing the ideas, or even later when he starts writing about the information gathered, the ideas collected are submitted to a stricter process of selection. This brings him to a more concrete level which, when expressed as a text, may make it necessary to introduce some kind of abstraction different from the one he started with.

Writing strategies

Generally speaking, the writing process implies that the writer is faced with contradictory goals, and that the cognitive limitations will impose different writing strategies (Flower & Hayes, 1982). The writer has to comply with the requirements of the presumed readership, while the available information and the text he produces himself as he goes along will all impose their specific restrictions on the continuing writing process.

Even the writing of factual texts involves creative activity, in that it is necessary to find, to organize and to develop information into a structured sequence of ideas. The formulation of the ideas as a text may throw a new light on them, compelling the author to see fresh aspects of the problems so that he has to revise his presentation.

Division of labour

The activities involved in the writing process can be carried out by one person or by several, in which case different people are responsible for the diverse activities. A division of labour is common in office work, whereby the manager generally accounts for activities 1–5 (from idea generation to translation into written text), while a secretary generally answers for activity 6 (writing) and 7 (checking spelling, formal aspects, etc.). In a printing office, the spelling of the written text is generally checked by one person. The retrieval and analysis of ideas can often be carried out as teamwork. Nowadays it is also becoming more common for the sequencing of ideas and their translation into a text to be a collaborative effort. This division of activities among several people may make iteration more difficult; for instance there will be less opportunity or motivation to rethink ideas in the course of the writing, in the way that is fairly usual when the same person both thinks and writes.

Implications for computer support

It can be seen that the whole business of proceeding from the ideas themselves to their formulation in a text is very complex. Several types of computer support could be suggested. Either the different processes can be supported separately, with the help of different kinds of aid—a situation which would be suitable when the production of the text is divided between several people. Or the different processes can be supported by some kind of integrated computer aid—a situation which would be of greater benefit to the writer responsible for the whole process from the collection of information via the development of ideas to the actual expression of these ideas in a connected text.

Various types of computer aids have already been envisaged (cf Danielsson, 1985, Bisseret, 1987), but I shall restrict my present analysis to the computer support systems which already exist, namely:

— idea-processors—mainly concerned with activity 3, the organizing of ideas.
— outline supports—mainly concerned with activity 4, the sequencing of ideas,
— wordprocessors—mainly concerned with activity 6, the writing of the text.

Let us see how these supports fit the activities. I shall analyse various tasks and some existing computer support systems below, in terms of their cognitive requirements. The analysis will focus on the functionality of the system in the specific task and the "user-friendliness" of the dialogue.

It should be noted that the intention is not to evaluate the systems or their interfaces. The analysis may be unfair, both in terms of the selection of examples (some existing systems will certainly have been left out) and in the analysis itself (some functions and some user-friendly details will not be mentioned). However, I hope that the analysis and examples will serve to show how a cognitive analysis of a task and of a computer support system can be carried out.

IDEA PROCESSING

The notion of providing computer support for idea processing is a fairly new one, and may even seem odd to some people who work with ideas. If we limit ourselves to one task, in which information is to be collected, analysed, and condensed, and the ideas presented in an orderly fashion, it might be easier to recognize the need for some computer support. Examples could be: a student prepares a thesis, a journalist wants to get an overview of a certain topic, some administrators are trying to make sense of the applicability of various regulations to a particular situation, or some politicans are preparing surveys of the current economic, social, or some other interesting situation.

The people behind the most advanced system for idea processing currently available describe the task to be supported as follows:

"The goal of all idea-processing tasks is to move from a chaotic collection of unrelated ideas to an integrated, orderly interpretation of the ideas and their interconnections"

(op. cit. Halasz, Moran & Trigg, 1987, p.45).

Task analysis

Let us start from this rather general statement as the expression of a model for the idea-processing task. We can then ask ourselves whether this task model is applicable to idea processing.

The quotation can be regarded as the statement of a problem-solving activity, which includes the formulation of the goal of the activity (an integrated, orderly interpretation of the ideas and their interconnections) and of the current situation (a chaotic collection of unrelated ideas).

First we should note that "idea-processing" does not contain the first activity in the writing process, i.e. information retrieval. "The chaotic collection of unrelated ideas" corresponds not to a lack but to an abundance of information.

Also, the goal of idea processing makes no mention of the goals of planning, writing and checking.

In the absence of empirical data, I shall try to analyse this task model in light of our knowledge of the writing process.

Can idea processing in fact be isolated from the activities of gathering information, planning, writing and evaluation? As we have seen, the whole task of moving from ideas to text involves these different activities recursively, which means that ideas are being processed during the writing and evaluating phases as well as in the "purely" idea-processing operation. Further idea generation may become necessary in the course of writing and evaluating, and new relationships between ideas may have to be sought in order to achieve a satisfactory sequence of ideas for the textual exposition. The activity of idea processing is thus intimately connected with all other parts of the text-production task.

The separation of idea processing and actual text production may be detrimental both to the production of the text and to the refinement of the ideas. If idea processing is separated from text production, the feedback circle may be broken. This may happen if different systems have to be called upon, so that easy transition from one task to another becomes impossible. In fact, however, a separate arrangement for idea processing and writing is not necessary. If the idea processing system is integrated with the text producing system and easy changes in the ideas and their relationships according to the needs developed during writing and evaluation are allowed for, the integrated system may be more of a help than a hindrance. It should be noted that a helpful system should support both the expression of each single idea in the text, the relationships between ideas, and the combination of the variously related ideas into a connected text.

Next, we could ask whether the description of the situation captures the essential nature of idea processing. First what is an "idea"? Can it be pinned down to a single "unit" which may be related in an "orderly" way to other units? Some people apparently have difficulty in defining their ideas, as can be seen from the following quotation from the same authors' observations on the users of the system:

> "They aren't quite sure how to segment their ideas and information into notecards ..."
>
> (Halasz, Moran & Trigg, 1987, p. 51)

Although we know very little about how people actually process ideas, our common sense hints that ideas start by being so vague that they can hardly be expressed at all, let alone segmented. As the ideas are worked on, they assume some nebulous form, change shape, evoke new ideas, get separated from one another, come together in new constellations, possibly giving rise to new ideas. In short, the development of ideas concerns not only the relationships between the ideas, but also their actual content. At the beginning, it may be incorrect to speak of an "idea". What exists at that stage is more of an "idea cloud" sometimes expressed in words, sometimes in pictures. The concepts may be vague and their definitions depend on haphazard examples popping up. All these fuzzy ideas and concepts may exist together at the start: whirling around, mixing together, refusing to be pinned down as expressed ideas. The danger of expressing the ideas too soon has been recognized by Moran, who coined the phrase "premature encapsulation" (1987).

Thus the development of ideas seems to concern more than just the relationships between ideas, as the above quotation suggested. The start is not "a chaotic collection of unrelated ideas". Ideas are seldomly generated in a chaotic and unrelated way. Rather, they are usually generated by association with one another, associations of which the thinker is more often than not unaware. The associations evoke new ideas, but they may also keep the thinker on well-established paths. In this second case, the ideas may run round in circles, blocked by invisible conceptual walls due to their own implicit relationships.

How then, should the spelling out of these spontaneous and implicit associations be tackled? We know very little about idea relations and idea generation. When is it likely to be helpful to try to make the relationships between the ideas explicit? Or when might such attempts lead to unwanted fixations? Obviously people find it difficult to make sense of the demand "to define the relationships", as the following observation on users of the idea-processing system illustrates:

> "They don't quite know how to use links to build relational structures or even whether such relational networks would be appropriate for their task"
>
> (Halasz, Moran & Trigg, 1987, p.52).

However, the processing of ideas is not complete once the ideas have been spelled out and their relationships expressed. The process of relating ideas to each other often involves further changes in them: when confronted with one another, ideas often have to be developed further, distinguished from each other, and explained; their consequences have to be considered and checked. The structure induces changes in its own parts, which indicates that the structure is more than the sum of its parts. In many cases a restructuring of the situation as a whole is required. This restructuring may lead to new insights, in which case we call it "creative" or it may lead to another well-known way of looking at things, in which case we speak of a "new perspective".

The changes in ideas which lead to changes in the structure as a whole may lead to difficulty in understanding what the structure is, and how it should be represented. This difficulty may be responsible for the problems observed by the developers of the system:

> "Most users start with an unorganized and poorly understood collection of ideas. Their first task is to design and construct a network structure that represents and/or organizes these ideas. They find this task to be problematic"
>
> (Halasz, Moran & Trigg, 1987, p. 51).

If all this is true of idea processing, how can a computer support system help? A computer support system must make something easier for its user, if it is to be accepted. It must be an aid, not a stumbling block.

As mentioned in the introduction to this part, there are many ways in which the computer system may function as a tool. One which could be relevant for idea processing concerns finding the ideas, once they have been formulated. Many people will remember those painful searches through notebooks, filled on trains and planes, or the despairing hunt for the paper serviette on which *the* idea of the day was jotted down during lunch. Would we not gratefully acknowledge a pocket computer, serving as our idea databank?

However, these situations come much later in the process of idea development than the initial quotation suggests. A thinker may well need support in storing and retrieving ideas which have already been expressed and related to each other in an orderly way. Instead of piling up on the desk, notes may be stored on a disk for easy retrieval. Let us see what concepts and operations are needed for the efficient use of such a support system.

Concepts and operations in an idea processing support system

The general philosophy behind the support for idea processing is that it should facilitate the access to previously formulated ideas. Let us suppose that these ideas are in the shape of written notes. Each note can be regarded as a node in a network. In order to get from one node to another, a link is needed. This link is defined by the user himself as the relationship between one node and another. It is thus easy to move from one note (and node) to another via the defined link.

Figure 40 illustrates some of my own ideas about moving from ideas to text in a network of ideas.

In order to see what is meant by the note "conceptual object" linked to "function of system", let us start by locating the node "function of system", and pointing at the node "conceptual object" listed there. Or if we want to see what concepts are included in the node called "function of system", we can start at the same node and point at the link "includes".

There is also another way of getting access to the notes. The network itself can be inspected by the user as illustrated here. In this case we can point at the links in the network in order to get access to new notes.

In the system presented here another kind of organization is also required for the storage and retrieval of notes. This organization is hierarchical, in order to facilitate the efficient storage and retrieval of notes, regardless of their network interconnections.

The following conceptual objects are essential to the computer support system:

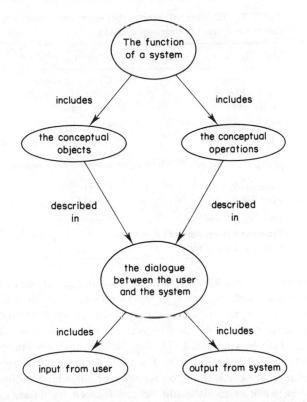

Figure 40 A network of "ideas" in the shape of the titles of "notes" related to each other as indicated by the links.

— A hierarchical file organization of notecards
— A network relating different notecards to each other by links
— A notecard containing
    — A title
    — A note, which can be a text as long as necessary
    — One or several links with reference to other cards.

On these objects the operations listed in table 7 can be performed (from the standpoint of the user). The operations performed by the system refer to the support which the user gets from the system, not the system operations necessary to get these operations to function.

It is easy to see that these objects and operations differ a great deal from what can be done with pen and paper (or by a simple wordprocessor, as will be seen later). With pen and paper it would be possible to write notes on cards (this is the model used for the system). But the idea of finding one card, given another, would hardly arise in a paper situation. The restrictions imposed by the

Table 7. Division of labour between user and computer system for idea processing

User	System
Write cards Write titles Write links	Create network on basis of titles and links
Check network Change network (whereby the cards are not changed)	Show network Create, delete links
Save cards in file Find file	Create file Show file
Find card from card Find card from network Find card from file	Show card

paper situation are so much greater that very few organizational principles are possible. Hierarchical and sequential organizations are feasible and so are piles of cards. But a network can only be envisaged for a very restricted number of cards, in which case it might not be necessary to use cards at all. The network could simply be kept in your head. The real advantage of a computer system would not come into play until you had a great amount of information corresponding to many more cards than you would ever consider handling manually.

Even if the network of cards could be constructed by hand, a duplication of the work would be needed: writing the cards and writing the network. The tentative changes in the network which can be performed in the system can of course be performed manually, but the easy access to cards lying "behind" the network cannot.

Thus an idea-processing system that works in the way described here can be compared to an information retrieval system. In the idea-processing system the basis for retrieval is specific rather than general: an idea can be retrieved from another idea via the link, or it can be retrieved from the network. But if the user does not know where to start, retrieval will be difficult.

From this description it can be seen that the system fails to support one activity that would be very useful to the development of ideas. Some ideas develop by being divided into several subideas. This happens for instance when concepts are distinguished from one another. This means that the new ideas created have links that are similar to those of the original concept with all the concepts above them in an ideas hierarchy. With concepts on the same or lower levels, some links will be the same as those of the original concept, while other links will have to be changed. Substantial support could be provided by a system allowing the links to be "inherited" by the new concepts, and allowing the user to indicate which links should be rewritten rather than simply copied. A similar system of automated link-generation would be even more useful, when concepts (nodes) are brought together under a common concept—i.e. when ideas are generalized or abstracted.

OUTLINE SUPPORT

Most writing teachers recommend the production of a table of contents as part of a good writing practice. Producing a table of contents emphasizes the top-down process of writing. Plan first and write afterwards. Not everyone writes this way, and not everyone who writes a table of contents follows it later. Producing a table of contents is as much of an iterative process as the organization of ideas.

Making a table of contents is a way of easing the transition from a structure of multirelated ideas to the sequential form needed for a text. In a table of contents the ideas are organized hierarchically. The sequence of ideas can be more easily checked in summary form, than after all the details have been spelled out. Moreover, it is easier to change the order of the ideas in a table of contents than in a full text.

Task analysis

The model for producing a table of contents is fairly straightforward.

The topic to be covered by a text can be subdivided into subtopics, which in turn can be subdivided, which in turn... until we get down to the actual sequence of ideas. Each subtopic can be represented by something other than a full text. By one or more words (as in a heading), or even by a whole paragraph explaining the content of the subtopic.

The task of producing a table of contents thus consists of dividing the whole structure of ideas into subtopics, labelling and explaining them and ordering them into a sequence which suits the topic and the readership (or audience).

The task may or may not include the actual translation from ideas to words, by incorporating a wordprocessing system in the outline support system. Since the table of contents is quite likely to be changed during writing, the support system will be more effective if wordprocessing and outline organizing are integrated. Such integration makes it possible to derive the table of contents directly from the written text, as well as writing the text by starting from the headings in the table of contents.

Conceptual objects and operations in an outline support system

What support in performing tedious or impossible tasks can an outline system provide? Headings are often hierarchically organized, with some more general, some more specific. When writing on paper, checking the levels and wording of headings is a tedious job. Getting headings consistent in the first place, changing them and still keeping them consistent, may well be more trouble than seems worthwhile. The support system should deal with the following conceptual objects:

— Topics, which are described by a few words only
— Rankings of topics and subtopics, indicating the scope of a topic and its relative position in the hierachical structure of topics and subtopics
— Comments to topics, which provide some further insight into their content
— Full text of topic.

The operations which are to be performed are shown in Table 8.

Table 8.   Division of labour between user and computer system for outline support

User	System
Write topic and subtopic	Organize topics and subtopics
Inspect outline at desired	Show only the details
level of detail	desired
Change order of topics and subtopics	Reorganize order and presentation
Write text with headings	Derive table of contents from text
Change text and headings	Change table of contents accordingly

If we compare this description of a possible outline support system with the support provided by a handwritten outline, we can note certain differences. First, in a handwritten outline it is difficult to limit inspection only to the level of detail desired at just that moment. With a long outline, covering several pages, it takes longer to get an overview of a handwritten version. Further, the reorganization of the outline in the handwritten version would generally require a good deal of rewriting. And the derivation of outline from the text has of course to be made by reading the text and writing down the headings. There are thus some gains to be made in inspecting the information and some rewritings to be avoided. These gains may be great enough to motivate the use of outline support systems for people who use outlines a lot. For "ordinary" writers, outline support hardly seems worth its cost.

TRANSLATING IDEAS INTO TEXT

The translation from ideas to text is usually carried out by human agents.

Suggestions do exist, however, for designing of computer systems to produce texts (cf McKeown, 1985, Tucker & Nirenburg, 1984). Such systems could be useful when a lot of simple texts are needed, for instance for varieties of equipment, for varieties of users, or for different languages. If nothing else, the necessity for translating technical instructions from one language to another would justify all the efforts being made to develop automated systems. Hitherto most systems aiming at translating from one language to another have failed.

Another idea has been to try to develop a computer system which can take as input a well-defined idea structure and an outline based on it, and then produce as output a sequence of sentences and words in the same language. Such a system would be useful for deriving natural language expressions in computer systems, perhaps for providing meaningful error messages or explanations in expert systems, or for describing the concepts of database systems to novices.

It is difficult to see how a system which translates ideas into text within the same language can be of any help to someone struggling with the problem of progressing from ideas to text; the user would have to do so much preparation of the ideas to be presented. Further, given the present state of knowledge, when it comes to generating language he would also have to check very carefully the text produced with the system. It seems that the preparations for using the system and the checking of its output must surely be more laborious than writing the text oneself. Added to which, the user gains nothing in terms of getting new ideas or organizing ideas differently when he is not writing himself.

One possible advantage which can be offered by an interactive translating system lies in providing the user with some alternative ways of expressing things and a chance to choose between them. People who have well-defined writing tasks, such as writing business letters could find some advantages in such a text generation system. They might be happy not to have to go to the trouble of finding new expressions for each new letter, but would be content to clothe their ideas in a couple of standard words or diagrams. Some managers today expect their secretaries to put their ideas into final shape, and although I do not like suggesting that secretaries should be replaced by a computer system which can formulate ideas as text, it has to be said that this is a possible way of using a text-generation system.

The drafting of legal documents has been tackled in a system developed by Sprowl et al. (1984). It is not impossible that such documents are so standardized that a system describing standard templates with slots for names, etc. could be useful.

A possible text-generation system would slot into the activity of writing rather as a ghostwriter slots into the thinking of the person possessing the information to be conveyed. In the ghostwriter case it does not seem impossible to separate writing from knowledge content, but this may be because the ghostwriter takes over much of the generation and organization of the ideas, as well—and most importantly—as the checking of the text. It seems rather unlikely that the translation of ideas to text can be wholly separated from idea processing and checking in any but the most trivial writing situations.

WRITING TEXT

Writing a text is an activity for which computer support has been available for a long time, and for which a good deal of experience has been acquired. As we have seen, the process of moving from ideas to text is an iterative one, in which ideas are generated, new ways of organizing ideas are found, and a new sequencing of the ideas may become necessary. This means that if the ideas are expressed directly as text without any intermediate steps, all these changes have to be made in the text writing phase.

In order to avoid constant rewriting, two alternative solutions are available. One is to plan extensively and not to write until the ideas are clear; the planning can take place with or without the support systems discussed above. The other is to start writing, but to use a wordprocessing system to help with the changes which will be necessary. And the less support there is for organization and sequencing of ideas, the greater will be the benefit of support in writing. However, even if the other types of support are available, of all activities discussed here, writing the text is probably the one with most to gain from a computer support system. The confessions of a great many authors suggest that the strategy of writing-and-changing-the-text is common. Authors are dedicated users of wordprocessing systems, once they have learnt how to handle them.

Let us therefore see how writing can be tackled and supported by a wordprocessing system.

Task analysis

A text is a sequence of letters, which ultimately make up words and sentences. This is true both in the paper-and-pencil world and in the wordprocessing world. There is no need to define ideas or relationships between ideas, no need to find a hierarchical order between concepts and thoughts. The sequential nature of a text is "natural", because since their early schooldays people have been taught to read and write texts in this way. Even though "a picture says more than a thousand words", there is very little training in picture drawing at school compared with the training in composing words from letters, and texts from words. Thus the simple model of transferring from one medium (be it a handwritten text, shorthand notes, or thoughts) to a printed version of the text, with various requirements as to lay out, should be enough to introduce the idea of a wordprocessor or text editor to a prospective user.

Wordprocessors support three different functions which are crucial to the handling of texts, i.e. travelling, viewing and editing (cf Yankelovich, Meyrowitz & vanDam, 1985). Travelling refers to activities necessary for discovering the place to be attended to (for viewing or editing). Viewing refers to the extraction of what is to be displayed, while editing refers to the changes which the writer wants to make in the text.

Conceptual objects and the operations of wordprocessors

Wordprocessors differ with regard to the type and number of objects and operations with which they are concerned, but all have a common "core" of objects and operations which are very closely related to the paper-and-pencil world.

The following objects are usually possible to manipulate:

    Signs, usually letters, numbers and delimiters
    Words
    Lines
    Printed page (not always)
    Screen page
    Paragraphs (differs)
    User-chosen part of text
    Text

The following operations are usually allowed:

    Delete
    Insert
    Copy
    Place (copy)
    Find
    Find and replace
    Go to (next or preceding sign, word, line, or page, beginning of text, end of text) (differs)

Most of these semantic objects and operations are already familiar to the users of typewriters.

One totally new concept has to be learnt, both here and in other interactive systems, i.e. the concept of the "cursor". The cursor is connected with the "travelling" function, which in a paper situation is usually performed by hand and eye. In a wordprocessing system the user's attention and the cursor's position may not coincide. The user then has to know how to get the cursor to the desired position.

It is interesting to examine a little more closely those objects and operations which differ from paper-and-pencil use. We have already encountered some examples of difficulties in learning wordprocessing systems, in the chapter on learning (Chapter 5). These difficulties can be attributed to the conceptual differences between the wordprocessing world and the paper-and-pencil world.

The first crucial difference concerns the problem of "figure" and "ground". On paper the text represents the "figure", and the paper the background. Thus all the paper showing between words and at the end of lines and paragraphs is no more than "background", and it is something that cannot be manipulated in the same way as the text. A text can be rubbed out and replaced by another, but the idea of "rubbing out" the paper behind the text, i.e. the background, is nonsensical.

At the same time the text "belongs" to a particular position on the paper. It "occupies" this place, which means that in order to change the text it is necessary either to rub it out and replace it by another text or to cut it out together with the paper it occupies. The paper limits the possible movements of the text. A novice wordprocessor user would not expect a text string which is too long to fit between the margins to move from right to left on the next line (so called "wrap around"), nor would he expect it to be moved to a new page. Also, the idea that new text can be inserted at a particular place without first making room for it, is foreign to a person who has only used a typewriter.

These differences stem from the fact that a wordprocessor treats the text as a sequence of signs which can be distributed on the screen according to the wishes of the user. The wishes of the user are expressed by the text he feeds in, as well as by the commands he gives. The sequence of signs includes all keypresses by the user (except those corresponding to commands). This means that even spaces produced by the space bar are regarded as "signs" by the system.

In the paper-and-pencil world, spaces are not signs. They are just the opposite: an interruption in a sequence of signs. Spaces are blanks on a paper; when you write manually, you do nothing to create them. You lift your hand and let a piece of paper shine through. On a typewriter you have to depress a key, but nothing is produced on the paper. The only visible happening is that the type-wheel moves forwards. The main impression is that the paper is left blank, without any signs. This difference between "sign" and "blank space" in the paper-and-pencil situation leads to difficulties in wordprocessing, when the blank spaces have to be used as "signs".

A possibly confusing situation arises when the system is used to type over an existing text—the so-called "overwrite" or "type" mode. When overwriting existing text, all keypresses (excluding function keys) delete the signs already existing, and insert the sign of the key pressed, including the blank sign. Pressing the space bar then gives the impression that the existing text is deleted. Another confusing situation occurs when the system is used in the "insert" mode, when the position of the signs on the screen is crucial. Then every sign, including the blank sign, will move the signs on the right of the current insert position one step to the right. As we noted in the earlier chapter on learning (Chapter 5) this effect is difficult for a novice user to understand.

Another difference between the paper and the wordprocessor situation is connected with the function of "finding" and "replacing". On paper you have to do the finding yourself, with your eyes. The idea of searching and finding a string automatically is quite new. However, it does not really conflict with anything people have learnt before, and should thus be easy to learn.

The "replace" concept may be more difficult, particularly if used for repeated "replaces". The difficulty here lies in finding a unique string. To the human eye the string to be replaced looks unique, simply because we do not conceive of the other possibilities. To replace all occurrences of "per" by "con" in order to change "perceive" to "conceive" may have quite disastrous consequences: persist will become consist, permutation conmutation, and person conson. To anyone unused to computers, the system is "blind" indeed!

Wordprocessing systems also impose particular requirements which novice users do not think of. One example is the necessity of telling the system which input string should be considered as part of the text and which is meant as an instruction to the system to change the text. To a novice user this distinction is unnatural. It is not a requirement included in the task as defined by a typewriter. It can therefore be expected that novice users will have difficulty in shifting from typing to editing and vice versa.

Human–computer communication and wordprocessors

The early wordprocessors worked on one line at a time. The user could "order" one particular line, edit it, and then get it back into the shape it should have. The edited line was always returned to the position of the last line shown when the request for the line was issued. This way of working was modelled on the way the paper-terminal worked: a new text or a new edit could only be placed at the bottom of the text, where the paper was empty. On a screen this arrangement is very confusing to a novice user. The unwanted lines are still visible, and the new version appears at the bottom, which makes the text very difficult to read.

This type of editing was tolerable when nothing better was available; it worked best for short texts, possibly for program texts. For the more complex needs of authors, secretaries, and so on a different kind of dialogue was necessary. When the screen-oriented editor arrived the users were able to get on paper almost exactly what they saw on the screen.

One difference persisted, however, which has not yet been solved: the difference between working at the screen and producing wonderful documents there and getting these splendid layouts and different fonts on the paper. There are very few combinations of computers and printers which can really claim that "what you see on the screen is what you get on the paper".

There is, for instance, the different size of the pages on screen and on paper, not to mention different papers. Unless the system has some kind of arrangement for calculating the length of the pages in print, problems will arise. Figures that have to be inserted may be cut in two, with half at the bottom of one and half at the top of the next. Unless the users are careful, headings may appear at the bottom of one page, and the rest of the paragraph on the next page. It may be difficult to place footnotes at the right place. Of course many wordprocessing systems try to get round the difficulties, but a novice user, who is not expecting the problems, will have to learn to take preparatory steps in order to make the transition from screen to paper.

Another common complaint from wordprocessor users is that the wordprocessor screen is usually smaller than an ordinary piece of paper (often no more than 23 lines, as against a typewritten page that can take around 60). This makes the overview of a text on a screen more difficult than it is on a page.

Let us now turn to the communication between user and system. A consistent set of commands is easier to learn and remember than one that is not consistent (see chapter 13). In the wordprocessing world there is at least one example of a system that functions very well but has a rather inconsistent set of commands.

This system distinguishes between "small" entities like letters and "big" entities like words by the use of different keys. If a user wants to delete a letter, the "ctrl" key should be depressed together with the letter "d". If a word is to be deleted, the "esc" key should be depressed together with the letter "d". This is thus a rule which can be used to learn the distinctions used in deleting. The same rule which distinguishes between "small" and "big" can now be used for other purposes as well. To delete a line you depress "ctrl" and "k", but there is no equivalent for deleting a paragraph.

Another distinction is connected with moving "forwards" and "backwards". In screen scrolling this distinction is captured by the same keys as the ones relating to "small" and "big" for deletions. To move forward one screen "ctrl" and "v" are depressed together. Following the "small" and "big" rule, the novice user may well expect that "esc" and "v" together would lead to a bigger move forward in the text; however, it leads the user one screen back. Thus the user has to learn a new rule for scrolling, which has no connection at all with the rule for deleting. He will also have to learn later that the "ctrl" and "esc" keys are not related to any particular semantic distinction, but simply to distinctions in a random way. It would be easier for the user if a completely new rule were invented to specify the distinction between "forwards" and "backwards". This rule could then possibly be used for scrolling as well as for deletion, for quick cursor movements up and down the screen, as well as for backward and forward search.

So much for the lack of consistency within one system. But a major problem for the users of several systems is that there are even greater inconsistencies between the dialogues used in different wordprocessing systems. The resulting confusion will be most pronounced in connection with the most commonly used functions, because these frequently recurring procedures are just the ones that sooner or later become automatic to the user. When he starts using a new system, in which new dialogue procedures have to be used for the same functions, his familiar automated procedures will be involuntarily evoked, as we saw in chapter 5,—even if the new system is intrinsically more user-friendly than the old one.

A particular difficulty arises in the communications required by the system for its own purposes. We have already noted that the system has to be told when the user intends to insert text or when he intends to instruct the system to do something with the text. Switching from inserting to editing is something that occurs fairly frequently in wordprocessing, and it is only to be expected that users changing from one system to another will easily confuse one way of making this change with another. Even if the solution may seem satisfactory in one system (for instance not having any "modes" for typing or editing, but solving the distinction by using menus), the very fact that systems differ will cause difficulties as soon as the user is involved with more than one of them.

Another aspect of dialogue concerns the actual words (or other designations) used for the commands (or in the menu). The actual designations should both embrace such semantic distinctions as are necessary, while also being self-explanatory. These two requirements sometimes collide.

To take one example: in the world outside computers users "write" and they have no need to distinguish between "writing" on screen, "writing" on paper outside the screen, "writing" into the internal memory of the computer, or "writing" to some kind of permanent storage. In order to capture the distinctions, different words have to be used. For screen writing, "show", "display", and "type" are often used. For paper writing, "write", "print" or "spool" are common terms, while for permanent-memory writing, "save", "store", and "file" are all usual designations. When writing into the CPU of the computer, the "return" or the "enter" key is often used. Looking at this list, we can see that the distinction can be captured well enough by using "display" for the screen, "print" for the paper output and "store" for the permanent storage. Note that it is not possible to take one word at a time and to find a "natural" word corresponding to its meaning. Instead the whole context has to be considered, with the various distinctions that must be made.

As things are now, almost all wordprocessing systems have their own distinct designations. A few examples: In one system the command "ctrl Y" means "delete the rest of the line", a command which cannot be undone. In another, the same command means "retrieve the recently deleted signs". The resulting confusion could be disastrous. In another case we have one system in which "ctrl l" means "rewrite the screen" and in another it produces an empty line. Here confusion between systems may not prove quite as fatal, but could still be extremely annoying.

Implications for human–computer communication

The following are some general recommendations for creating a good dialogue in a wordprocessing system.

1. The communicative language should emphasize the distinctions which are performed in the functions chosen. This means for instance that two words which in natural language are close synonyms should not be used to designate quite different functions. In a wordprocessing system "write" and "type", for instance, should not be used to activate the system processes of "writing on the screen" and "typing on paper".
2. The communicative language should also emphasize distinctions which are required by the system but not recognized by novice users. In a wordprocessing system, the distinction between "insert" and "edit", for instance, may easily be confused.
3. The communication should build on consistent rules for handling the distinctions. As we have seen, it is better to have one rule referring to the distinction of "small" and "big" and another for the distinction between "forwards" and "backwards". In this way different functions can make the same distinctions with the help of the same rule.

Effects of wordprocessors

For "ordinary" people computer aid in writing may come to represent as big a change in writing strategies as learning to write at all once did. Most people in the Middle Ages were unable to write, and had to use professionals to write even their most personal letters for them; education in writing has made all kinds of writing available to all (educable) people. So far computer aid in writing is not available to all, but we can already speculate about its effect on the writing world.

At present the most common computer aid is the wordprocessor. Its main virtue is that it makes it very easy to change a text. This aspect of wordprocessing has already been mentioned in the testimony of experienced wordprocessor users (cf Severinson-Eklundh & Sjöholm, 1987), many of whom reported that the wordprocessor had changed their writing strategies. They now often write texts directly on the wordprocessor, which they did not use to do when they wrote by hand or on the typewriter. Also they now do more work on their actual wording and make more minor changes in the formulation of their text.

The use of wordprocessors does not always encourage writers to make revisions in their texts, however. Daiute & Kruidenier (1985) report on a study of the use of wordprocessors by seventh to ninth-grade schoolchildren. Some of the students were told explicitly to reflect on their own writing, by being asked questions such as "Does this paragraph make a clear point?" The researchers found that the use of the wordprocessor did not in itself change the students' tendency to revise their documents. However, the group prompted by the questions revised their texts to a greater extent than the group using the wordprocessor without any prompting to check the result. Some other studies have tried to discover whether wordprocessors affect linguistic style in a positive way. Again, it might be expected that the opportunity for revising would also provide a chance to change formulations which had not been well thought out from the beginning. In a study reported by Card, Roberts & Keenan (1984), subjects were asked to write some texts with the help of a wordprocessor and others with paper and pencil only. The time taken to finish the texts was the same, but it was found that the number of changes made with the help of the wordprocessor was about five times as high as those made when writing by hand. There was no difference in the stylistic quality of the texts; a little less than half the changes were judged to have made any stylistic improvement.

In an informal way journalists have also reported that changes do not always lead to better results. They felt that changes were often made in the wording in two consecutive sentences, for instance, without adequate attention being paid to the relation between them. This made for a disconnected staccato style. Sometimes the language was no longer even correct, e.g. words might be used in the wrong order. We should remember that this informal account may refer to the effects of wordprocessors used in stressful situations (delivery deadlines), but the possibility of such effects is worth noting.

It has been suggested that the use of wordprocessors seems to promote minor changes in formulations rather than major changes in the text itself, such as moving paragraphs from one part of it to another (Collier, 1983). Big changes of this kind are technically speaking easy enough to do on most wordprocessors, but because of the small size of the screen it is so difficult for the writer to get an overview of the text, that the context is easily lost. We might well wonder whether such big changes would be made on a typewriter either. Cognitive limitations are probably enough to restrict writers to the narrowest contexts when revising texts in full. Major changes are more likely to be made at the outline or ideas stage, when the writer has not yet got bogged down in the details of words and sentences. Thus it seems that major text revisions will be helped not by computer aid in the shape of wordprocessors but by aids of the other kinds mentioned here, such as idea processors or outline support systems.

SUMMARY

The aim of this chapter has been to analyse the cognitive aspects of computer support systems for the subtasks involved in translating ideas into text. The purpose of the cognitive task analysis was to see how the task as a whole could be broken down into subtasks. We have asked ourselves what subtasks can be carried out by a computer system in a way that eases the performance of the task as a whole. In particular, it has been suggested that any subtasks that are tedious, difficult or impossible to do by hand or mind alone, should be delegated to a computer system. Creative and stimulating subtasks (however defined!) should be left to the human subject.

Several different subtasks can be identified, and suggestions have been made as to which of them can be carried out by computer systems. It can be claimed that the progression from ideas to text is such an integrated affair, that any partition into independent subtasks will hamper the generation of ideas as well as the expression of ideas as text. At the same time, it has to be recognized that the computer aids suggested are able to carry out tedious but necessary subtasks, as well as subtasks which might never be considered if the support systems were not available.

A support system for processing ideas does that part of the job that involves storing ideas and retrieving them when needed. The concepts required by such a system, i.e. "ideas" and "relations between ideas" may be difficult to grasp before ideas have been fairly fully worked out. It thus seems likely that computer support in the processing of ideas would be most valuable when the ideas have become stable enough to be expressed in words and the relationships between them clear enough to be written down in explicit form. At this stage in the processing of ideas, the tedious and sometimes distracting process of finding and surveying ideas which have already been formulated, can receive beneficial support from a computer system.

Support in creating and altering outlines facilitates the work of revising and listing headings, but is unlikely to be of much use unless it is integrated with a system which also facilitates writing and changing the text (i.e. a wordprocessing system).

A system for translating a well-thought-out idea structure into text could help people who have to work on technical texts without any literary aspirations. The old dream of making automatic translations from one language to another may never die, and may even be revived in the design of systems for generating texts from ideas.

Lastly, the most useful computer aid in this field so far enables the writer to write and without difficulty to change a text already written. A wordprocessing system relieves the writer of the boring task of rewriting whole passages of text simply because a few minor points have to be changed. It also performs other boring parts of the job, like checking the spelling or exchanging some frequent term or word for another wherever it appears in the text. In order to perform these useful functions, the system requires new concepts and distinctions, which could be difficult for a novice user to acquire. The most important concepts that the user must learn stem from the fact that the screen is not always simply a "background" to the text, but that blank spaces between words may well represent meaningful "signs" to the computer system, and from the fact that the system has to be told when it is receiving text to be written and when it is receiving instructions about what to do with the text already written.

At present the wordprocessing function is one of the most common ways in which computer systems are being used in the writing process. Consequently the human–computer communication aspect of this function strikingly illustrates one of the drawbacks of the uncontrolled development of computer systems, i.e. the lack of conformity that faces the user. In different wordprocessing systems the same functions can be performed in as many different ways as there are systems. Not only does the way the text is displayed differ (from the edited rows detached from the text proper to the "what-you-see-is-what-you-get" philosophy), but even the words used to drive the system (in commands or menus) vary for no apparent reason. Radical clearance in this jungle of communication practices would make room for healthier growth in the use of wordprocessing systems.

Finally, wordprocessors seem to lead the writer to perform more text changes than before. These changes most often concern only minor parts of the text, and do not necessarily lead to a better style. Wordprocessors do not seem to adequately support big changes, such as the restructuring of relationships between ideas or the sequencing of these.

Chapter 9

From Question to Answer

INTRODUCTION

Since computers are at present the best media for storing and retrieving simple data, it is natural that they should be used for these two purposes. What could be more obvious than designing systems to answer questions about stored data? People who need information for solving a variety of problems have seen in electronic storage a quick way of satisfying this need, and systems designers have been required to store various kinds of data. Repeatedly, however, people have been disappointed to find that the reality does not come up to their expectations.

I shall analyse below some problems related to this business of asking and answering questions. We will find that the problems themselves are such that any hope of solving them simply by way of computer information storage is certainly exaggerated.

In order to understand the problem of seeking and providing information, let us start from a very simple situation. Suppose we are standing at a crossroads, and we don't know which road to take to get to a certain destination. The road signs give no hint, and we have no map. Someone comes along and we ask him which road to take to reach our goal.

A common definition of information is related to situations of this type. The information seeker and the information provider both know that there are certain possible alternatives. The information provider reduces the number of alternatives to be considered. If he can reduce them to one, then he can give a definite answer. In this very simple situation, information can be defined as "reduction of uncertainty". The technical calculation of uncertainty follows the following formula:

$$H = \log_2 N$$

where H = the entropy (uncertainty) of the information and N is the number of (equally probable) alternatives.

From this formula we can see that in a sense we get "more" information if we receive a correct answer when there are five possible routes from the crossroads than when there are only two.

This simple situation can be taken as a reference point in our examination of what is needed in order to ask questions and to answer them. First, the questioner in the crossroads case knows his destination and knows that he does not know what road to take. Second, the questioner knows about the possible alternatives. The answerer knows both the destination and the road, and also perceives the same alternatives as the questioner. This means that much information can be given at little cost.

A common example of such a simple situation occurs when we call the speaking clock. The questioner knows the alternatives (different times of day), and knows whom to ask. The question is implicit (what is the time *now*?) in his dialling the requisite telephone number. The answering machine "understands" the question as a result of being called at a particular time. The answer can then simply be played back from prerecorded numbers, the combination of which changes according to a calibrated clock mechanism. Most people would hesitate to call such answering machines "databases".

As soon as we leave the simple situation in which questioner and answerer see the same alternatives, neither the question nor the answer can be easily defined any longer, and the following problems may occur.

1. The questioner and the answerer may not have the same frame of reference as regards information. We could compare this with the situation in which the person at the crossroads asks someone else over the telephone which road to take. In the worst possible case the answerer does not even know where the questioner is. In a somewhat more favourable case he may not know exactly what the roads look like, and is therefore unable to understand what the questioner is referring to when he says: "There's one road to the right which is fairly straight."
2. The questioner does not know exactly what he wants to know. This is a situation that is fairly familiar to students and to experts. In most cases of information search the information being sought is by definition unknown. The request: "Tell me what I need to know in order to solve my problem" is far from well-defined, and this ill-defined nature of the question causes problems not only in envisaging the question but also in evaluating the answer to it. Not even an expert questioner may always be able to tell whether or not an answer provided is relevant to the problem.
3. The questioner does not know how to formulate his question so that the answerer will understand it. This is a problem even between people who speak the same language, as has been found in many situations in which experts try to help people. The problem is further aggravated if the answerer is a computer system with its own idiosyncrasies. This problem has so far received most attention in research on database search.

Let us now see how computers have been used to handle information needs.

Computer systems for handling data have developed from the conventional type of handling fairly well-defined concepts (databases) through human indexing of more vaguely defined concepts (information systems), to the so-called "knowledge engineering" of very complex concepts that are difficult to define (knowledge bases). The designations "information" and "knowledge" do not accord with our everyday definitions of these words—and certainly not with the philosophical distinctions! Thus a short description of the way the words are used in a computer context would be in place here.

The term "data" or "database" is often used to refer to objects or concepts which are described in terms of some generally agreed distinctions, often quantitative ones such as age or salary, or simple qualitative ones such as address or sex. This means that a database user should be able to handle data easily, provided only that he knows the distinctions used to describe it. However, as we shall see below, even this simple situation may cause difficulties when it comes to formulating questions and evaluating answers.

The term "information system" is often used to describe systems for handling objects or concepts that are not very well-defined, for example scientific articles which may be classified by some expert in the field (when an indexing procedure is followed), or by the author himself using keywords, or by his actual wording in the text (when a full-text search is possible). In all cases the questioner must understand what distinctions have been used (in the indexes or in the texts) and be able to envisage how his particular information need could be matched to the indexes or wording. It is so difficult to find a match between the information need and the information hidden in the system that the user is often given special support by another person (a documentalist).

The term knowledge base, finally, is used to describe systems which represent not only complex concepts and heuristic rules to handle problems, but which also offer possible manipulations on the concepts, such as drawing conclusions, making predictions, decisions, etc. A questioner who does not know the structure and content of the knowledge as defined by the system, has little chance of understanding the alternatives offered by the system. Therefore knowledge bases that are to be used by human beings must be provided with a very complex "negotiation" procedure, whereby the information need of the user is defined by an interaction between the system and the user. We shall encounter these problems in the next chapter.

The technical and human problems in the defining and handling of databases, information systems and knowledge bases, depend on the complexity of defining the existing alternatives and designing the permissible questions and possible answers. The farther we move away from "data" towards "knowledge", the more complex is the world that we want to be able to ask questions about. This means that not only the computer representation of the data or knowledge becomes more complex, but so too does the communication with the user in order to provide answers.

Let me start by analysing the database search situation.

DATABASE SEARCH

For our present purpose a database can be defined as a collection of data which can be accessed only by the active questioning of a user. This distinguishes database search from the use of knowledge based systems, where the system is more active and information is developed in interaction between the system's questions to the user and the user's questions to the system.

The use of a database presupposes a need for information. A business manager requires information in order to make a decision, a journalist collects information to write an article, a scientist searches in order to find where information is lacking. The information-seeker's need may be clear and precisely specifiable, or it may be initially vague and specifiable only after it has been satisfied. The need is expressed to other people in natural language, and the stored material is also represented to a great extent in natural language. The expected answer may be a text or figures, to be arranged later in tables or graphs.

The process of deriving information and synthesizing knowledge is clearly circular and cumulative, which means that the same database may operate differently for different people and at different stages in the cycle. It may not even be the best solution for the user to retain the original content in the database at different stages. He may want to introduce his own synthesis in addition to the database, for instance, to make its use more efficient in subsequent cycles of the information-synthesizing process.

Let us look at the problems from the point of view of the user. First, the information need has to be matched to existing data; secondly, a query has to be formulated in the query language offered; and finally, the data obtained have to be evaluated with reference to the information need.

Matching information need to existing data

Data does not turn into information until it answers a question. Thus, the value of a database can only be measured in terms of the information needs of potential users.

Let me take an example. The local council in a small community wanted to find out how many children would need a swimming school during the summer. Since no data was available, they sent out a questionnaire to the local inhabitants to find out how things stood. This worked well, and a swimming school was started with the number of instructors well matched to the number of children needing their instruction. The following year the question of putting up a new building for school-starters came up for discussion, and since the age of these children coincided with the age of the children attending the swimming school, it was decided to use the data on swimming-school pupils as a base on which to plan the new building. Construction began and everybody was happy until school started. Then it turned out that far fewer children started school than had been expected. Why? The simple explanation was that many people lived in the community in the summer only. This may appear an obvious mistake, still it shows something of what has to be considered when we search a database.

Another example: It had been decided for reasons of planning to try to find out how many people living in Sweden did not have Swedish as their native language. Such people might require special help, perhaps extra lessons at school, special radio or TV programs, and so on. The databases available had no information on "native language". So this had to be defined in terms of the data that was available, which included data on where people were born and where their parents had been born. On the simple assumption that people born abroad did not have Swedish as their native language, and a second assumption that the children whose parents were born abroad did not have Swedish as a native language either, the shocking information emerged that barely 50% of the Swedish population had Swedish as their native language! A false conclusion, certainly, but one derived from existing databases.

An exaggerated belief in the usefulness of databases can be discerned in the current tendency to store all possible "data" in a computer for possible future "use". Since computers can store an enormous amount of data, this costs very little. Some researchers, for instance would like to see all the data from all studies in their field stored in computers. Here, however, we have to ask ourselves how this data can be turned into information. Can data from a study conducted by one researcher be helpful to another? The answer will depend on the question posed by the first researcher and on the question the second researcher wants to ask. How can it be decided whether the stored data matches the later need for information, and who can judge this issue?

This problem has been analysed by Belkin (1978). Belkin suggests that the core problem consists in "facilitating the effective communication of desired information between human generator and human user" (p.58). It is obvious that one major problem lies in the differences in perspective between the data generator and the information searcher. Information is generally needed by professionals with complex problems for which there are no ready-made answers in any database. Thus it cannot be expected that the relevant information can be found by direct means. Rather, it has to be inferred from such data as is available.

The importance of prior knowledge

It seems obvious that a user who knows something about the database has a much better chance of matching his information need to the database than one who does not know anything about it. A series of experiments conducted by Lena Linde and Monica Bergström (Linde, 1986, Linde & Bergström 1988) confirms this expectation. In these studies, subjects were prepared for a database search in some different ways. One group was trained by searching in tables, where the names of the columns differed from those used in the later table search, i.e. these subjects were trained in the formal aspects of the database. Another group was trained in drawing inferences from statements referring to the database, i.e. they were being familiarized with the content of the database. It was found that the subjects who had become familiar with the content of the database spent less time on their search when they were told to search online than the subjects trained only in table search; the former group also needed less help.

Search strategies

Since the user cannot know exactly what is in a database (otherwise he would have no need to ask!), it is rather rare for him to reach his goal after a single question. Rather, the search in the database often consists of a sequence of questions and answers. The user thus acquires some knowledge of the database and finds out what kind of information can be obtained from different kinds of question. The user can adopt various strateiges in choosing the sequence of questions. He can either approach the topic broadly, by posing questions covering different aspects of the subject in what is called a breadth-first strategy. Or he can approach the topic by asking questions which intersect each other successively, i.e. according to a depth-first stragegy.

In a database where the questions are arranged to intersect with each other successively, only the depth-first strategy is possible. For some users, however, this may not be the best approach. Some users may prefer to get an overview first and then to decide. This working style is precluded in a database system which requires an intersecting approach. But the strategy can be efficient in many situations. In particular, a breadth-first strategy can provide the information about the database that the user may lack. A depth-first strategy is only efficient if the user already knows from the start where to begin.

In a study of pupils searching for data in a very simple database, Beishuizen (1988) found that different pupils use different strategies with equal success. Beishuizen therefore suggests that a database should give users the opportunity to employ their preferred working style.

In another study, conducted by Lena Linde and myself (Linde & Wærn,

1985), users' strategies in handling an incomplete database were studied. We found that the more efficient users (in terms of number of questions posed in order to solve a problem) often started by asking for an overview of the concepts in the database. This can be regarded as a breadth-first strategy. Since the data was both unknown to the users and incomplete, this strategy was the most efficient one.

FORMULATION OF QUERY

Most human-factors research in the field of database search has focussed on query language and the difficulty of formulating questions in such languages. In order to understand this difficulty we should perhaps consider some of the historical background.

Early in the history of databases, data was retrieved from the database by computer specialists. The user came with his question and the computer specialist wrote a special-purpose program for acquiring the requisite information from the database. In the 1970s this general procedure was facilitated by the construction of higher-level language, intended to be used by people who were not professional programmers. The query languages were thus constructed to help programmers avoid writing a new program each time somebody wanted some information from a database. For natural reasons the early query languages were thus designed to fit the needs and thinking of the programmers rather than those of new users.

The difficulty in mastering the query language is to some extent independent of the difficulty in matching the information need to the database. Even if a user knows exactly what question to ask (in natural language), the formulation of the question in the query language can cause problems. Many of the studies that have been made deal with just this situation: a user (generally in the laboratory) is instructed to find some information in a database. The information to be sought is described in the form of natural language.

Much of what has already been said about communication between human users and computers naturally also applies in the case of database query languages. However, certain special aspects should perhaps be considered, e.g. the logical problem of defining the information desired, the concept of the data "model", the procedural/declarative distinction, and the syntactic form. An overview of the human-factors aspects of query languages is given in Reisner (1981).

Logical problems

The query language is constructed to help the user to get information that is as concise as possible. This means that the user will get what he asks for, neither more nor less. Compared to a search in a paper-based medium, such as a telephone directory or a pile of index cards, much less information is obtained from a database search. On paper we usually find a lot of redundant information; when we look for a person's telephone number in the directory we also find his address which may or may not be useful in the present context. In a database search no side information is given, unless it is explicitly asked for. On the other hand there are several ways in which we can approach the database: we can find not only the telephone numbers of everybody called Andersson, but also (if the database contains the same data as the directory) all the telephone numbers of people living at a particular address.

The absence of redundancy is useful, if we know what we are looking for. In such a case we will not be told more than we ask for. At the same time, the conciseness requires that we formulate our query very carefully. If a questioner wants certain aspects only of the data to be included, this must be expressed by combining the requirements on the information in some way. The usual way of doing this is to use Boolean operators:

1. Intersection to mark that we want two requirements to be fulfilled simultaneously. Example: Which students have studied software and have an average grade below 2.5?
2. Union to mark that we want either one or the other requirement to be fulfilled. Example: Which have an average grade below 2.5 OR have studied software for more than 5 years?
3. Negation to mark that we want everything EXCEPT something particular. Example: Which students have not taken the course in software?

We can also combine negation with one of the other operators, whereby more complex situations arise.

4. Intersection between a positive and a negative set. Example: Which students have taken the course in software 1 but not in software 2?
5. Union between two negative sets. Example: Which students have not taken the course in software 1 or in software 2?

The examples come from a series of experiments, performed by Cecilia Katzeff, on students' logical reasoning in database search (Katzeff, 1986a, b)

We know from research on human reasoning that some of these combinations can be troublesome. In particular, people who are not logically sophisticated find it difficult to understand that the natural language meaning of "or" is ambiguous (can be inclusive or exclusive), and this can lead to problems in a database, in which only the Boolean inclusive "or" applies. Moreover, we know that people have difficulty in understanding the effect of a negation. This means that we may expect users of a database to have some slight trouble with examples 2 and 3 above, but to have much greater difficulty with examples 4 and 5. By "difficulty" is meant here both difficulty in expressing the question in logical form and difficulty in evaluating the outcome of the search.

The expected difficulties were demonstrated in Katzeff's studies. However, Katzeff also showed that it was possible to give users a model of the logic of the database and that this made it possible for them to handle their search with less confusion even in complex situations. The model consisted of Venn diagrams, in which positive and negative sets were marked.

The familiar logical difficulties thus have to be allowed for in considering database search, and there are various ways in which this can be done. Either the traditional Boolean search model has to be abandoned, or some restrictions made as regards the permissible combinations. The most usual approach at the moment is to restrict the permitted Boolean operations to simple intersections, which means that a depth-first strategy is being imposed on the users. We have seen that this search strategy may not be suited to all users, particularly those who have little knowledge of the content of the database. Another solution is to teach the users what intersection, union and negation really mean. Such a course is possible for some users at least, as Katzeff has shown, but it is probably only worth attempting in the case of fairly sophisticated users who want to conduct complex searches.

Data models

In order to express a question in a query language, the user must have some conceptual view of how the data is stored in the computer. This conceptual view is reflected in the query language, but does not need to correspond to the way the data is actually stored. There are three well-known data models, i.e. the relational model in which data is regarded as represented in the form of tables, the hierarchical model which sees the data as forming a hierarchy, and the network model, in which it is assumed that the data is stored in the shape of nodes and internal relationships. All these data models are used by people in natural situations, and have also been found in experiments in which people have been asked to sort words describing different concepts (cf Durding, Becker & Gould, 1977).

The suitability of the data models varies, depending on the data to be stored and the kind of questions which are asked.

When facts are being kept for the purpose of keeping track of goods and deliveries, personnel and salaries, or patients and treatments, for instance, a table structure is generally used. A table of facts may look like this:

Table 1a.   Characteristics of the sensory system

Personal names	Department	Function	Salary
Brown	Hobby	Marketing	15.000:–
Jones	Flowers	Decorator	10.000:–
Brown	Food	Cashier	9.000:–

Such a table provides information in answer to such questions as: "Tell me the names of all the people with marketing functions", or "Tell me where all the people who are called Brown are working and who earns more than 20.000:–".

Thus a table model is useful for data which easily lends itself to two-dimensional representation. The table approach then provides a comprehensive and structured overview of the data required.

A hierarchical form of database presentation is often used in public databases, concerned with information about news, sport, theatre, etc. Here the hierarchical form seems to provide a natural way of sorting out at an early stage everything which might possibly be irrelevant. It might be thought that people looking for a particular football match are unlikely to be very interested in getting information about theatres and vice versa. At lower levels a table approach might be more useful. After the first level of hierarchy, we have to consider what the next suitable level could be. Place? Or time? Or the name of the league?

The drawbacks of the hierarchical database may be that users feel lost in such a big base, that they do not know "where they are" if the hierarchy is not familiar to them, and that they will have difficulty in "navigating" through the base. Such problems are common in most public databases, as Young & Hull (1982) for instance have reported in a study of casual users interacting with Viewdata.

A network approach can be useful when the data has no clear structure. The concept of "hyper-text", which was discussed in chapter 8 in connection with the processing of ideas, is one example of this approach which has recently become increasingly popular. In a hyper-text organization, the data is represented in the shape of nodes and links. Each node can contain different kinds and different amounts of information. A node may contain a full text or a picture, or it may simply consist of a heading relating to several texts.

Studies of different data models in databases have not been able to prove that one model is "better" than any other. Brosey & Shneiderman (1978) report that queries, formulated in a hierarchical model are better understood than the same queries formulated in a relational model (table format). However, the database in this study had a natural tree structure. Other studies (Lochovsky & Tsichritzis, 1977, Ray, 1985) have found that less experienced users wrote more correct queries when using a relational model.

These divergent results could well make a conscientious system designer despair. But in fact the differences are not difficult to explain: the subjects were not given the same tasks (comprehending versus writing) and the databases were probably different too. It is quite probable that a particular data model fits a particular set of data better than another, and that users find it easier to write queries which suit their particular information needs. However, we do not know how much would be gained or how much effort it would take to create and learn new query languages for new databases. Most researchers in this field are too impatient to conduct meticulously controlled studies of all combinations of users, databases, and query languages. There are so many other things competing for the system designer's time and energy that such studies are unlikely to be considered worth the effort.

The procedural/declarative distinction

The distinction between "procedures" and "declarations" in database search has provoked a certain amount of discussion, but has still not been clearly defined. According to Date (1977) a "non-procedural" query states "what the result of the query is, not how to obtain it". It has been suggested that a procedural language should be easier to learn than a non-procedural, because people conceptualize the computer search as a sequence of steps: first the computer finds the table, then it looks for columns, then it looks for the information desired in that column (cf Reisner, 1981). In a study conducted by Welty & Stemple (1981) it was found that users made more errors when using a less procedural language (SQL) than when using a more procedural one (Tablet). However, this difference was obtained only in the case of complex queries.

As new approaches to database search are developing, the distinction between procedural and declarative is emerging as something that is difficult to define and not really relevant to the question of user-friendliness. The new notion of virtually "navigating" one's way through a database suggests a procedural approach, whereas the various logical languages that are being developed promise advantages from adopting a declarative approach. It may well be that "navigating" and "declaring" have to be separate in search activities, and that both are necessary: navigating for finding what should be declared, and declaring when no navigating is needed.

Syntactical aspects

The syntactical aspects of query languages concern the form in which the queries have to be written. Most commercial query languages require a very restricted form that deviates radically from natural language. The question has therefore been raised as to whether it is possible to communicate with a database by asking questions and receiving answers in natural language.

As early as 1978 some natural language interfaces to databases were described (Waltz, 1978). The dialogue samples sound natural enough, as the following example shows:

User: How many Phantoms required unscheduled maintenance in April 1975?

System: Thirty Phantoms. Do you want to see them?

User: No. Did any of these require radar maintenance?

System: Yes, three of them. Do you want to see them?

. . .

. . .

User: Is it true that both Phantoms were fron the same squadron?

System: I assume you mean "from" instead of "fron". Yes, both planes were from the same squadron (Waltz, 1976, p. 21).

Even if it is possible to create a natural language dialogue which really does seem natural (see also Weizenbaum, 1966), several researchers are very hesitant about recommending natural language as the vehicle of communication between a human user and the computer system. Full natural language capability cannot be achieved at a reasonable cost, or within a real-time interaction situation, or for any but a very restricted domain. Thus the user will probably become confused by having to learn the exceptions in the computer system. There is a risk that the system's capacity will first be overvalued, because natural language facilities may remind the user of a human assistant, and that when the user detects the limitations, the system may instead be undervalued as a result of disappointment.

There are certain other aspects in database search which render natural language less useful than more formal languages. If we still want to be able to make logical combinations, natural language will be too vague for the logical rigour required. In particular the natural language use of "or" and "not" are ambiguous. It is even possible that people who have to express themselves in a language which is not natural may be compelled to think more carefully. Careful planning and afterthought are required to obtain and evaluate information from a database!

Turning now to the more formal query languages, we find a distinction between languages which work in the two-dimensional space of the computer screen and those which work with linear strings. "Query by Example" is an example of space-oriented language in which the user has a table to fill in, and the information sought is left out, while SQL is an example of a linear language.

To illustrate this let us compare two query language expressions to the following question:

"Find the names of employees in department 50."

The following is the formulation in Query by Example:

Emp	Name	Deptno	Sal
		50	

As a contrast, a formulation of the same question in a linear string in SQL is the following:

SELECT NAME
FROM EMP
WHERE DEPT NO = 50

(Examples from Reisner, 1981, p. 14.)

Earlier studies showed that the time required to learn Query by Example was about a third of the time needed to learn SQL. This does not mean, of course, that all two-dimensional languages are easier to learn than all linear languages. There may be other differences between QBE and SQL which are as important as the difference in dimensionality. For instance, the Query By Example highlights the data model and reminds the user about the relevant data fields—two important aspects in learning and using query languages.

The problems which arise in connection with learning a formal database query language vary, depending on the language to be learnt. At the very beginning, everything will be difficult: the sequence of descriptors to be followed, the exact words to be used in describing fields and requirements, and punctuation and relational signs. Since the query language is a variant of a programming language, users who are not trained programmers will find particularly difficult those aspects of the language which include remnants of the "computer model". As for all interface languages, the need for "meaningfulness" in commands and "internal consistency" is important. One of the biggest problems, of course, lies in the differences between the various query languages. Transfer between languages is not easy, and knowledge of another language may even be a drawback because of the different conventions used.

There are some aspects of formal languages which users could be relieved from. Among these is the need to spell correctly and to use exactly the right word. In a study of minor mistakes made, Reisner found that the most common errors of the users who were not also programmers was using the wrong kind of ending, e.g. SELECT NAMES instead of SELECT NAME (Reisner, 1977). Other common errors were spelling mistakes and the use of synonyms (PERSONNEL for EMPLOYEE). Since we know that people often make mistakes in details both when remembering and typing, such errors were predictable. An easy way of solving the problem is either to correct the errors automatically (if it is clear what is meant) or to settle them in a dialogue with the user (if the computer finds alternatives). Spelling correctors and synonym lists are nowadays incorporated in some database systems.

Evaluating the result of a database search

Every answer from a database search has to be evaluated by the user and involves him in decisions: Is it relevant to his purpose? Where should he go next in order to find more (or better) information?

A decision-making approach to database search has been suggested by

Fischoff & MacGregor (1987). These authors point out the fallibility of the human decision-maker. Moreover, in chapter 4 above we have noted how bad most people are at integrating information according to formal models. A particularly relevant piece of evidence relates to people's confidence judgments; the user's confidence in the outcome of a database search determines his future actions. This means that some psychological insight into people's ability at gauging their confidence to the "real" uncertainty is helpful. It has been found, for instance, that people are generally overconfident; that is, they believe they are right more often than is in fact the case, the reason being that they often disregard or underestimate the impact of negative evidence (cf Fischhoff & Beyth-Marom, 1983, Nisbett & Ross, 1980).

The tendency to trust the result of a database search may be strongest in people who are not accustomed to this kind of search. Subjects studied by Katzeff (1988) were found to have different strategies for checking the answer yielded by the search. The most common strategy was to accept all answers which were not error messages from the system. Another less common strategy was to check whether information received corresponded to what was expected. The least common strategy was to check whether any information was included which should not have been according to the description. It should be noted that the subjects were not used to database search, and that the experiment took place in the laboratory, so that the risk of getting false information was not felt to be serious.

If the results can be generalized to other situations, they suggest that database users may run the risk of seeking and accepting data which "looks" relevant and failing to search for other kinds of data which could supplement or contradict that already found.

Because of weaknesses in everyday human thinking users would probably benefit from training in the evaluation of search. Thus, Fischoff & MacGregor (1987), for instance, suggest that they could be warned that a "database is probably harder to use than they think". A more efficient method might consist of training users explicitly in confidence judgments, as weather forecasters in the United States are trained, for instance (Murphy & Winkler, 1977). Another technique which has proved successful in other circumstances (Koriat, Lichtenstein & Fischoff, 1980) is to ask people to reflect on why they could possibly be wrong (and why other alternatives might be right).

Effects of databases

When the opportunity to store data in computers first arose, the usual overoptimistic hopes sprang up about the marvels offered by new technology. It was predicted that all the knowledge of the world would be available to everybody. Every home would have access to all the libraries; every schoolchild would learn how to access databases. Knowing *how* to search was considered more important than knowing *what* to search for.

We can always hope, of course, that humanity will become more knowledgeable as knowledge becomes more easily accessible. But, as I have tried to show above, data is not knowledge. Data does not even imply information. In order to transform data into information, some sort of question is needed. In order to make use of the data in databases, knowledge is required. It is not enough to know about what databases exist or know about query languages. Users must also know something about the subject matter covered by the database. Otherwise they will not be able to ask questions which serve their information needs. Nor will they be able to evaluate the answers they receive to their questions.

And so the effects of databases will probably echo those we have already seen in the case of libraries. People who already know a lot will get to know still more. But a great deal of training will be needed in mastering both the tool and the content.

SUMMARY

Databases can be defined as systems possessing the facility to store and retrieve data. Data is distinguished from information and knowledge by its application to a particular problem. Data turn into information when they answer a question.

In order to use a database efficiently, users have to match their own need for information to the data in the database. This means that they have to know what kind of information they can expect in the database. Their prior domain of knowledge is thus important. They also have to be able to choose an approach to the system which fits not only their own preferred search strategy but also the design of the database. To be able to put a complex query to a database system, users have to be able to cope with the common problem of formal logic. Further they have to understand exactly how the query should be formulated, something which can be fairly demanding in certain query languages. Finally, they have to evaluate the result obtained. Their opportunities for evaluating the search outcome and the search process depend on the system (is it easy to conduct supplementary checking searches?) as well as on themselves (do they know what is needed in order to check a result?).

Chapter 10

From Problem to Solution

FROM DATA TO KNOWLEDGE

The step from data to knowledge is a big one. Since we have defined the concept of information above, it should be appropriate to attempt a definition of knowledge here. According to one dictionary (Edwards, 1967), "Knowledge is justified true belief". Each of the words in the definition can be debated, i.e. what is justified, what is true and what is belief? However, in the context of using computer systems to represent human knowledge, this definition fits rather well.

A computer system intended to represent human knowledge is based on what an expert perceives as "true beliefs". Moreover, the system should have the chance to "justify" these beliefs (knowledge).

The possibility of capturing all the expert's knowledge in a computer system also implies that, by itself, the system should be able to solve the problems which the expert can solve. The idea of designing a system which can solve problems on its own is an intriguing one. It has also been proved to be possible, at least for some types of problem. This field has also attracted many researchers and system developers, and it is known under many names: expert systems, knowledge-based systems, rule-based systems, and knowledge systems.

It should be noted that each term by no means stands for a unitary phenomenon. They have each been applied to very different kinds of systems. In many practical applications simple functionalities have been offered under these labels, such as decision-making aids based on a simple weighting of alternatives against each other. These applications are regarded as rather trivial by the more theoretically minded researchers, working with artificial intelligence as a basis for knowledge systems. However, few of the systems based on ideas connected with artificial intelligence have been used in real-life situations. Most knowledge systems based on artificial intelligence concepts and methods have been developed at universities or research institutes to demonstrate what can be done.

I shall here use the term "knowledge system" to denote the whole class of systems which are based on rules for representing and handling knowledge. The term "expert system" will be used for a more restricted class of knowledge systems, to be defined later. I shall analyse the problem of offering knowledge systems here, basing my exposition on the different claims and counterclaims that have been made in this area. To start with, a few words should be said about artificial intelligence.

ARTIFICIAL INTELLIGENCE AS A BACKGROUND TO KNOWLEDGE SYSTEMS

The task of representing and utilizing knowledge in problem solving is one aspect of the whole problem of artificial intelligence, which differs from other kinds of programming in two ways. First, artificial intelligence is applied to problems which are regarded as requiring human intelligence: the production and comprehension of language, the interpretation of picture, induction, deduction and other forms of problem solving. Secondly, artificial intelligence adopts certain particular methods for solving these problems such as symbolic programming, propositional calculus and algorithmic or heuristic search.

Intelligent problem-solving systems were originally designed as fully automated systems. Possibly the first and certainly one of the first "intelligent" systems was the Logical Theorist designed by Newell & Simon (1956), which proved able to solve all the problems in Russell's *Principia Mathetmatics* as well as various new problems in the same domain. Other systems such as the General Problem Solver were also suggested for "simulating" human intelligence (Newell & Simon, 1961).

Some problems encountered by artificial intelligence

The biggest controversy connected with intelligent problem-solving systems concerns the possible simulation of human intelligence. Naturally, the automation of intellectual functions which have been considered specifically "human" challenges our conception of ourselves. This challenge will be further discussed in chapter 17. Even though the successes have sometimes been impressive, failures also appeared quite early. Hopes for the full automation of what we call "human intelligence" were not fulfilled. As one frustrated commentator put it: "AI's record of barefaced public deception is unparalleled in the annals of academic study" (*New Scientist*, on the back cover of the book by Dreyfus & Dreyfus, 1986). Perhaps hopes had been exaggerated and the problems underestimated.

What problems, then, are connected with the automation of human intelligence? I will limit myself here to a few aspects, namely self-consciousness, common sense and rule-based symbol processing, all of which are relevant for an evaluation of the potential of knowledge systems. Interestingly enough, criticism has come mainly from philosophers or people who have themselves been involved in designing artificially intelligent systems. Psychologists have been very quiet on the subject.

It has frequently been claimed that it is impossible in principle to design an artificial system which also possesses self-consciousness. A self-conscious system understands what it is doing and does not only react to meaningless rules (cf Searle, 1980). Without self-consciousness a system cannot tell that it knows a particular fact until it performs an act connected with this knowledge, and it certainly cannot tell that it does not know such a fact, until it has failed in a search for it. Nor can the system tell what strategies it is following in its problem solving without self-consciousness.

Up to a point, of course, a system can be built to include rules which inspect its own rules and their outcomes, as is the case in learning systems. The philosophical question still remains: is the system aware that it learns?

The next criticism is also based on a comparison between human and artificial intelligence. It has been questioned whether it is feasible at all to design systems which require "common-sense reasoning" or natural language comprehension (Dreyfus, 1972), and critics invoke the difficulty (or impossibility) of designing "context-free" systems, for either language comprehension or problem solving. We all know that words have different meanings in different contexts. We have also seen in Chapter 4 that the same basic problem has quite different psychological characteristics in different contexts. For a human being, a problem of logic expressed in abstract symbols is more difficult to solve than the same problem expressed in terms of a well-known everyday situation.

We have seen that people think in terms of analogies with what they already know, rather than in terms of context-free rules which are applied to an interpreted situation. This means that systems which simulate human thinkers would have to be equipped with an enormous amount of knowledge. The amount of knowledge is not necessarily a problem in itself—systems are growing bigger and more rapid every month; the problem lies rather in specifying the knowledge that people actually use and how they access that knowledge in each particular situation.

The last criticism which I shall mention here is based on a doubt as to whether people actually do reason at all with the help of symbols or whether they follow rules in their reasoning (see e.g. Dreyfus & Dreyfus, 1986, Winograd & Flores, 1986). People's problem-solving activities could equally well be explained in terms of "direct action" in the world, i.e. without necessarily any symbolic activity. Humans have an amazing ability to perceive patterns, and their capacity for parallel activities in the brain is greater than any existing computer can match (Dreyfus & Dreyfus, 1986). Thus the reason why people seem to be so bad at formal reasoning may be that it is simply not their natural method of thinking. People can learn rules and can even automate them, as when they learn foreign languages for example. But this is different from actually following rules in the process of reasoning.

Computer systems designers have responded to this last criticism with systems that simulate neural networks. For psychological reasons it seems certain that such systems will meet the same problems as we discussed above in   ⌐ with common-sense reasoning. We simply do not know what shou' networks. The problem of the representation of knowledge c⌐ even if we accept that knowledge may exist in the form c⌐ their connections.

Thus, two kinds of criticism have been raised. One conce⌐ question of what the computer in principle can or cannot do. ⌐ ⌐e otner concerns the parallel (or rather non-parallel) between human thinking and computer problem solving.

It is of course difficult to tell what is possible or impossible in principle, and what is only impossible because of practical limitations. We might claim, for instance, that most of the tasks attacked by artificial intelligence could in principle be performed by traditional computing methods. However, very few people dreamt of programming heuristic problem solving in Assembler or Fortran, although some fairly advanced formula calculations were performed in those languages. The practical problems of programming and running the programs were simply too great to encourage even the most adventurous computer enthusiasts. We can thus say that the advent of new computer languages, new computing methods, and more efficient computers led more people to believe that the gap between fantasy and reality could be crossed.

Let us now turn to the question of the possibility and desirability of designing systems which function in the same way as human beings. A common answer to this question is to quote the analogy with aeroplanes. So long as flying technology approached its task by trying to simulate the flight of birds, the attempts failed. Once the technology freed itself from the bird model, success was reached—which does not mean that no knowledge was gained from the study of birds.

With this analogy in mind, we can now ask ourselves whether or not knowledge systems should function as human beings. In some instances it may even be better that they do not (for instance in applications greatly dependent on formal reasoning). In these cases a stand-alone system may perform better than a human being. It could also be asked whether systems intended to support people in their problem solving have any need to function exactly like humans. Would it not be better for the human user to be supported by functions which he finds difficulty in performing, rather than working with a system that simulates the methods humans use to overcome their cognitive weaknesses?

A related question concerns the failure to distinguish adequately between the computer as a TOOL for problem solving and the computer as THE problem solver. At universities, in particular those involved in the development of "intelligent tutors", "intelligent help systems" or "natural language interfaces" tend to explore ways of producing a system that could solve the problems of tutoring, providing help or communicating without any human intervention.

An equally interesting challenge would be to develop systems which interact with humans in an "intelligent" way. The challenge lies in assuming that artificial intelligence and human intelligence differ in some essential way. Such an assumption calls for a special approach to this interaction, including a particular way of partitioning the problem-solving task. For instance, someone who is good at common-sense reasoning and language comprehension could take over those parts of the task which require these capabilities. The computer could then take over lengthy calculations, or processing according to "unnatural" formal rules, searching in big problem spaces, etc. This suggested approach has naturally to be elaborated and tested in detail. One problem that could arise concerns communications between human and computer about part results. How can the two parties be taught or designed to understand each other, if their basic models for calculation are essentially different?

Some of the difficulties and limitations of knowledge systems discussed below may well be due to the fact that the basic problems of task-partitioning and problem-solving communication have not yet been addressed.

Knowledge systems as experts or tools

Let us now look at the situation in which someone has a problem which he wants to solve, but he lacks some of the necessary knowledge. We can envisage two rather different ways in which he would need help.

On the one hand he might want to use the computer as most people ordinarily do, i.e. as a tool for solving the problem. In this case the knowledge sought plays the same role in the problem-solving process as a mathematical calculation or a statistical prediction. The user calls for the knowledge or inference which he thinks is required in the particular situation.

On the other hand, the user may need some more active help, which could be provided by a human expert. He would be willing to accept advice and recommendations, and would expect to learn something himself in the process. This time, the computer acts as an expert, with the consent of the user.

This distinction is an important one. The two approaches reflect the expectations with which the user addresses the system, and they affect the way in which he will understand the system and be able to benefit from its knowledge. This in turns means that a knowledge system and its interaction with the user must be designed according to the purpose envisaged by the user. A knowledge system intended as a tool should allow the user more freedom than one which is regarded as an expert. A user expecting to find a tool would not be pleased with a highly controlled dialogue, because he wants to take the lead. A user expecting to meet an expert, on the other hand, would expect not only good advice but also comprehensible explanations.

Hitherto most knowledge systems have been designed to fulfil an expert role, although some are now being designed as tools. Among these are the so-called interface systems, which serve as interface to data which are not directly accessible to the user. Such systems can be used for example in advanced process control.

Under the next heading I shall mainly focus on knowledge systems built to function as experts, i.e. on what are known as expert systems.

EXPERT SYSTEMS

Expert systems are concerned not with automating all kinds of human intelligence, or with content-free human intelligence (such as formal logic), but with human expert knowledge in some particular domain.

The list of tasks addressed by such systems is already impressive, and can be expected to grow.

Some variants can be mentioned:

— Process control, in which the computer takes in data from a process and processes the data independently. Human beings are usually involved only in supervising the process control.
— One-shot decision, planning, and configuration, in which all input data can be given at the start and no further interaction is required. An example of such a system is the very successful system for configuring VAX computers, called X-con.
— Computer problem solving, in which the computer requests data from a human user as and when it is needed. This case is the prototype for the systems called "expert systems".
— Human problem solving with the support of a computer system. Here the human solves the problem, and the computer checks the solution and gives further advice or recommendations if the human solution is not correct (or suboptimal). This case is exemplified by what is called "critiquing systems". The various attempts to develop "active help systems" for computer users are an example of this approach to knowledge systems.

These variants have been chosen to reflect the very different allocation of tasks between computer and human used in current developments of knowledge systems. In the first variants on the list, i.e. process control and one-shot decision-making, the computer solves the problem on its own, with very little intervention from the human user.

As long as everything works correctly, this use of knowledge systems resembles the use of other computer supports such as statistical or other calculation programs. However, if an error occurs, perhaps a situation not foreseen by the programmer, then somebody has to be able to diagnose and correct it. This can be a major problem, as various incidents in process control have shown.

In the two following variants, the system interacts fairly frequently with the user. In the following pages I shall concentrate upon such kinds of system.

Applications of expert systems

In what situations can expert systems be of use? Obviously it is not worth addressing a problem with the help of a knowledge system, if there is a simpler way of solving it. If there is already an algorithm for solving a problem (such as differential equations, bayesian calculus, etc.) there will be no need for the complicated development of a knowledge system. The same applies if there is somebody who could do the job; if the problem is simple enough to learn, why not teach somebody to solve it, instead of building a knowledge system to support him?

On the other hand, the problem should not be too complex. It is not possible to build an expert system for a problem domain about which our knowledge is inadequate. An expert system cannot go beyond existing knowledge. Even if the building of such a system may sometimes help in defining existing knowledge a little more clearly, it cannot repair the gaps which remain or tackle the inevitable compromises which experts in an inadequately elaborated field have to face.

A more practical problem concerns the knowledge which is to be handled in the system. After all, an expert system must be enclosed in a computer system, and current programming methods must be used in order to represent and use the knowledge.

The limitations of computer memory will prevent the storing of common-sense knowledge. Memory limitations will also determine the extent to which inferences can be generated and followed up. Inferences are generated exponentially, which means that special measures are needed to limit them. This applies to the knowledge rules as well as to the metarules for processing knowledge. Naturally the size of the database and the time and space required for processing it always depends on the computer equipment currently available, and the limits to what is practical will probably be pushed much further even while this book is being printed. At present it is being claimed that a problem which occupies a human problem solver for one to two hours is about the right size for an expert system to cope with.

All these constraints refer to the feasibility of building and using expert systems. Let us now consider the possible uses of systems, assuming the practical constraints have been allowed for.

First, an expert system can be useful when human expertise is scarce or not easily available. Perhaps a catastrophe has occurred in some distant spot, as may happen for instance in war, during an earthquake, a great fire, or a tropical storm. Normally no expert is at hand, and yet expert help is required to provide such things as medical help and transportation, or possibly evacuation plans, rebuilding plans, temporary housing, and food and water supplies. In such situations people who have some limited knowledge (local doctors, administrators, etc.) could be supported by knowledge systems able to give advice about what to do in this specific situation.

Existing medical diagnosis systems, such as MYCIN and its followers represent a somewhat less dramatic case. The typical case is the doctor with ordinary medical training who can call on specialized expertise to help him to diagnose a particular disease. This idea, whereby people located far from the centres of knowledge have access to more centralized knowledge, is of course applicable to other areas apart from medicine; banking and legal advice are such possible applications. Or a mechanical engineer may require knowledge of some particular manufacturing details, or a social scientist some special statistical advice.

Expert systems can also be useful when a human expert retires, with the risk that his knowledge will disappear with him.

We can also envisage expert systems being used for simpler purposes. People wanting to fix their own cars or TV sets may find a knowledge system more useful than a handbook, which is often difficult to read and understand.

Thus the usefulness of expert systems which can solve problems of this kind can hardly be denied. The question then remains: can we design expert systems which allow human expertise to be used in problem solving in such a way that the user remains in control of the situation?

The conventional procedure in building expert systems

Although expert systems represent a rather recent trend in the history of computers, a particular procedure for its development has already been suggested. I shall refer here to the procedure as presented in Hayes-Roth, Waterman & Lenat (1983). This volume seems to be one of the basic handbooks, but in developmental work it naturally needs supplementing by more technical books geared to the particular knowledge involved and the particular computational tools used. Much more has been written on expert systems since 1983, but I have not found anything which radically deviates from the general philosophy of this book.

The key tasks for developing an expert system are described as follows:

1. The knowledge has to be acquired, which includes the identification of the knowledge domain, the defining of the characteristics of the problem and of the concepts and rules required to represent the knowledge.
2. The expert system is designed, which means that structures are suggested for organizing the knowledge.
3. The knowledge is programmed into the system, which means that the knowledge base and the inference engine are implemented.

4. The system is tested and refined by revising the concepts and rules where necessary.

As can be seen, these tasks are mainly concerned with the problem of how to get at the knowledge possessed by an expert, and how to represent the expert's knowledge in an expert system.

This means that the interaction between the expert and the knowledge engineer is one of the most important activities in constructing an expert system in this exposition. Consideration of the user is built in "at the top" of the system, once the question of problem-solving performance has been dealt with. A further, separate problem concerns the interface to the user, including the request for data, offering of suggestions and explanations of requests and suggestions.

This conceptualization of the design procedure is better suited to knowledge systems regarded as experts than to systems regarded as tools. If the procedure starts from the expert, it is difficult to look at the problem from the user's angle and to decide what he really needs from the system. The expert-based system assumes the lead, and it is difficult to reverse the roles and to let the user state what he wants to know.

The bottleneck problem in acquiring expert knowledge

The problem most widely discussed at present is, how can we acquire the knowledge from an expert to be used in an expert system? This has been called the "Feigenbaum bottleneck" problem, since Feigenbaum seems to have been the first to write about it (1980). The situation is usually described as follows. A knowledge engineer interviews an expert in order to capture his or her knowledge. This knowledge has then to be formulated with the help of a system which stores and processes the knowledge, a so called expert system shell. The acquired knowledge is then tested against the expert in an iterative procedure.

The bottleneck problem has several causes. The first concerns the expert's inability to express his own knowledge. The very essence of an expert's knowledge often lies in its being so automated that the expert himself is no longer aware of it, which means of course that he cannot pass it on to another person. The problem of verbalizing knowledge has frequently been discussed. For instance, a distinction has been drawn between "explicit" and "tacit" knowledge (Polanyi, 1969), whereby "tacit" knowledge is knowledge which is not expressible but which is still used implicitly. A similar distinction has been drawn between "declarative" and "procedural" knowledge (Anderson, 1983), whereby procedural knowledge is regarded as knowledge which is so highly automated that it is no longer accessible to introspection. Other researchers have challenged the very idea that people can express what they know (Nisbett and Wilson, 1977).

Various solutions to this problem have been suggested. For instance, the system itself can be made to infer the knowledge required from the expert's behaviour—i.e. the system could "learn" the expert's knowledge from examples given. The greatest problem about this approach according to Hayes-Roth (1984), is the critical importance of the initial choice of knowledge representation, since current automated learning systems cannot refine their representation languages themselves. Other problems in automated learning are connected with unexpected errors in the data received; a system would prefer error-free data, in order to avoid probabilistic hypotheses. The system's restricted ability to utilize domain knowledge to guide learning constitutes another difficulty.

One way of solving this problem, namely of spelling out implicit knowledge, is to make things easier for the expert by not requiring him to describe every single aspect of his knowledge. Some implicit knowledge can be inferred from the expert's way of handling concepts which are crucial to the particular domain. Psychological scaling techniques can be used, as suggested by Cooke & McDonald (1987). Other psychological approaches to eliciting or interpreting human problem solving include variants of Kelly's repertory grid (Kelly, 1955), or verbal records as work actually proceeds (Ericsson & Simon, 1984) or dialogue (O'Malley, Draper & Riley, 1984).

Another problem related to the expression of knowledge is knowing where the knowledge should be applied. It is impossible for an expert to predict all the future situations in which his knowledge could be useful. A similar sort of situation applies to databases: knowledge can be represented in a system, but even so it may not be useful in a new unpredicted situation. We can even say that one of the most useful aspects of an expert's knowledge is knowing when it is applicable—an aspect which is of course impossible to implement in an expert system.

Let me take a simple example. Suppose that we have a system for the medical diagnosis of stomach disease. We encounter a sample of people with a particular digestive problem, and it turns out that they all come from an environment which has been subjected to heavy radioactive pollution. Is it possible to use the expert system here? Unless the expert has predicted this particular situation, the system itself cannot decide whether it is applicable. The diagnosis and advice derived can be quite wrong because no account has been taken of the critical situational factor.

Another problem related to the acquisition of knowledge for expert systems concerns the mismatch between the expert's knowledge and the representational language required by the expert system shell. It is very possible that a single representation will not be sufficient to cover all aspects of the expert's knowledge. A characteristic feature of human knowledge is that it is not usually consistent. The examples and rules may have been derived from different contexts, which may not be possible to express in the same frame of reference.

Finally there is the question of the knowledge engineer's understanding of the expert domain. The engineer has to know at least something about this domain, if he is to be able to understand what the expert says (or shows) to him. Thus, the knowledge engineer may miss or misunderstand some of the expert's knowledge. He may also have a tendency to interpret what the expert says either in terms of his own knowledge or in terms of what is required by the expert system's shell. This particular problem can be solved by getting rid of the intermediate knowledge engineer and letting the expert express his knowledge himself in the expert system. However, at present the handling of the expert system shell still requires too much technical knowledge to make this approach feasible.

It might perhaps be possible for the expert to interact with the shell in natural language, or in some technical language which is natural to the particular expert domain (graphs, formulas, etc.). Naturally all the disadvantages of natural language that we have previously discussed will also apply to the natural language interface to an expert system shell: the vagueness of natural language, and the difficulty to spot the particular meaning in a particular context increases the risk of errors. Above all, in this weak communication form, the expert would not be challenged to question crucial conditions and distinctions. But a more technical language, better suited to the problem addressed would not only reduce the risk of errors; it would also make the support system so much more specialized that an expert might be required to develop it.

The problem of representing knowledge

The problem of acquiring knowledge from the expert is intimately linked to the problem of representing this knowledge. A knowledge engineer often works iteratively with the expert and the expert system shell. He has to translate the knowledge acquired into the shell, and then to test the reasoning that follows from this knowledge against the expert. If the system's reasoning is not acceptable to the expert, something has to be changed—either the knowledge elements provided by the expert (the concepts and procedures), or the strategy used to process this knowledge.

The expert system shell does not generally allow for more than a couple of ways of representing knowledge, procedures, or strategies, which means that it may not be possible to fit all the expert's knowledge into the frame of the expert system shell. As some expert system developers have put it: "It was only after a considerable development effort that we discovered how poorly suited ... was as a shell for the radio domain knowledge" (Kidd & Cooper, 1985).

A further problem in representing knowledge arises from the fact that some types of knowledge are more certain than others—something which is often captured in expert systems in the shape of probability ratings of the suggested rules. However, studies of the way people judge uncertain events have shown that humans are very bad at assessing and using probabilities (cf chapter 4). And experts are no different from ordinary people in this respect. Further, experts resemble other people in rarely volunteering negative evidence, even if such evidence would be very valuable in diagnosing a fault, for instance.

The problem of knowledge representation concerns not only the expert's knowledge, but also the possibility of capturing his knowledge in a way that can be useful to other people. The expert's model of the task and the user's model may not coincide, and may even conflict. An expert system should thus be able to bridge the gap between the expert's model and possible user models.

Thus we also have to consider how an expert system diagnoses and handles different models. It may be necessary to incorporate different user models at the system design stage, so that various kinds of possible ignorance or even misconceptions can be handled later.

It might facilitate the knowledge representation process if the expert system were to know what kind of user knowledge could be expected. A human expert works from the advice-taker's knowledge (or lack of knowledge), rather than dictating every detailed procedure to be performed. In a similar way an expert system could note any areas in which the user lacked crucial knowledge or risked misunderstanding important facts or drawing the wrong conclusions. What is needed is an ability to predict possible variations between users, and a capacity to diagnose the knowledge of a particular user from his reactions to the system. This is an area in which we can hope that expert systems and computer-aided instructional systems will cross-fertilize.

Interactive problem solving

Let us now turn to the case in which a user interacts with a knowledge system that fulfils the role of the expert. In the ideal case, the expert system would function as an experienced person, to whom the user only turns when necessary and with whom he can communicate naturally (although not necessarily in a natural language). People after all only turn to human experts when necessary, and would communicate with them either in a natural language or in the technical language required by the context. The inexperienced person would expect to be given advice when he needed it, and otherwise to be left alone.

However, descriptions of existing expert systems do not correspond to the expectations that arise from interaction with human experts. In building knowledge systems the expert traditionally decides what problems to address, whereas a human expert might try to find out what problems the inexperienced person is facing. Only when the user's problem can be predicted by the expert serving in the expert system, will the system's approach correspond to the interaction between the human expert and his advice-seeker. If on the other hand the user's problem has not been predicted, the user will either have to change his mind about the problem or use the system in a roundabout way. From the designer's point of view it is easier to steer the user than to build a system flexible enough to respond to the diverse problems of different users.

This means that many demonstrations of expert systems involve an interaction with users which can seem rather patronizing. The following is an example from Johnson & Jordan in Hayes-Roth (1984). The interactions are numbered for subsequent reference. (System output in capitals, user input in lower case.)

1. DO YOU WANT INSTRUCTIONS?
   no
2. I UNDERSTAND THAT THERE IS THE POSSIBILITY OF A SPILL IN WHITE OAK CREEK. DO YOU WANT TO VOLUNTEER ANY INFORMATION?
   yes
3. DO YOU KNOW WHAT SUBSTANCE (OR TYPE OF SUBSTANCE) MIGHT HAVE SPILLED?
   yes
4. PLEASE NAME THE SUSPECTED SUBSTANCE(S) (IF YOU NEED INSTRUCTIONS TYPE HELP; TERMINATE BY TYPING DONE)
   oil of vitriol
5. OIL OF VITRIOL = SULFURIC-ACID?
   yes
   WARNING!! POTENTIALLY HIGHLY CORROSIVE AND YIELDS TOXIC COMBUSTION PRODUCTS.
   WEAR PROTECTIVE CLOTHING.
   (SULFURIC-ACID) (5.0)

In this particular example we clearly recognize the patronizing manner: the user seems fairly experienced, since he does not require any help. He can produce the name of the substance without any difficulty. And yet the system gives him unsolicited advice, which a human expert would hardly do. If the user knows the name of the spilled substance, and if he knows its chemical components, then he could also be expected to know that the substance is dangerous. We see that the system designers have not made any attempts to assess the user's knowledge or needs.

Another example from a sample run of the same expert system illustrates a further aspect of expert systems, i.e. their explanation facility.

4) PLEASE WALK UPSTREAM ALONG THE CREEK LOOKING FOR THE OUTFALL FROM WHICH THE LIQUID IS DRAINING. IF YOU FIND ONE, PLEASE ENTER THE OUTFALL NUMBER.
   why?
5) THIS WILL AID IN DETERMINING THE SPILL BASIN.

IT HAS ALREADY BEEN ESTABLISHED THAT THE LOCATION WHERE THE SPILL WAS FIRST REPORTED IS ALONG-CREEK

THEREFORE IF THE OUTFALL FROM WHICH THE LIQUID IS
DRAINING IS KNOWN THEN

IT IS DEFINITE THAT THE OUTFALL FROM WHICH THE LIQUID
IS DRAINING IS THE SPILL BASIN.

(RULE001)

When the system asks the user for information, he may question this information request, as happened here in response to question 4. Interaction 5 explains why the information was needed. If the user wants to continue using the system, he had better answer the question under 4.

It should be noted that these examples derive from a demonstration of how to build expert systems, rather than from a full-fledged expert system. In this particular demonstration, the user side was neglected. But we might well ask whether such neglect is not all too common in similar demonstrations, and perhaps even in systems built for practical use.

The example was taken from a demonstration of an expert system, where the division of labour in the task consists of letting the user feed in the data which the system requires and letting the system carry out the problem solving. This can hardly be regarded as collaborative problem solving. If the user does not know what problem solving approach the system is using, he will be at a loss after a couple of questions about the problem analysis (short-term memory limitations). The resulting short-sightedness will leave him unable to interpret or evaluate the explanations that the system supplies. Thus an expert system is only helpful to a non-expert, if its problem-solving approach corresponds to that of the user.

The following is an example of how problem-solving approaches may differ. In diagnosing patients, some doctors start by formulating a hypothesis that seems most plausible, given the data available. They then continue to collect further data in order to support or reject the first hypothesis. Their hypothesis allows them to be very selective in their choice of data to collect. If the hypothesis is then rejected, they formulate another which seems plausible in light of the new set of data. This is an efficient way of working, when there is a lot of data that can be collected, and when relevant hypotheses can be formulated. Let us now compare this hypothesis-testing reasoning with a method which starts from the data and draws inferences from it, without considering any plausible hypotheses. At each observation, various diagnoses might be suggested, and the combination of observations may either restrict or increase the number of diagnoses, depending on the observations that are collected.

It is possible to realize either line of approach in expert systems. But a user who approaches the problem by formulating hypotheses would find an observation-driven approach inefficient. And a user with an observation-driven approach would not be able to feed a hypothesis-driven expert system with the hypotheses required.

It thus seems that happy cooperation between expert systems and human users calls for compatibility between the approach used by the two parties. This idea has been supported by the results of an experiment, showing that incompatibility between the user's approach (forward chaining) and the system's approach (backward chaining) led to a decline in performance quality of between 30 and 60% in the use of a simple decision support system (Lehner, 1987).

KNOWLEDGE SYSTEMS AS TOOLS

Let us now look at the possibility of using knowledge systems as tools. One example of this is the use of the systems known as expert interface systems, which aim to enhance a user's ability to utilize an external data source. Such tools can be used for example in centralized sensor integration and display control, or in real-time command and control decision-making support (cf Lehner, 1987).

In this kind of situation the expert system can be used to advantage even when its approach is not compatible with the approach used by the human user. When the users in an experiment (Lehner, 1987) were given information about the system's aproach, they performed even better when this approach was incompatible than when it was compatible with their approach. The reason was that the approaches supplemented each other in providing grounds for the decision subsequently reached. When the subjects knew about the system's approach, they could use it to advantage. In another study Lehner found that subjects who were given direct access to the system's data could use this to counterbalance their ignorance of the system's approach. Finally, Lehner found that it was necessary for users to understand the system's approach in order to identify any inconsistencies.

Thus it seems that a user employing a knowledge system as a tool would benefit from an understanding of the system's internal workings as well as from an overview of the data used. Naturally this would make heavy demands on the user, but in this case the knowledge system is after all only a tool and the user is supposed to be the expert.

USER INTERFACE TO KNOWLEDGE SYSTEMS

Communication

The last problem we will discuss in connection with knowledge systems is the one that at present commands the least attention. It concerns the interface between user and system. Because the two parties may be employing different approaches and models to the task, and because the user has to be able to evaluate the system's questions and advice, more attention should probably be devoted to making clear to the user both the system's representation and approach.

In balancing between the user's need to understand the system and the system's need to understand the user, it may be easier to let the user do the adaptation. For this reason many demonstrations of expert systems use a dialogue which is rigidly circumscribed, asking for input from the user when the system needs it.

For expert users, such a dialogue is too restrictive. They need some way of feeding in their own questions and requirements. How can such a need be met? It might be most natural for the users to input facts in natural language, and in the form and order which seems to them to fit the problem. However, users do not always know what concepts the system is employing. In such cases, existing and required information can be presented in terms of a network of concepts and relations, and the users can mark the places where they could volunteer information. At those places a menu of input options could be displayed. This is the solution proposed by the Prospector system, and it has also been advocated by Kidd & Cooper (1985) among others.

Explanation facilities

Another important aspect of knowledge systems concerns their way of explaining the advice given and the questions asked. As we have seen, explanations can be given verbally in a form which is a slight reformulation in natural language of the rules actually being used. Such explanations may not always be easy for the user to understand, particularly if several rules have to be combined in the explanation.

The verbal exposition of rules is difficult to review because of the sequential and linear presentation. Instead, the structure behind the rules can be graphically depicted in form of the network of nodes and relations used in deriving a conclusion. Such an overview could be helpful to the knowledge engineer working on the development of the system, as Poltrock, Steiner & Tarlton (1986) have suggested. An example from a system developed by Henrik Eriksson at the University of Linköping is shown in Figure 41. As can be seen, this kind of overview can be helpful to the end user without extensive training. But even graphical exposition fails to solve the problem of having to explain many interactive rules.

Other problems arise in explanations which refer to calculations based on the probabilities attaching to the rules, as in calculating Bayesian a posteriori probabilities for instance. It is difficult to see how any explanation, either verbal, mathematical or graphical can be formulated to counterbalance the human tendency to underestimate the a posteriori probability in a realistic situation.

In the case of both content-related and formal rules, some knowledge about

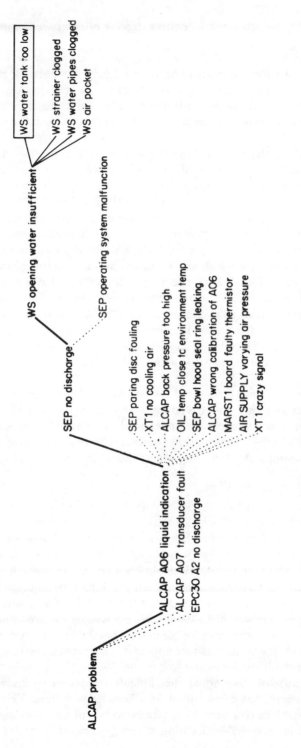

Figure 41 An exposition of rules and facts in graphical form.

how human experts explain their reasoning and advice would be valuable. For instance, we can expect human experts to explain not only by stating their rules, but also by trying to provide other kinds of explanation. A good teacher, for instance, tries to formulate metaphors or analogies to support the more special rules. More abstract rules can also be referred to, to make it possible to generalize.

Explanations are also needed about the way the system itself works, i.e. about the inference strategy that is used. As we have seen, information about the strategy greatly helps the user, particularly if the approach employed by the system is alien to the user's own approach to the problem.

Naturally the designers of knowledge systems have been aware of the need for—and the lack of—good explanation facilities. Clancey, in particular, tried to develop a teaching interface (called GUIDON) to the medical expert system MYCIN. The many failures on this front led him to look for possible reasons (Clancey, 1983). He found that since a good deal of knowledge is not explicitly stated in rules but is implicit in the ordering of rules or clauses within rules, no explanation based on rules alone can ever be sufficient. Instead, strategic knowledge and knowledge needed for justifying the advice have to be included in the knowledge base. Principles and generalizations are important, for instance, because they provide a framework within which the validity of a rule can be checked.

The problems that have obstructed the development of explanations have also led to the conclusion that only a system which reasons as humans reason, can provide explanations which can be understood by users. This brings us back to the problem of whether a computer system can be built to reason in a similar way to human beings. All I can say about this at present, is that the issue has not yet been settled.

Conclusion

We have seen that three approaches can be used in designing knowledge systems. One is to design a system which can work on its own, according to its own principles and without much interaction with human users. These systems need not concern us here, since they do not touch on human cognition.

The other two approaches have cognitive implications. The first is the system-as-expert approach, in which the expert system is designed according to principles which should as far as possible simulate a human expert's way of functioning. The second is the system-as-tool approach, in which the system is supposed to complement the human user.

In the first approach we noted the difficulty in acquiring knowledge from the expert in a way that can be used in a knowledge system. This is not only because the expert cannot express his knowledge, but also because not all his knowledge can be captured by existing expert system shells.

In the approach that involves simulating a human being, the problem of individual differences arises. Not only may there exist differences between human cognitive processes in general and the processes used in current practice in knowledge systems, but there are also differences between people—between knowledge engineers, task experts and knowledge system users. We do not know what kinds of difference are liable to cause potential users the most problems. People can after all learn a lot.

A particularly serious problem concerns the relation between existing systems knowledge and the possibility of deriving explanations from it. It has been argued that intelligible explanations can only be derived from a system which reasons in a way that is similar to that of its prospective users. This argument is plausible only if the system itself has to derive the explanations from the rules (or both the explanations and the reasoning from the same knowledge base as suggested by Swartout (1981) among others). The explanations could be linked to the rules by the expert himself, however. The linkage does not have to be automated.

Obviously a knowledge system that can operate as a tool complementing a human user's problem solving must fulfil a great many requirements if it is to be useful. First, it should capitalize on the user's strengths as well as on the computational strengths of the computer and the expertise of the expert. Secondly, it should be able to show and explain results in a way that can be checked by human users. Thus the system has to keep a model of the knowledge domain and of the user's knowledge.

SUMMARY

Knowledge systems represent a plethora of different kinds of problem-solving support, ranging from stand-alone automated decision-making systems to highly interactive problem-solving tools. Since very few systems are actually used in practice (except for demonstration purposes), conclusions about knowledge systems must be based on the tentative suggestions built into the demonstration systems and projections of these into the future.

In this chapter we have considered some cognitive aspects of knowledge systems. Knowledge systems can be used either as tools (like most of the computer systems we have talked about up to now) or as simulated experts. At the present time most knowledge systems can be classified as simulated experts. An expert system can be useful if knowledge is sparse and difficult of access.

The problems connected with expert systems include acquiring knowledge from experts, representing this knowledge in a computer system, and finally communicating it. At present the easiest way of solving the design problem seems to be to regard the expert system as a directive system, which solves the problem by employing the user solely as a source of information. This kind of system guides the user through the dialogue, giving advice and providing explanations. The user himself plays rather a passive role. He supplies the information that the system needs, and he can ask for clarifications and explanations to help him to evaluate the advice offered.

Given this approach to an expert system, the biggest design problem will be in getting the knowledge from the expert. However, from the user's point of view, the biggest problem lies in the possible mismatch between user and expert knowledge. The concepts used, the strategy for handling the task, and the way of evaluating the importance of various facts or the probability of certain statements—all these are major sources of possible misunderstanding. This difficulty can be handled to some extent by engaging the users as well as the experts in the development of the expert system. Users may also have to be educated to understand the particular approach adopted by the expert system, to get an overview of the data used by the system, and to evaluate the results and explanations offered by the system.

The use of knowledge systems as tools requires that even greater attention be paid to the difference between expert and user models and to the allocation of labour between user and system.

Chapter 11

From Function to Form—On Computer Support in Design Engineering

INTRODUCTION

The use of computers in industry is diverse and, as everywhere else, is on the increase. Industrial work ranges from market analysis, through planning and economic forecasting, to design and the actual manufacturing of a physical product. This wide range of activities may profit from many different kinds of computer support. Unlike offices, which are concerned with symbolic information (numbers and texts), industry must be concerned with physical objects as well. This means that the very particular requirement of the products manufactured will influence the need for computer support. In industry the same information-processing problems arise as in offices, but other problems connected with the function of the product itself, its manufacture and any need to modify it during its life-time will also occur.

I shall not try here to cover all the problems involved in industrial operations, where computers could be of help. Instead I shall concentrate on one particular activity, i.e. the design of a product. Since the design activity depends to a large extent on the product designed, I shall also concentrate on the design of mechanical equipment. Electronic circuit design and architectonic design will not be discussed here, however interesting they may be.

THE DESIGN PROCESS

It is commonly held that the nature of the design influences 80% of the price of the product (Helldén, 1986), but the design activity itself accounts for only a very small part of the price. Recognition of this fact has focussed much interest on the design process itself. What happens during the process? What conditions are favourable to the development of a good design?

The design process is a complicated one, for which few systematic analyses have been performed. I shall present below some suggestions put forward by experienced designers and some of the findings from research performed in this area.

Different levels

First, it has been suggested that the design process works on different levels. Three main levels can be distinguished:

1. The conceptual level, at which the functions of the product are specified and where the first general ideas about the corresponding physical shape of the product are created.
2. The concretization level, at which different parts of the product are specified, and their physical shape worked out in greater detail. Different relationships between the parts are also conceptualized and worked out.
3. The detail specification level, at which all parts of the product are worked out in detail and their relationships specified.

Different phases

Secondly, it has been suggested that design proceeds in stages. The following stages have been derived from Pahl & Beitz (1984) and Helldén (1986):

1. Task clarification, when the problem to be solved is formulated, and the main goal of the design project is specified.
2. The concept phase, the purpose of which is to check the feasibility of a design project. In this phase, planning, general investigations, information retrieval, etc. are carried out. For complex projects, this phase can be very extensive. Economic feasibility must be tested, current regulations and patent issues must be investigated. Questions of technical feasibility must be answered. In this phase only principles and systems are specified, but no details or assemblies.
3. The preliminary design phase, where basic technical solutions are designed and chosen. In this phase layouts and the preliminary designs of parts and assemblies are worked out. The feasibility of the proposed designs is tested and the best alternative chosen. The result of this phase is a conceptual design.
4. The detailed design phase, in which each part is designed in detail. The result of this phase is a prototype design. This phase is also integrated with the detailed design of the production system.
5. Refinement phase. In this phase the prototypes are refined in order to get a product that can be marketed. Here the production system is finally specified.
6. Modification phase. In this phase improvements are continuously made as a result of feedback from vendors and product users. Modifications also have to be made when the production system changes.

Although the levels of design activity suggested above to some extent correspond to these phases it is important to note that each phase may incorporate design activities at the different levels (cf Warren & Whitefield, 1987).

It should also be noted that the design process is not as sequential as the suggested phases might indicate. Rather, iterations may occur in each phase and over several phases, until a marketable product has been derived. As Håkan Helldén puts it: "The great problem is to decide when the product is really finished" (op cit. Helldén, 1986, p.9).

The need for iteration is due to the multitude of factors which have to be considered. The value of many of these factors cannot be determined until a first specification of some other factors has been suggested. Thus economical feasibility, for instance, is dependent on the existing manufacturing system, but this can be modified to some extent, if a big enough amount of the same product is to be manufactured. Also, although a particular manufacturing system poses some very particular restrictions on the product to be designed, enough options often remain so that several alternatives can be considered in the conceptual design.

Different activities

In all its phases the design process includes a variety of activities. The following have been described by an experienced designer (Helldén, 1986): drafting, computing, simulation, retrieval of information, technical discussions and administration. Helldén suggests that the order in which the activities are mentioned is a crude estimate of their ranking in terms of the amount of time devoted to each of the different activities.

Now it should be noted that the actual work performed by a particular designer is to a large extent due to the organization of work in the company. A designer may have a specialized work task, whereby he works either with a particular product (horizontal integration) or with a particular phase in the design work (vertical specialization). In most countries vertical specialization is the most common (cf Wingert, Duus, Rader & Riehm, 1984). This is not the case in Sweden, however, and it is from this country that most of the examples below will be taken.

In a study of designers in three different companies, the activities in Table 9 were suggested, (Löwstedt 1986). The table also shows the mean percentage of time devoted to each activity by a sample of designers estimating their work over a ten-day period.

Even if it is difficult to interpret this table in a general way—the companies differed from one another in certain ways, for example, and the time period chosen may have favoured one activity over another—we can see that the activities suggested correspond well both to the suggestions by the experienced designer and to the description given of the stages above. The figures indicate

Table 9.   Average time for different activities in design work

	Percentage of total time
Administration and planning	10
Retrieval of information	11
Problem solving	18
Computing	6
Drawing and changes	32
Assembling information	8
Checking	6
Other	9

that the designers investigated represent horizontal integration rather than vertical specialization. At the same time, the estimation that about one-third of the time is devoted to drawing agrees with other estimations based on Swedish designers.

Conclusion

To sum up: the design process appears to involve two main kinds of activity—one concerned with technical problem solving and one concerned with the communication of ideas and results. The technical problem solving is performed by information retrieval, decision-making, simulations and checks; the communication is performed by drawing. The communication aspect of a drawing can be compared to that of a text—the idea cannot be understood until it is expressed. At the same time the drawing supports the technical problem-solving by making visual checks possible, thus revealing weak points. This relationship between problem-solving and communication must be born in mind, when considering the supports which might be beneficial to the design process.

IDEAS ON COMPUTER SUPPORT FOR DESIGN

As we have seen above, design is concerned with progressing from the vague idea of a desired function to a specification of how this function can be implemented in a real product. Design can thus be regarded as information production, which means that the computer can come in as an information-processing tool. Where can the computer be of help in the design process?

Let us suppose, as before, that the computer functions as a tool, helping the user to perform his task more quickly and/or better. This also means that the computer supports the user with information-processing tasks, which humans find difficult. As we saw in the chapters on human cognition, such tasks include inferences based on formal logic, the integration of several information sources, and decision-making under uncertainty. But this brings us to a difficult trade-off decision. It is important that people are not altogether deprived of tasks which involve difficult information-processing of this kind. We know that people develop from encountering difficulties. Rather a way must be found whereby the computer supports human problem solving without replacing it. Thus what is desirable from a human point of view is that the computer takes over those aspects of work which the human professional finds cumbersome or boring, but not those which can confirm and develop a user's competence and creativity. How this division of labour is to be brought about has not yet been discovered.

A scenario for computer support

To be able to discuss ideas for computer support, we first need a scenario for the design activity envisaged. We have seen that the first four stages of design aim at producing, testing and modifying a prototype. For this goal a concrete object, a physical prototype, is needed. In a scenario the real physical prototype is replaced by a prototype in the computer. The computer is perfectly capable of storing geometric information about an object (i.e. information about the physical shape). To this geometric description information about the object's technical properties, such as weight, material, tensions during use, etc. could be linked. By storing all the information relevant for the product, including the behaviour of the product during manufacture, we obtain a product model which can substitute for the physical prototype in some problem solving contexts. (Kjellberg, 1982).

Let us then suppose that we have access to a product model in the computer. If the product model is to be genuinely useful, we also have to imagine that the computer can represent the manufacturing processes and the manufacturing system. In such a scenario we can envisage the work of the designer taking place mainly at the computer. Planning, idea generation, product development, and testing—all the activities involved in design can be performed at the computer, with the product model and the models of the manufacturing system and manufacturing processes as its data or knowledge bases.

Different supports for different activities

What kind of computer support seems likely to be useful? Since the design process involves so many different activities and can vary so much depending on the degree of novelty in the design, the support envisaged must be correspondingly varied.

Three types of design process can provide us with a point of departure for discussing computer support:

1) Variant design, where the design is a variation of some previous design. The simplest case is exemplified by parametric design, whereby a new product is designed by way of variations in given parameters.

2) New construction, where the design itself is new, but the existing product system is regarded as fixed, and where most of the characteristics and the demands on the product are known.

3) Development work, where both product and product system can be designed, and where some of the characteristics and demands on the product are not known.

A first step towards an overview of different kinds of support that might be needed for different activities and different types of suggested design is shown in Table 10 below. The activities are listed in roughly the same order as they occur in the different phases of the design work. As I pointed out above, it is natural for the activities to be repeated in several rounds. In the table an earlier listed activity is generally a precondition for the next one. Sometimes different activities can also occur in parallel. The most important activity that proceeds in parallel with others is communication, which can serve as information retrieval, information judgment, decision support, etc. Here the communication activity is placed at the end, to mark the fact that the finished design has to be communicated.

Note that in all cases it is assumed that facilities for storing product models and models of manufacturing processes and manufacturing systems are available in the computer. In the case of designs already completed, it is assumed that the product models are available in a database. For design in progress, the product modelling facilities allow specifications at different levels of detail, as well as incomplete and tentative specifications (cf Helldén, 1986).

We can now consider in a cognitive perspective some of the requirements that such computer supports must fulfil. I shall focus primarily on analysing the support needed for the creation of new design and development work. Variant design already has computer support which seems suitable enough, although some details can be improved. Below I shall discuss support mainly as regards its appropriateness to the task. Interface problems connected particularly with design work, such as graphics, will be discussed below, under the heading of "Experiences of CAD".

Information retrieval and the assessment of relevance

Information retrieval is regarded as one of the most important activities in designing a new product. Since design has to take account of the existing manufacturing systems, information about the characteristics of the present system—capacity, current work load, etc. as well as details of the machinery—should be readily available. For genuine development work some kind of ideas pool would also be useful.

From a cognitive point of view the need for all this information imposes a

Table 10. Overview of possible computer support in future design work on product models

Type of activity	Type of design		
	Variant design	New design	Developmental design
Information retrieval	Database of existing products	Database over product system, previous designs	Database Idea pool
Judgment (Importance)		Expert advice	Interaction analysis
Creation of alternatives		Idea pool Associative networks Interactive graphics	Idea pool Associative networks Interactive graphics
Integration of information		Decision support	Decision support
Inferencing		Logical, pragmatic inferences	Logical, pragmatic inferences
Prediction	Calculations	Calculations Simulations	Calculations Simulations
Search among alternatives		Expert rules Design rules Interactive graphics	Expert rules Design rules Interactive graphics
Checks	Calculations	Simulations Interactive graphics	Simulations Interactive graphics
Diagnosis of error	Database checks Checks on input and calculations	Design history Expert advice	Design history Rules for own expertise
Communication		Conferencing system with graphics	

very heavy load on the designer's working memory. This memory load can be eased in various non-exclusive ways; the task should be modularized, so that different parts of it can be undertaken separately. The information should be carefully selected, so that the designer gets only such information as is relevant at the moment. And last but not least, the designer should be given ample time to learn and digest the information in order to form "chunks" which can be used in getting an overview of all the complex information.

Experts at the task may be able to advise about how to modularize the task and about what is important in different parts or at different stages. But they will not be able to tell anything about the timing of the information. The amount of time needed for a particular designer to acquire an overview of all the complex information will vary enormously, depending mainly on the designer's experience of the particular product and of the relevant manufacturing system.

What kind of computer support would be useful in this situation? First, of course, a good database retrieval system is mandatory. In this system all information about previous products and designs, and about the current manufacturing system should be easily available.

A database system calls for initiative on the part of the designer. The designer has to know what type of information is needed, and when, which means that he also has to be able to perform the required modularization of the problem. If the designer has neglected to ask for potentially important facts, the database will be silent on this. A knowledge-base system with information about possible modularizations, and with weights given to the facts according to their importance at different stages would help the designer to check whether everything important at that particular moment has been considered.

The combination of a "passive" database and an "active" knowledge base could prevent the possible dulling of the designer's knowledge and skills. A knowledgeable designer would be able to find his way efficiently, and in a manner suited to himself, by using the database. The less experienced designer might find the expert's advice about modularization and relevance instructive.

In genuine development work, expert knowledge may be lacking. Here other ways of finding information must be sought—ways that resemble research more than design as such. Experiments can be performed on a basis of old ideas; the results of these can be analysed in various kinds of interaction analysis (e.g. factor analysis, cluster analysis, path analysis, or discriminant analysis) in order to discover the relevant factors in the particular situation.

Integration of information

Once information has been gathered it has to be integrated for further use, either in order to create alternatives or to decide between alternatives when such are available.

It is fairly well established that people in general have difficulty in integrating large amounts of new information. The designer will face the problem of integration when he has collected all the information required for each modularized part. The facts will consist of suggestions for technical solutions (from prior designs and the ideas pool) and practical constraints (from the data about the manufacturing system).

The integration of information can be based on normative rules, where such exist and are applicable, as suggested by Suh, Bell & Gossard (1978) and Suh & Kim (1985). A simple solution can be found in a linear combination of independent variables. However, in design it is often impossible to keep different functions independent of each other. An experienced designer can have worked out some useful principles for combining complex interacting variables. This knowledge can then be used as heuristic rules to support the required integration for less experienced designers.

Creation of alternatives

Creative work often implies creating many alternative solutions. In order to stimulate creativity the productive phase can usefully be separated from the evaluative phase. A computer support system for the creation of alternatives should then promote the finding of alternatives as well as keeping track of alternatives once they have been found.

Designing a product may differ from other kinds of creative activity in the interaction between function and form. Not only technical knowledge but also the visual image has its given place in the creative process. The sketch of the envisaged object gives the designer an opportunity to check immediately the feasibility of the product. It should also be noted that in the case of some products, the aesthetic quality is important. Here again, the picture is the most decisive information medium.

How can the production of alternatives be encouraged? People are often stimulated by seeing similar problems and "almost" solutions. Access to problems and solutions can be facilitated by working together with other people (with or without computer systems), or by having previous problems and solutions stored in a database. The finding of similar problems, principles and solutions can be helped by databases, built as semantic and associative nets. For design work it is not enough for these databases to be presented in verbal or numerical form. Since the visual part of the design activity is so important, means of visualizing the solutions as well as the envisaged designs must be easily available.

Other ways of stimulating the production of new alternatives have been suggested, e.g. by analysing functions, manipulating simple models, and studying mathematical expressions (Helldén, 1986). Such information could be made available in a computer support system, where the designer can sit down and "play" with different product models, working back and forth between analytical analyses and concrete realizations. It is worth repeating here that the tension between function expressed as mathematical and technical constraints, and form expressed as pictures, can be extremely valuable as a source of new ideas.

Inferencing

When the information has been integrated and alternatives created, the designer has to derive appropriate conclusions. It is here that "inferencing" occurs. Starting from different characteristics of the information retrieved, the designer has to infer what the different alternatives may lead to before he can decide between them.

People do not appear to be very good at drawing inferences, in particular if these inferences have to be based on logical or probabilistic rules (cf Chapter 4). Thus it might seem a good idea to develop computer systems to support this weaker aspect of human information-processing.

Inferencing can be based either on normative rules (logic, mathematics and statistics) or on heuristic rules (expert knowledge).

But although it could appear well-advised to design computer systems to support the drawing of inferences, there is a major problem here, connected with the user's ability to evaluate the result derived by the computer system. If the user is weak on drawing adequate inferences, he will have very little to guide him in evaluating results. Thus the problem is a question not of a possible loss of knowledge on part of the designer, but of a lack of evaluative tools. Since we still want the designer rather than the computer to be responsible for the design, the designer should also be able to check results arrived at.

In a "real" world, this problem would not arise. Any errors that may occur in the computerized processing of information (in input, computation or output) would be easily detected by submitting the product to a test run. The problems of testing in a totally computerized system will be discussed below under the heading of "Checking".

Predictions

The case of predictions is very similar to the case of inferencing. Laboratory experiments have shown people to be bad predicters, particularly if the predicted outcome is probabilistically determined (cf chapter 4). Thus, one reason for using a computer support appears obvious.

The difference between prediction and inferencing lies in the fact that prediction requires a criterion. In the design situation, it is the company decision-makers or the designer who decides what criterion should be used. The company decision-makers set up certain economic and marketing criteria; the designers can then formulate and test criteria concerned with manufacturability and the length of the product's life.

So long as the predictions can be based on agreed computational principles, there should be no difficulty about suggesting computer support. After all, computers are good at computing. The crucial thing for the designer will be to establish the values of the variables which have to be included in the formulas.

When there are no normative rules, however, the prediction situation is more uncertain. The use of experts may be advisable, provided the present situation is more or less the same as the situation in which the expert has acquired his expertise. Predictions are notoriously dependent on the particular situation.

Here again we find that a designer who is less familiar with the particular product to be designed may find it difficult to use a computer system based on the knowledge of an expert. How can the designer ever find out whether the expert rules are based on the same conditions as those obtaining now? Only if all the conditions that ought to be considered are actually spelled out, will he know. But more often than not expert rules are based on the fact that all the relevant conditions are NOT known. If all the relevant factors were known, a normative rule could be formed and the calculations performed accordingly. The situation is more tricky, the less that is known about the planned design. This means that predictions in development work will be much more difficult to perform than predictions connected with new designs.

Search among alternatives

Once alternatives have been produced and their implications in terms of functionality, manufacturability, cost, length of life, etc. have been calculated, the search for the best alternative begins. This search can be performed in two, essentially different ways. Either it can be based on the specification of the product itself, in which case we can speak of deciding between alternatives, or it can be performed during the actual design process by trying out alternative paths sequentially. In this case the search can be regarded as a problem-solving process.

In either the deciding or the problem-solving case human information processing capacities may fail. In decision-making people try to simplify the decisions, which does not always lead to the best choice. In problem-solving people may become entangled in vast problem spaces and may be unable to find the best solution path. Thus computer support in choosing between alternatives, in terms either of described products or the path to follow at a particular point in the design process, should be useful.

However, it is no small problem to design an adequate decision support system for different tasks and different people. It is much easier to support the choice between alternatives which can be defined by independent variables than to support the choice between interacting or holistically defined alternatives. Analytically minded people may find an analytical decision support system useful, while those who are more intuitively inclined may find such systems more of a hindrance than a help.

There has been no formal evaluation of decision supports for designers. However, there is reason to believe that the decision will at some time involve holistic evaluations (functionality, aesthetic quality, etc).

Let us now consider possible support in selecting a path to follow during the design process. Here a computer support will probably have to rely solely on expert strategies for solving design problems. There is no theory of the design process, and certainly no normative rules about "optimal" or "good" design processes. It is therefore necessary to study expert designers, in order to discover a good strategy for proceeding through the design problem space. However, very few studies have yet been made of designers working on "real life" problems in real time and covering the whole design cycle. After all, a complex design (where computer support would be most needed) extends over a considerable period, and involves a lot of different activities. The problem of acquainting oneself with the expert's knowledge will thus be immense if not insurmountable.

Worse than the vast range of expert knowledge, however, is the fact that experts probably differ in the way they handle the design problem. Strategy variations have been found even in very simple tasks, constructed for the study of strategy variations among expert designers (Wærn, K.-G. & Haglund, 1985). Some of the designers worked in a way which can be described as trial and error, some planned their work carefully before starting. There was no difference in the resulting efficiency or in the design actually produced. But the expert rules, and thus the advice, derived from these strategies would be quite different. It is also likely that the different strategies would not all suit any particular designer equally well.

We can thus conclude that the search among alternatives is intimately connected with strategy considerations. And these may be very prone to personal "equations". More research is needed to find out whether there is a strategy which is efficient and also useful for all designers, or whether it can easily be determined which strategy will best suit one particular person.

Checking

Let us now suppose that the previous activities have led to the design of a prototype, in this case a product model. Now the suggested product model has to be tested to see whether production can start.

The idea of testing a prototype is of course to see if all relevant factors have been appropriately considered in the design of the product. By testing the prototype under realistic conditions we can see whether it would collide with surrounding parts, whether it would break under normal strain, whether it can be easily assembled, etc.

Using a computerized product model all the ordinary prototype tests can be performed, provided all the data for the tests are specified in the product model. However, there is one difficulty about using a computerized product model of which the designer should be aware. The product model may contain errors which are not due to mechanical weaknesses and which would not be possible in a "real" model. Such computer-derived errors could range from simple input errors whereby incorrect variable values have been fed into the product model, to errors in the conceptualization of the relationship between function and form, or to errors concerning the model for integrating information.

Input errors are easy to detect, so long as the variables refer to geometrical properties which can be visualized on the screen. Variables connected with technical data are more difficult to check directly, but can be detected by cross-checking input and/or data used.

In the case of conceptual models, possible errors may be much more difficult to detect. The tests to which a real product may be put may elude the product model. In reality there are so many variables to be considered that it is only too easy to neglect some of them. Relevant variables will be considered, but who can say what will be relevant in real life? Should transportation effects be calculated? And what about the effect of storage in different places?

It will never be possible to discover that the models are wrong, if the same computational models are used for testing and for design. The most obvious solution then lies in having different computational models for construction and testing. But this is rather a clumsy solution (particularly if it is difficult to derive a computational model), and one which is not even capable of saying which one is right, if the results differ.

Perhaps, then, computerized checks on computerized product models can be performed when the product and the contexts in which it it will be used are well known. For new products or new contexts, however, a real prototype would still be necessary. Testing with a real prototype will also give the designers an opportunity for acquiring feedback about their product model. Their simulated checks can be compared with the real-life tests. If different results are obtained, there must be an error somewhere. In trying to diagnose the error we have to decide whether the error lies in the computer system or in the real-life test.

Diagnosing faults

Most designs for new products go through several cycles, during which the first prototype has to be changed as a result of one or more faults discovered in the test.

A great deal of work then has to be devoted to diagnosing fault. In the simplest cases, the diagnosis is based directly on experience of the product and the product system. The material may be too weak, the tolerances too low, or the assembly too complicated. This kind of error can easily be fed into a computer as a source of information for future designers and controllers. However, professionals working on product control today do not feel the need for computer support in such simple cases.

In other cases, diagnosis may be more difficult, as vain attempts at remedying the fault may show. In such cases, some computer support could be useful. Although the exact form it should take is difficult to specify. It might be enough to have access to a database of previously detected errors, together with their diagnoses and remedies. Or it could be useful to have access to expert rules for diagnosis and recommendations, as has been suggested in the case of various expert systems for diagnosis. In the case of more advanced technological products it would certainly be helpful to have access to a more specified technical theory of the kind being developed for ball bearings or aeroplane frames for instance.

Communication

No designer in industry works "in splendid isolation". Either he has to collaborate with other designers as often happens in big design projects, or else, in the case of more restricted designs it may be enough to work with planners and manufacturers. Because of this need for collaboration personal communication lies at the very heart of design operations. Information is often gathered from meetings; ideas are often created during conferences.

Some of this communication has already been formalized. Between the designer and the manufacturing system, the drawing is the formalized means of communication, hitherto mostly in the shape of ink drawings on paper, produced either manually or by computer. Parametric designs can be communicated simply in terms of the values of the parameters, hitherto also generally presented on slips of paper.

When information about the product is stored in the computer, the computer serves not only as a storage or information-processing tool, but also as a medium of communication with the help of computer networks or terminals connected to a mainframe.

In this way the information stored in the computer can easily be used directly in the production process, as is generally the case nowadays when numerically controlled machines are used. This means that it is no longer necessary to set up the machines manually, since the information needed can be fed into them direct. Someone will always be needed to supervise the process, however, which means that the use of terminals and screens in the manufacturing process is to a great extent a question of supervisory work.

In our scenario for the future, in which information about the product resides not only in a drawing but also in a full product model, communication aimed at other purposes is also possible (cf Kjellberg, 1982).

Communication among collaborating designers can be facilitated by the presence of a product model in the computer. The designers can try out different ideas together, and get immediate feedback. That such collaborative work benefits from the use of a computer has been demonstrated at Xerox Parc, where designers of interfaces for simple machines collaborated through a computer-based environment for fast prototyping. The interface to be designed was simulated, and the designers were able to test different functions and ways of working together (Henderson, 1986).

At present there are few computer systems which directly support collaborative work. And some problems are immediately predictable—for instance, who should be able to change the database, and when. What if several people want to make different changes at the same place? However, the potential of the computer as a tool in collaborative work is also obvious, not only to me but, judging by the interest shown at the first conference on "Computer supported collaborative work" (held in Austin, Texas, December 1986), to many other people as well.

It may also be necessary for people working in different places to be able to communicate with each other more quickly than letters allow. Hitherto the telephone (and telegram) has been the main means of quick communication. As a result of distributed computer systems, electronic mail systems and electronic conferencing systems are growing increasingly popular. If these systems are to be useful in collaborative design contexts, they must include facilities for showing pictures as well as text and numbers.

Since I believe that much can be gained by human collaboration, I predict that designers who learn to use electronic communication will experience more job satisfaction and produce better designs more efficiently than those who are confined to working alone, however sophisticated the computerized knowledge-based tools they may aquire.

Integration of computer tools

The possible computer tools suggested above would not be sufficient if they were to remain isolated from one another. To be really useful in a design context, the tools must be integrated. What does such integration involve?

From an information-processing point of view it means that all the support systems can access the same product-model database and can feed their results into it. In other words the designer should not have to feed data more than once into the product model, which also means that the results of one information-processing activity (perhaps the search for information) can be used in another (perhaps the integration of information) without any intervention on the part of the designer. Naturally, the designer should be able to inspect the result and to change it if necessary, but the result which has been affirmed by the designer should be usable in other information-processing activities. This requirement imposes heavy strain on the architecture of the computer system as a whole, but it would be outside the scope of our present subject to pursue such complications here.

From the designer's point of view, integration means that all the different kinds of computer support should be available at the same workplace. An overview of the envisaged scenario is given in Figure 42.

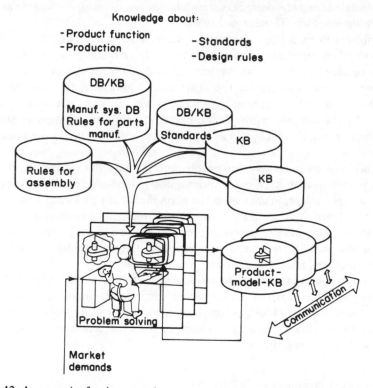

Figure 42 A scenario for integrated computer support for mechanical engineering. (Source: Kjellberg (1982, 1985).

From a cognitive point of view, such integration requires that the different support systems are consistent with one another. In this case, consistency has at least three different aspects.

One concerns the content of the knowledge-base models used in support of information retrieval, information integration, etc. Above all, the content should be consistent with the product model. This also ensures that the contents of the different support systems are consistent with one another. This means that the data required by the product model should be handled in a compatible manner in all computer support systems. A three-dimensional product model would then require consideration of its volume properties by all supports. A two-dimensional drawing support, for instance, would be of little help to the designer working with a three-dimensional product model, and would require much unnecessary extra cognitive effort for translating the data.

Another aspect of consistency concerns the strategies suggested by the different support systems (for instance for information integration, the creation of alternatives, search among alternatives). Strategies should be allowed to vary, particularly as regards the level of the design currently being used by the designer. They should also be allowed to vary according to the preferred working style of the designer. However, within these required variations the different computer support systems should be consistent with one another. This means that a designer at the conceptual stage should not be recommended to do fine tolerance tests, or that the designer at the final stage should not be recommended to look for general functional principles.

The more difficult of these recommendations, namely of suiting the suggested strategy to the designer's preferred working style, must be a matter for further research. For instance, is it necessary for a designer who prefers to check each step carefully before starting to work, to enjoy computer support which proceeds in a similar way? Or would such a designer be helped more by a support system that performs the checks automatically, so that the designer can start working at once? What kind of support is needed for a designer who prefers to adopt a trial and error approach?

The third aspect of consistency concerns the interface. If one designer is expected to work with several different computer support systems which are accessible from a single work-station, the interfaces to these systems should certainly be as consistent as possible with one another. This does not necessarily mean that the input and output devices should be exactly the same. Sometimes graphical input is needed and sometimes alpha-numerical, and the same of course applies to the output from the computer. However, it does mean that the handling of the systems should use the same terms of communication in commands or menus, and that the effect of a command with the same name should be the same in all support systems. It also means that the feedback from the system should be consistent, for instance that the drawing of a figure on the screen should follow the same conventions, and that the possible numerical checks should be given in the same scale of measurement. There is enough data on the detrimental effect of interference to warrant a strong recommendation for consistent interfaces (cf chapter 5).

EXPERIENCE OF CURRENT CAD SYSTEMS

Let us now turn from the design of ideal computer support for mechanical engineering, and look at things as they are in practice today. A great many designers already use computer support which is known as Computer Aided Design or CAD. What are present CAD systems like? How are they used? And what do different users feel about them?

Let me quote a definition of CAD from Wærn, K-G. (1988a):

> "Computer aided design is an activity in which design engineers, draughtsmen and drawing assistants use specialized interactive computer systems to assist them to formulate and solve technical design problems and to communicate the resulting problem solutions. The communication usually takes the form of drawings and part lists, but may also consist of computer-readable data for use in automated manufacturing, e.g. by numerical control machines."

General characteristics of CAD systems

Current CAD systems vary a good deal, but their main common feature is their use of interactive graphics. All CAD systems include facilities for the input of data intended to specify geometrical properties (points, lines, curves, etc.), and for the output of information in the form of figures on a graphic screen, as well as other kinds of information related to the design. The resulting representation in the computer database allows for searching and updating of the geometrical properties produced thus far.

First let us compare CAD systems with ordinary wordprocessors. As regards easily performed modifications, current CAD systems resemble wordprocessors. A wordprocessor provides little support for finding information, or for organizing it once it has been found (cf chapter 8). But it is a very efficient tool for avoiding the dull and inefficient work involved in typing the same text over and over again, just because minor changes have been made in the wording. Similarly, CAD systems delegate the simple re-drawing and changes to the computer system, thus leaving the designer free for other activities.

In its combination of graphic facilities, numerical calculations and text-processing facilities, however, a CAD system is much more complex than a wordprocessor.

A two-dimensional drawing is the kind of product which may resemble text most closely. However, even here the advantages of graphics can be exploited in a way that is not relevant when only text is involved.

In a wordprocessor there is seldom any need to look at the text in mirror-writing, backwards or upside down, whereas if we are designing an object we may find facilities for reflecting parts of the drawing or turning the object at different angles extremely helpful. Complex, symmetrical objects can be drawn as a single part which then can be reflected, turned upside down and moved about in order to produce the object desired. Similar efficiency can be obtained at the drawing board only by drawing one part (for instance the upper half) in detail and omitting details in the repeated parts. A copy machine can be used for finishing the drawing if necessary.

Another difference is that most CAD systems arrange the data on different but interrelated "levels" or "layers" (terms differ between systems). For instance, the primary geometry may be stored at one level, the secondary at another, texts at another, and so on. In this way, by choosing the appropriate level, the user can work with selected parts of the database without disturbing the rest of the contents. In addition, most systems also offer the possibility of temporarily "blanking" unwanted lines off the screen—again without disturbing the real database contents—in order to obtain a simplified picture of the detail under consideration.

Still more obvious is the advantage of storing geometrical properties to form pictures, if the properties can be made to represent three-dimensional objects. A user of a wordprocessing system would never need to look at a text from its edge or to cut it into slices. But such possibilities can be very useful when producing a design of a complex three-dimensional object.

To start a three-dimensional design the designer usually defines the object by drawing separately the standard views of it. The computer then represents the inputs internally in a form which corresponds mathematically to the definition of a three-dimensional object. This means that later the computer can present views of the object over and above those which were produced to start with, which gives the designer unique opportunities for checking the design. By turning the computer-produced object around and looking at the resulting shapes on the screen, the designer can check the design visually, in much the same way as he could with a prototype.

The three-dimensional representation also allows for different ways of processing the object, to check visually a variety of manufacturing effects such as drilling, planing or milling.

At this point it becomes necessary to distinguish between three degrees of sophistication in three-dimensional CAD systems. In one type (commonly referred to as the 2.5-D system) points of the design object can be defined along its edges only (as laid out by the user). This gives a "wire-frame model" of the object. Since only edges are defined and not volumes, the design may result in "impossible objects", as illustrated in Figure 43.

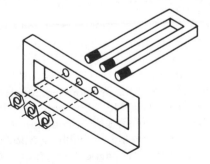

Figure 43 A wire-frame model allows the design of impossible objects.

Another type of system admits points to be constructed on the defining surfaces of the object. By using the system's graphic facilities, e.g. shading and colouring, pictures obtained from this kind of system may be made to look very natural and "real". The third and genuinely three-dimensional type of CAD system allows for any point of the volume of the object to be defined ("solids"). Only this kind of system allows for complete three-dimensional design work, including computations of gravity centre, and predictions of the effect of different manufacturing operations.

The geometrical properties of the design can also easily be supplemented by numerical measures on the different dimensions. In all current CAD systems it is possible to carry out the final dimensioning of the design, which is necessary for using the design in the manufacturing process. The dimensioning work can take quite a long time if it has to be done at the drawing board. The dimensioning work is carried out with great precision by the CAD system, a virtue which is highly esteemed by experienced designers. The measuring capacity of the system can then be extended to measure different parts during the actual work of design, measures which can then be used for checking purposes.

CAD systems in use

This general description of CAD suggests that the system is best suited to supporting the drawing operations in the design work. Current 2- and 2.5-D CAD systems (the most common at present) can be said mainly to support communicative activities and to offer very little help in the other kinds of activity mentioned above. Since drawing represents about one-third of a designer's work, a CAD system is well worthwhile.

In most companies the introduction and use of CAD is generally motivated on economic grounds, although economic calculations of CAD installations show that the systems have not usually resulted in the hoped-for increase of productivity (Löwstedt, 1986). In some companies, the justification for introducing CAD could be said to be some kind of preparation for the future, or the provision of training in computer literacy.

Thus CAD is mainly used by companies which believe that its efficiency or the competitive advantage of using computers at all will bring them economic benefits. Enthusiastic and progressive people who encourage the introduction of CAD may also facilitate its efficient use (Löwstedt, 1986).

Sometimes CAD may allow for the development and testing of designs which would not otherwise have been possible. This applies particularly when complex interacting parts are being designed. Thus the design of large-scale integrated electronic circuits for example, would probably not be feasible without CAD. Some designers have pointed out the particular virtues of CAD in checking and refining ideas for new designs of complex geometrical objects. The designing of a new propeller or the design of a new kind of ball-bearing for a big windpower plant have been cited as examples.

At what stage during the work of design is CAD used? In light of the special features of CAD systems—easy changes, easy visual checks, precise measurements—it could be expected that CAD would be used mainly in the detailed design phase. Since it is not possible to control all possible factors affecting CAD use in different companies, a frequency analysis of different kinds of CAD use does not tell us much. However, we can get some idea of CAD use from a non-systematic sample of CAD users in different companies (Wærn, K-G., 1986). By observing three or four designers in each of four different (mainly small) companies, it was found that CAD was certainly not used only during the detailed design phase. In this sample several quite complex tasks in the preliminary design phase were also tackled with the help of CAD. None of the tasks studied could be classified as belonging to the concept phase, however.

This finding agrees with the general view of CAD's usefulness. CAD is useful for producing drawings, but the thinking involved in solving the technical problems has to be undertaken outside the CAD system. The reason for this may be either that the CAD system is not very well suited to the concept phase, or that those who generate concepts do not have access to CAD systems. The capacity of the CAD system to specify details can of course become a drawback in the concept phase, where no specification of details is wanted. However, a clever designer would certainly be able to specify geometrical principles in the system, without getting bogged down in details. There is nothing to say we should specify all the dimensions of a shaft, for instance, when it can be specified simply as a line or as a cylinder in the concept phase (Helldén, 1986).

We can now look at the CAD system as a tool in light of the needs of the individual designer. The data has been taken mainly from two different investigations, Löwstedt (1986) and Wærn, K-G. (1986).

Experience of functional aspects

As far as the functional aspects of CAD systems are concerned, designers' opinions accord well with the advantages mentioned above. Designers appreciate the time gained from being able to compress their drawing operations and not having to repeat similar parts of the designs. They also comment favourably on the fact that they have less need to redraw pictures because of minor changes, and they claim that this reduction in the actual drawing accounts for most of the gain in efficiency. Most designers find CAD's dimensioning facility useful, on account of its precision in particular. Precision is also mentioned as an overall advantage of CAD systems compared with working at a drawing board.

Some designers using three-dimensional CAD systems comment on the opportunities opened up by this type of system: being able to view complicated surfaces in three dimensions, and keeping control over changes in a complex object in three dimensions. The system is appreciated even for two-dimensional work because it enables the designer to test different solutions to the same problem.

There are some functional aspects which the CAD users find less satisfying, however, most of them connected with the information retrieval facility. Since a great deal of CAD work is based on utilizing previous designs of different parts, it is essential to have easy access to such designs. However, the information retrieval capacity of current CAD systems is not very good. Earlier designs are generally only available via the drawing number allocated to them, which means that this number has to be retrieved first. Depending on the type of organization of drawing files used in the particular company, this retrieval can sometimes be fairly tedious (Wærn, K-G., 1986).

The precision cited as one of the advantages of CAD can also prove a disadvantage. Some designers mention the temptation to exaggerate the necessity for precision, just because the CAD system makes it so easy to attain. Precision may be sought for its own sake, rather than as a way of acquiring a good design. According to some researchers, e.g. Finne (1982) and Cooley (1981), this may be a natural consequence of the way in which CAD is introduced into traditional design work, namely as a means of increasing industrial efficiency and productivity.

A deficiency (rather than a disadvantage) in the system is that at present it is not much use for sketching purposes, mainly because of its awkward interface. As one designer puts it:

> "It is similar to playing piano and designing at the same time. When you work with the pen, you can think constructively: sketch and try out a construction. When working in CAD you have to think of keys and commands all the time. At CAD you are not a designer".
>
> (op cit. Löwstedt, 1986, p. 138).

One facility that deserves praise as well as some fear is connected with calculation. Most CAD systems provide opportunity for calculating the necessary technical data (for instance the tolerances of different parts of the object under construction). Without CAD these calculations are performed by hand with the help of some kind of calculator. When they are integrated into CAD, however, they can be performed much more easily, but without the designer even knowing the formulas which have to be used. According to some designers, this could mean that a human calculating skill might wither away (Löwstedt, 1986).

Experience of system handling

The interface of CAD systems varies somewhat from one system to another, but there are some features in common. All systems must have some facilities for graphic input, which means that there must be some way of easily moving the cursor around on the graphic screen. This is usually arranged by a device capable of performing two-dimensional movements easily, such as a pen on a tablet, a track-ball, a mouse, or a thumb-wheel. On top of this the designer needs an alphanumerical keyboard to input figures (to be used for calculations or specifications of the design) and text (for giving commands or for writing descriptions of the drawing).

Also, all systems must have some facility for graphic output. This can vary from simple monochromatic screens to advanced colour screens, from two-dimensional pictures (with more or less advanced perspective rendering) to three-dimensional screens, where the object is seen as a full three-dimensional object, and not only rendered in some perspective. At present the most common output is a screen with a simplistic three-dimensional rendering, often showing the lines which in a real object would be hidden from the eye (see Figure 44 below). Naturally the screen area is considerably smaller than the area of a conventional drawing board.

To this graphic screen one or more alpha-numerical screens can be added. These screens are then used for the non-graphic communication between the system and the user (which can also be done in windows on the graphic screen) and for keeping track of the program as it runs.

But there are also some conspicuous differences between the interface of the CAD system and the "interface" of a drawing board.

First, most CAD systems are not suited to free-hand sketching and drawing; instead the designer should be able to call upon ready-made command routines in order to produce different kinds of lines for building up a figure. This makes work with a CAD system much more "indirect" and abstract than work on a drawing board. This "distance" from the actual drawing is what designers find most disturbing when they try to use a CAD system for sketching. One designer described the clumsiness he felt as being "like trying to play a cello with a long bow from a distance of two metres."

The typical CAD system may thus confront its user with involved menus or complex sets of functional keys or commands, just to call up lines, circles, or other primitive design elements stored in the CAD geometric database. An example of a menu showing the different options can illustrate the complexity involved. (See Figure 45).

In a detailed study of work with a CAD system (Wærn, K-G. 1986) it was found that about 50% of all the operations performed ("operation" defined as a simple unit of activity) consisted of preparing and controlling the drawing in the system, while the remaining 50% were concerned with actual drawing. These figures show just how many system-handling operations are necessary in current CAD systems.

However, after some training with the CAD system, the designer is no longer so disturbed by the complexity of the graphic input. Expert CAD users can go a long way towards automating the purely system-handling routines.

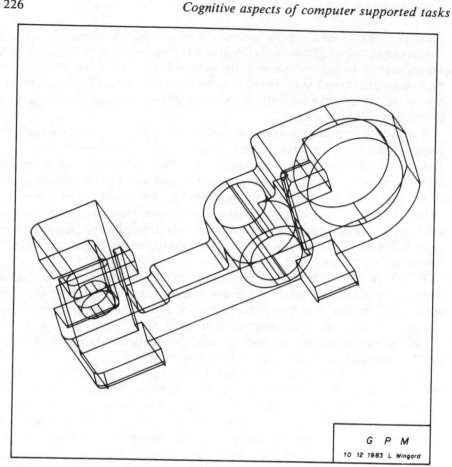

Figure 44 An example of a picture with hidden lines showing.

There are other aspects of CAD systems, however, which continue to be troublesome even after long experience of the system. One of these is connected to the small size of the screen compared with a drawing board. The small size is particularly awkward when the designer wants to make various checks on the drawing. When information about the size of angles and radii or the results of calculations are to be shown together with the drawing, the screen will certainly be too crowded. Extra manipulation of the screen is therefore needed, e.g. the temporary "blanking" of lines and text, in order to create enough visual space and conceptual clarity—manipulations which occupy some of the designer's attention.

In compensation for the small size of the screen, all CAD systems allow the designer to look more closely at parts of the design by "zooming" in onto a particular spot. In this way the part can be enlarged as much as necessary for inspection and correction. There are two kinds of zooming which can be

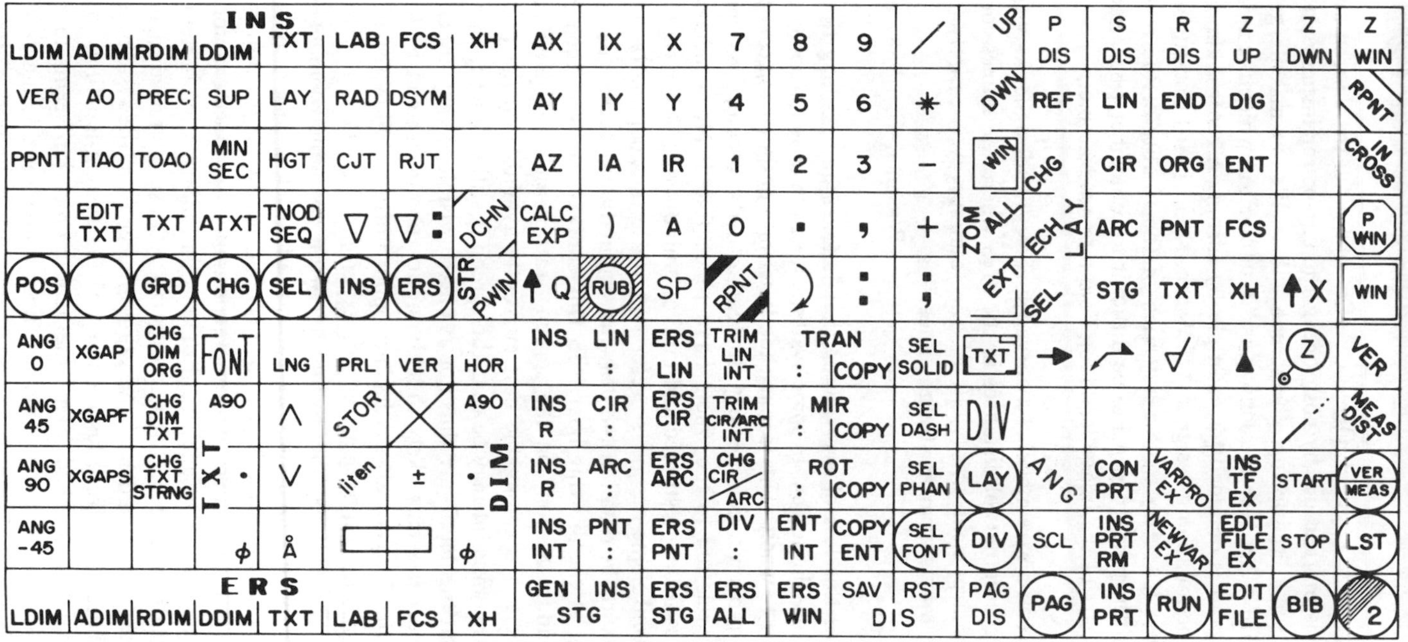

Figure 45 An example menu for graphic input in a CAD system.

performed by a CAD system. One is "static" zooming: the desired area of the screen image is marked out by positioning the cursor for instance at diagonal points. After some "redrawing" the screen will then show an enlarged picture of this area. The other type of zooming is "dynamic", in which the enlargement is continuous and is obtained for example by turning a control knob. A fairly common complaint among designers (cf Wærn, K-G., 1986) working with static zooming is that it is easy to lose any idea of the totality of the object while zooming in on the part. It seems to be difficult to remember where each line in the enlarged part of the image leads to. To quote an example:

> "In the case of a wire model of a curved surface, the designer may want to check the correctness of distances in the area where the splines converge. With an enlargement of, say, 40 $\times$, the total survey is entirely lost: all the splines may appear as straight lines."
>
> (Wærn, K-G., 1988a op cit.)

One reason for this loss of overview is that it takes quite a long time for the system to redraw the screen. In some systems it can take as long as five minutes to go from part to whole. This is much too long for a designer to keep the details of the design in his working memory. Instead, other strategies for remembering the details in relation to the whole have to be found. No wonder designers complain about feeling restricted and kind of "blindfolded" when thay are using the CAD screen! Some designers prefer not to use the zooming facility, trying instead to look at the detail in the drawing originally produced, just as they do when working at the drawing board. In this context, many of them complain about the "bad resolution" on the screen—rather an astonishing complaint, since the screens are among the best currently available on the market. The reason for this complaint may be that the screen is still smaller than a drawing board, and that the details are thus not as clearly visible as they are on a board.

In this respect it seems likely that dynamic zooming should be less disorienting, since the designer always has an opportunity to follow the path of the lines that are zoomed onto. In a study of experienced CAD users shifting from one system with static zooming to another with "dynamic zooming", the new facility was frequently mentioned as a major advantage, (Wærn, K-G., 1986).

Another part of the system's interface is concerned with the information for the designer about the system. This metacommunication (see chapter 15) consists of error- and help messages from the system, information in manuals, and other aids outside the system. Even an expert CAD user will need such information. Sometimes unexpected error messages emerge from the system, sometimes the designer needs to refresh his memory of the system-handling routines, or to find new handling methods. This metacommunication seems to be one of the most common sources of trouble and irritation among designers. Of 26 designers interviewed, 20 complained about difficulty in understanding the error messages, and 19 complained of difficulty in finding and understanding adequate information in the manuals (Wærn, K-G., 1986). The most frequent complaint here was that the error messages and manuals are in English (Swedish-speaking designers were being interviewed). Furthermore, the error messages were found too cryptic and likely to contain references to other sources, instead of simply saying what was wrong. Designers thought the manuals were too big and it was difficult to get relevant information from them. The problem was solved by asking somebody else who knew the answer. Unfortunately this person was not always available.

Finally, the most common complaint was concerned with the long and irregular response times of the CAD systems. This complaint turns up in all studies that have so far been made of designers' experience of CAD. The long response times are largely due to hardware problems. Since the CAD system involves big geometric databases and the recalculations necessary for redrawing, rescaling, etc. are extensive, the response times are bound to be long if the computer CPU is small, or if several terminals are connected to a single time-sharing system.

From a cognitive point of view, any delay of feedback is detrimental if the feedback is needed during a sequence of mental operations. However, long response times are not always a source of irritation. If the computer takes its time to store a finished drawing in a file, this will not cause the designer any particular problem. But a long response time for zooming in and out of drawings or for refreshing the screen will certainly disturb the designer's regular flow of thought.

Experience of access aspects

At present users of CAD systems often find that access to CAD work stations or terminals is restricted. Naturally it is not possible for all designers who want to use CAD to have CAD equipment of their own in their office; this would not be an economical way of using the equipment. But this restricted access to CAD sometimes makes it less advantageous to use CAD throughout the design process.

Several designers claim that the use of CAD has changed their working strategy (Löwstedt, 1986). When they worked at drawing boards, they would plan and lay out their design on the board. Now, using CAD, they plan much more fully before entering the system. Also, because it costs so much to use CAD, they try to use it as efficiently as possible, which also means using it more restrictively.

One aspect of CAD that still causes problems is connected with interruptions caused by system breakdowns. If the CAD system is used as the main tool in producing a design, a breakdown will prevent the designer from going on with his work on that particular design. This causes irritation, but it also generates a new strategy, namely always having some other activity on the go, which can occupy the designer for the time it takes to fix the breakdown. Depending on the location of the breakdown in the design process, the effect may be more or less hampering to the problem-solving activity. The possibility of breakdowns may also induce extra precautionary action such as filing or keeping notes outside the computer—all of which takes time.

Experience of training in the use of CAD

It is obvious that designers who are going to use a CAD system will need a lot of training in how to use it. Not only does he have to know what functions a system can perform and how to handle it, but he also has to understand the different methods that could profitably be used and when to use them.

The need for training in CAD use has been assessed in several studies (Ebel & Ulrich, 1987, Löwstedt, 1986, Wærn, K-G., 1986, Wingert, Duus, Rader & Riehm, 1984).

When CAD users are asked to estimate the time they find necessary for getting to know the system and learning the most elementary facts about it, their average estimation is around two weeks (Wærn, K-G., 1986, Wingert, Duus, Rader & Riehm, 1984). This "first elementary phase" consists mainly of learning to handle the system's interface. Even after this phase interface handling is probably still not automatic.

To be able to perform in the system in a way that corresponds to working manually at the drawing board, some designers estimate that about 300 hours of training are required (Löwstedt, 1986). Another interesting question in this study concerns the time needed for keeping up one's skill in handling the system, which seems to call for a few hours each week. When the same designers were asked how much time would be needed to develop the skills for handling the system, they estimated it at more than 15 hours work a week. In another study (Wærn, K-G., 1986) most designers estimated the time needed for achieving a "full mastery of the system" at between six months and a year, at least. These figures provide a striking illustration of the difficulty involved in progressing from the most elementary system-handling to full mastery of the system's facilities.

In all studies designers complain that they receive too little instruction in the ideas underlying CAD in general and in handling the system for their own particular purposes. They also find the time allotted to training in the use of the system to be too brief. The main reason for this is the pressure on the companies to produce as much or even more as before CAD was introduced.

What, then, is particularly difficult about learning CAD? The first obvious answer is that it seems to be difficult to decide *what* actually has to be learnt. Ebel & Ulich (1987) list the following new skill requirements: computer literacy, higher mathematical and analytical skills, notably a good comprehension of the principles of analytical geometry and of the application of coordinate systems, combined with an open mind.

The same review gives some data about what is actually taught in different countries. The following are mentioned:

— basic training in information technology, which seems to be conducted best in vocational schools rather than in companies;

— special CAD training, comprising for instance the architecture and functioning of CAD-systems, the management of hardware and interface, and the generation of drawings and the basic geometrical elements and designs required;

— special training in CAM, particularly aimed at draughtsmen and comprising knowledge about the characteristics of NC machine-tools, the preparing of parts and programs, and the coordination of systems for CNC machine-tools;

— traditional training in draughtsmanship and analytical geometry.

To judge from the problems described by CAD users, training is still inadequate on a number of points.

It seems to be difficult to understand the relation between *data* and *geometrical entities* (Wærn, K-G., 1986). Designers feel uncertain, because they have no control over the way their drawings are stored; they even feel that errors of which they are unaware can be introduced into their drawings.

Particular system-handling operations, which are not at all relevant to the drawing-board situation, can be difficult to learn. Wærn, K-G. (1986) made an intensive study of a system and found that the way the system required a drawing to be partitioned in order to achieve the most efficient data processing was a source of particular difficulty. The partitioning to the "levels" in the system was to some extent standardized and the layers could be used to some extent according to the designer's own choice. In both cases novices had difficulty in remembering what kind of information was available, and where—mainly because 256 levels were available! For experienced users, this aspect of handling the system caused no particular difficulty.

The designers always seem to be unable to utilize the advantages the system offers. At a very early stage, this emerges from the complaints of some designers about the difficulty working with whole figures and groups, when they are used to working with simple lines at the drawing board.

However, the difficulties experienced in two-dimensional modelling can hardly be compared with the very different situation that a three-dimensional system represents. The first difficulties reported mainly concerned learning to use the extra three-dimensional facilities—like turning the object round and looking at it from different angles. The solution to this problem is very well expressed by a designer, as follows:

"It is as if you had a fish in an aquarium that has a lot of sides—you can look at it from any side and see it differently, but it's still the same fish."

(op cit. Wærn, K-G., 1986, 1988a.)

Considering that three-dimensional modelling in current systems has to be performed by drawing two-dimensional views, it is not surprising that designers find the three-dimensional task much more demanding, particularly where spatial imagery is concerned.

A problem which will be more noticeable in the future concerns the updating of knowledge as a result of minor improvements in current systems, and the retraining required when a company changes from one CAD system to another. In both cases, the company hopes to gain some advantage from the change at as little cost as possible in terms of retraining.

CAD companies and CAD educationists have probably not yet become aware of this new situation. Traditional training is provided, which may not be fully adequate for experienced CAD designers. They may not need to learn more about computers as data-processing devices, capable of translating geometrical properties into computer-manageable data. They will also be well aware of the advantages and disadvantages of whatever computer system they have previously used, as far as functionality is concerned. What they need instead is training geared to the differences between the new system and the old.

Some preliminary data on the introduction of a new system to CAD users already familiar with another system are presented in Wærn, K-G. (1988b). The new system is naturally more advanced than the old one, which means that more functions are available and that a fully three-dimensional modelling capacity is now provided. The data derives from the first stage, during which the two-dimensional capacity only is learned.

All the designers interviewed found the new system very much better than the old one, as far as functionality was concerned. They had some difficulty in learning the new system, connected—as expected—with the differences between the systems. Some of the more obvious differences concerned the actual procedures for handling drawings. Some command procedures were the exact opposite in the two systems. For instance, when the trimming of unwanted lines was ordered, one system deleted the lines pointed at, while the other retained them. This was a source of irritation to start with, but the users soon learnt to accept the shift in orientation. The same applied to other minor procedural differences, which can be regarded as "low-level".

The main difficulty lay on a higher, conceptual level. For instance the new system required a completely new way of handling the partitioning of the design. Whereas the old system had involved one partitioning only (into "levels"), the new system allowed for several partitionings. The designers found this difficult to learn, since the previous mental model of "levels"—which could be readily envisaged as a pack of transparencies—had to be replaced by a totally different set of concepts.

Finally, it is interesting to note that despite being basically positive towards the added functionality of the new system, the designers also seemed to fear its complexity. Some even declared that they would never be able to learn all the details of the system. These claims were made in an interview on the third day of their introduction course on the new system. In a further interview about 8 weeks later, a similar attitude was expressed, but now at least some users sounded more confident about it. The following is a typical comment:

> "Of course I don't know all the tricks and gimmicks. There's so much in it, you know. Probably never will. But I know enough to see how to go on—pick things out that suit my purpose. At least I think I do. You learn as you go. And that's the kick, for me anyway."

Experience of the effects of CAD

Finally, we should look briefly at the possible effects of CAD on the competence of design engineers.

In the early days of CAD systems fears were expressed that their use would increase productivity at the expense of the designer's professional skill (Cooley, 1981), because CAD would cause a fragmentation of the design and drawing work.

In so far as CAD is used in a vertically specialized work environment, this fear might be justified. If each professional worker uses CAD for performing a particular part of the design work only, perhaps one for the development part and another for the finishing part, it is easy to see that competence in other parts would soon deteriorate. But given the horizontal integration generally obtaining in Sweden, the effects of CAD have to be related to the totality of tasks which a CAD user performs.

In current studies of CAD workers in Sweden very few designers have expressed any fear of losing their competence. The fear they do express on the other hand, is related to a great extent to the organization of work. In departments where the work is divided between layout and detail drawing, people are more concerned about the use of CAD. The risk that the use of CAD will lead to detailed constructions rather than new construction is imminent (Löwstedt, 1986).

In another study (Finne, 1982, 1988) it was reported that the use of CAD led to greater concentration on design work. This was connected with the separation of creative and routine work, which in turn was mainly due to the restricted access to computer terminals and the character of the CAD system itself. The new technique also made greater demands on precision and called for more control over pace of work, because more decisions were now necessry and the rate of the work as a whole had been stepped up. However, as Finne points out, these circumstances may have depended on the way the work was organized in this particular company. It may be possible so to organize work, that the negative consequences do not necessarily follow.

In the same study it was found that CAD itself, rather than the fragmentation of the design work, made for greater complexity and made more planning necessary. This may also have been because—as the same study indicated—the people who preferred complexity and planning were also those who accepted the CAD work to start with. However, this by no means suggests that CAD, a priori, in any way hampers the tackling of complex tasks. Nonetheless, at present most planning is conducted outside CAD and before use of the CAD system has started.

On the subject of professional knowledge the same designers believe there will be a shift from knowing the *solutions* to design problems to knowing *methods* for achieving such solutions. It is difficult at the moment to tell whether this is a positive or a negative shift in competence.

Some consequences that may be inevitable are connected with tasks performed by people other than the designers (Finne, 1982). First, the CAD system takes over most of the work previously carried out by draughtsmen. When the skill previously aquired by these people has become superfluous, they will have to learn something else. In some companies they have been trained in certain aspects of designing and have been given simple design jobs. If design is divided into simple and advanced work performed by different people, the risk will be that the "simple" designers are never able to progress by way of challenging jobs, while the "advanced" designers can never relax by working on a simple task. A similar fate may overtake the NC (Numerical Control) programmers who become redundant when the design is fed directly into CNC (Computerized Numerical Control) machines.

Another competence threatened by the introduction of advanced CAD systems is also mentioned in Finne's analysis. The work of the process planner may gradually become superfluous as the designer successively takes over more of his work. We can thus expect a concentration of complex work in the hands of the designer, who will then need very advanced computer support to help him to handle the resulting complexity.

SUMMARY

In this chapter we have discussed computer support in mechanical engineering, with particular reference to mechanical design.

The design process is complex and takes place at different levels: conceptual, concretization and detail specification level. It also passes through different phases: the concept phase, the preliminary design phase, the detailed design phase, the refinement phase and the modification phase. The first three phases generally include work at different levels, until a satisfactory design has been achieved.

For the various activities connected with design, different computer supports can be envisaged. We have looked at a scenario of future computer support, whereby a product model of the design product can be stored in a computer database, with all the technical details required, and including information about the relevant manufacturing process.

In new design and development work, computer support may be desirable for many different activities. It has been suggested that the following activities, which are all part of the design process, could benefit from advanced computer support: information retrieval, the creation of alternatives, the integration of information, inferencing, prediction, search among alternatives, checks, the diagnosis of errors and communication.

Current computer support consists mainly of Computer Aided Design (CAD). Experience of current CAD systems indicates that these systems mainly support the communicative activity of the designer and offer very little support for the other types of activity mentioned above.

CAD systems are generally appreciated by experienced designers, mainly because they ease some of the more tedious work of redrawing and take over time-consuming routine activities such as calculations and dimensioning. They also produce more precise drawings for less work.

On the negative side, it is difficult to use CAD in the concept phase, mainly because of the awkwardness of the interface which does not allow for easy sketching.

Apart from the sometimes awkward input, the CAD interface is generally well suited to its task. The small size of the screen poses some problems, however, in that the designer either is unable to see the details in the overall view, or loses the overview over the design when zooming into the details.

It seems that people need a good deal of training in the use of CAD systems, particularly training specific to the task they want to perform with the help of the system.

CAD's effects on the work strategies and professional skill of the designers depend on how the use of CAD is organized. Under vertical specialization, CAD may jeopardize the competence of CAD-users. Under a horizontally integrated work organization, CAD seems to result in greater job complexity. In this situation, CAD appears to call for more planning and to step up the pace of work; it also seems to encourage the separation of creative and routine activities.

One evident problem which arises when computer support is introduced in an industry, concerns the division of labour between different professions and between professional workers and computer systems. Draughtsmen and NC programmers may well be replaced by CAD systems. Process planners may also become superfluous, which means that all responsibility will fall on the designer. This problem will have to be addressed in future work on developing and introducing computer supports in industry.

Part III. The Interface Perspective

Introduction

When a novice computer user finds out that a computer system can help him with a variety of tasks, he may well be impressed and enthusiastic about the opportunities offered by the system. On getting closer to the system and learning the complexities of its handling, however, most computer users experience some disappointment.

System designers, users, and those concerned about human factors all have a common interest in facilitating the transition from WHAT can be done to HOW it should be done. The design of the user interface has therefore attracted a lot of attention.

While this topic merits all the attention it has received, a word of warning is in place. In some instances the very importance of the problem has persuaded system designers and human–computer interaction researchers into considering the communication problem in isolation. Some of the wrong questions have been asked, such as: What communication method is "best"? Or: Is communication method x "better than" communication method y? These questions can never be answered adequately for the following reasons. First, the "quality" of communication would have to be defined; secondly, the implicit general nature of the question would have to be changed to become much more specific. We should be asking instead about the particular needs that characterize a task, so that the properties of the communication could be adapted to them. The needs of the particular user must also be taken into account.

The requirement of some tasks are obvious. For instance, nobody would suggest that a user should input text by selecting each letter from a menu and pointing at it. Common sense is sometimes enough to help us to decide on the requirements of the task. Other task requirements are more subtle; for instance it may be necessary to move the cursor in order to select a position for the input. What kind of device would we, as users prefer for this?

Some of the user's needs are also obvious. Systems designed to be used by children avoid involved keyboard input and complex explanatory texts. But what about using foreign languages in systems designed for use by engineers? Or requiring users in industry to formulate specific, non-meaningful commands to the computer system? In both cases, we saw above that problems have arisen showing that the particular user needs have not always been adequately allowed for.

We can thus state that interface design should always be considered in relation to a particular task. The task and its corresponding concepts do not totally constrain the interface design, however. There are also some general recommendations on designing the lower levels of the communication.

This part on the interface perspective aims at covering these general recommendations. Communication style, lexicon and syntax will be covered, as well as the physical aspects of input and output devices. Finally, the design of metacommunication will be addressed.

Chapter 12

Communication Styles

Different styles can be chosen to support the communication between user and computer system. Those most in use currently are the following:

— menu selection
— form fill-in
— command language
— natural language
— direct manipulation.

It should be noted that the different styles are not mutually exclusive, and it is quite possible to use them in combination. For instance, a common combination includes direct manipulation and menu selection. First however, we should look at each style separately.

I should like to acknowledge here my main source of information regarding the different communication styles, namely Ben Shneiderman's book: Designing the User Interface (Shneiderman, 1987). The following presentation constitutes a small part only of all the useful insights contained in this work.

MENU SELECTION

Menu selection means that the different opportunities for handling the system are presented to the user in a list of options. The user selects one of them (using some sort of pointing device, to be discussed later); the system then performs the chosen action and the user observes the effect.

An obvious requirement here is that the options in the menu should be self-explanatory. This is not always the case, however, as can be seen in the menu presented in Figure 46.

The options in a menu can be described either in words or pictures (icons). Although it is sometimes said that a single picture says more than a thousand words, this only applies to pictures which are well chosen in relation to their

C − BLOCK GET	Y − DEL TO EOL	P − PRINT FILE
G − BLOCK PUT	K − DISK SYSTEM	X − SCROLL DOWN
B − BOLD PRINT	Q − USER 2	A − SCROLL LEFT
W − CURSOR UP	F − INSERT MODE	S − SCROLL RT

Figure 46 An example of a non-self-explanatory menu.

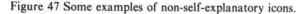

Figure 47 Some examples of non-self-explanatory icons.

meaning. The examples in Figure 47 illustrate the opposite case.

Menus are generally helpful for novice users (provided the options are self-explanatory). If the options are well organized, a menu can support the user's decision-making in the system. The use of a menu reduces the number of keystrokes needed to feed instructions into the system, which can be helpful for users who are not good at keyboard work (for instance children or the handicapped). On the other hand, if several instructions are to be given, it is certainly quicker to feed them directly from a keyboard than to have to look at a menu, move some pointing device to the option desired, and then select it.

It should also be noted that menus which appear on the screen occupy precious screen space. Most users complain that the screen is too small already. For this reason various ways of handling the non-transparency of menus have been tried out. Menus can be "pulled down" or "popped up" only when needed, and they can be placed in different windows, which in turn can overlap. Menus can also be located somewhere else altogether, perhaps on a special screen or tablet separated from the main screen. In cases like this the user has to shift his attention away from the place where the action is.

In a complex system the number of options to be presented can be very great and using a menu means that the options must be divided in a relevant and useful way. The appropriate grouping of options and their distribution in each menu presents a real challenge to system designers.

Several studies have been focused on the organization of menus. If there are a great many items a hierarchically organized menu will be useful. This kind of organization requires a good deal of knowledge about the user's task so that the groupings at each level of the menu will seem natural and comprehensible to the user, and so that the levels in the menus correspond in a natural way to the requirements of the task (cf Robertson, McCracken & Newell, 1981).

When the menu is being divided into different levels, the question arises of how to trade breadth (number of items presented at each level) against depth (number of menu levels). Some researchers have studied the speed with which a particular item is selected from menus organized in different ways. Their results indicate that users perform this task more quickly in a hierarchical organization with a few levels only and with more alternatives at each level than in an organization with a lot of levels and only a few alternatives at each level (cf Dray, Ogden & Vestiwig, 1981, Kiger, 1984, Landauer & Nachbar, 1985).

FORM FILL-IN

This type of communication is generally employed when users have to enter data in a particular format. It is particularly suitable when the same type of data has to be entered, perhaps about merchandise (type, number, price, stock, delivery), people (name, date of birth, address) or books (author, title, publisher, year). The form fill-in can help in placing the data to be entered, so that the user does not have to watch the screen too carefully.

Again the designation of the fields into which the data should be entered must be self-explanatory. The user will need to know the kind of data that is permissible in each field (the computer can only make a very rough check), and how to handle the input device. This type of communication thus requires that the user should know both the task and the system.

It should be pointed out that the task of form filling is usually regarded as something that should not take up too much of a single user's time.

COMMAND LANGUAGE

A command language provides a way of expressing instructions direct to the computer. It can be compared to an "empty" menu. All the information which is given in the menu is hidden in a command language. The users have to learn the semantics, i.e. the concepts to be used in terms of the objects to be handled and the operations to be performed, the syntax, i.e. the rules governing relationships between commands and their parameters, and the vocabulary to be used.

Thus a command language calls for a lot more learning on the part of the user than a menu does. Nonetheless a particular task can often be performed more quickly by giving commands than by looking at menus and pointing at options in them. Thus it might be expected that command languages would be preferred by frequent users of the system who will be involved in many complicated interactions with the computer. However, it has been found that in certain situations even proficient users prefer menus to commands (Potosnak, 1984).

Much of the research in the field of human–computer communication has been concerned with the design of command languages. Since many of the problems arising in connection with menus, commands and natural language interaction are similar, I shall discuss them later under the headings "semantics", "syntax" and "lexicon".

NATURAL LANGUAGE

An extended variant of command language involves what has been called the "natural language" approach to human–computer communication. At present, it is a question not of a full natural language but of a very restricted set of possibilities which may sometimes resemble natural language.

The idea is that the system should be able to "understand" sentences provided by the user as well as producing intelligible sentences for the user.

We met some natural language dialogues before, in the chapters on database search and expert systems. Let us here look a little closer on the requirements of these from the system and user side.

In order that a system shall understand a natural language input from a user, the system has to be able to "parse" the sentences typed in (i.e. recognize what is the subject, the predicate, and the object). It should also be able to recognize some synonyms.

However, the vagueness, the flexibility and the richness of natural language makes it impossible to embrace all the common ways of using natural language. People sometimes write "ungrammatical" sentences, and certainly use ambiguous wordings. Further, in natural language use, the context helps clarify ambiguous expressions which may otherwise be difficult to interpret.

For instance, the following instruction for washing your hair is perfectly intelligible:

> "Wet hair. Put shampoo into hair and work until it lathers. Rinse and repeat twice."

And yet a formal system having to read such an instruction would be in trouble. Not only would it have difficulty in understanding the criterion "until it lathers", but it would also have problems in understanding the meaning of "repeat twice". Does it mean wetting the hair a second time?

But of course we do not often talk to a computer about washing our hair. And there may be cases in which information sought and provided is precise enough to be handled without extensive reference to world knowledge or context, and in which computer systems with natural language facilities may be helpful.

Natural language systems have been directed towards information seeking and games, and recently towards expert systems. In all these instances it has been found that people readily overestimate the system's understanding ability. Since the system accepts some of the natural language formulations, users will expect it to accept even more. Then, when the system does not "understand", users may be asked to explain themselves better and often get irritated by the clarifying dialogue they have to go through before the system understands. One of the problems of natural language interaction thus seems to be learning the restrictions of the particular natural language interaction; and different systems may of course have different restrictions.

That natural language does not solve the problems involved in database search has been amply demonstrated in an investigation by Ogden & Sorknes (1987). Studying questioners who had no formal query training, these researchers found that only 28% of the subjects' first questions resulted in a correct result.

Another drawback of natural language interaction is the amount of typing that has to be undertaken. For a user who is a novice at the keyboard, menu selection would be quicker. For a proficient computer user, a command language which does not require so much typing would also be quicker.

Systematic investigations which have compared natural language interaction with other kinds of communication style have not found any particular advantage in natural language interaction (Hauptmann & Green, 1983, Small & Weldon, 1983).

We also have to ask ourselves how far the user understands the system's expressions. Some natural language interaction systems are able to form sentences which could be produced in ordinary language. As long as the interaction is short and concerns a topic with which the user is familiar, there should be no difficulty in understanding the sentences. But when long involved explanations are required, natural language on its own will probably not be enough. Although no systematic investigations have been published, recent developments in expert systems suggest that natural language explanations are not considered to be sufficient. Instead, explanations expressed as a tree drawn from various more or less interdependent sources of information in graphic form have been suggested (Bocker. Fischer & Nieper, 1986, Poltrock, Steiner & Tarlton, 1986), as we have said in chapter 10.

DIRECT MANIPULATION

The idea of "direct manipulation" was introduced by Shneiderman as early as 1974. The method has since been implemented in several systems (cf Shneiderman, 1980, 1987, Hutchins, Hollan & Norman, 1986).

According to this communication method the user can move and transform objects on the screen as if they were real objects. In a direct manipulation environment, the user can "lay out" papers on the screen, grasp them with the help of an instrument of some kind and move them over the screen to change their position. The objects can also be enlarged or reduced by dragging at one corner.

This manipulation of objects hardly merits the name of "communication", since it is so direct. The user gives no instructions, he simply acts. Direct manipulation has been described as "what you see is what you get", an expression that has served as a goal to be achieved by many system designers. The directness of direct manipulation has been praised by several writers, for instance in terms of the "principle of virtuality" (Nelson, 1980), or the "principle of transparency" (Rutkowski, 1982).

Direct manipulation is being increasingly employed in almost all kinds of computer applications, from simple desktop personal computers for the production of texts and pictures to database search and finally to complex computer aided design.

Direct manipulation suffers less risk than any other communication style of appearing meaningless and demanding to the user, so long as the task to be performed can be described by concrete objects. This means that system designers must be creative; they face a challenging task, which is certainly worth the effort. Most users who have worked with direct manipulation systems become fascinated by the ease with which they can be learned and find them both useful and entertaining.

However, there are important reservations; not all tasks can be described by concrete objects, and not all actions can be performed direct. Let us take the buffer concept as an example. This concept is used to support the activity of "cutting" and "pasting". How can hidden storage be depicted and acted upon directly? A possible conceptualization is the "clipboard" onto which we put the material to be worked on. However, on a clipboard we usually put several scraps at the same time. If the computer clipboard does not allow this, as is the case in some computer programs, the metaphor does not hold.

Actions on variables (which by definition are not concrete objects) are another example of operations which are difficult to represent by direct manipulation. Thus programming cannot be supported by direct manipulation when it is a question of iterations or recursions over the values of variables. However, programming can be supported by direct manipulation in other ways, as the so-called "visual programming" systems have shown. Graphs and flowcharts are natural supports for programmers, which can of course be enhanced by direct manipulation. Programming by example is another intriguing development, whereby the programmer gives a concrete example of input and output to the system, which then derives the program from his example (or examples). Such programming can also be supported by direct manipulation.

In a penetrating analysis of direct manipulation interfaces, Hutchins, Hollan & Norman (1986) give the following warning:

"Beware the over-specialized system where operations are easy, but little of interest is possible".

In other words, although it may be possible to design a system of easy direct manipulation for a single very specific task, as soon as the user wants to do something more than this the system is no longer efficient. This has been a common complaint about the direct-manipulation support afforded by small personal computers for wordprocessing and drawing. These systems are satisfactory and even fun in situations like text editing or drawing. However, programmers find these systems very clumsy to use, and not at all suited to their particular tasks.

COMPARISON BETWEEN COMMUNICATION STYLES

From the above it should be evident that it is difficult if not impossible to compare different communication styles in any general way. One style is useful to a particular purpose and person, another to another task or user.

Direct manipulation seems to be the preferred style at the moment. It is not only easier to learn (for the relevant tasks!) than other kinds of communication, but it also seems to give users more satisfaction—an important aspect for home or school use, and why not also in a work context? It is difficult to explain why it should be more "fun" to drag a square over the screen in order to enlarge it than to give a command to the same effect. Maybe the feeling of direct control and the successive change effected, give rise to a special feeling of pleasure.

Another reason for the popularity of direct manipulation is that more of the people now using computers are either computer novices or are using several different systems intermittently. Only a frequent user of one particular system will remember the different commands necessary to handle a command-driven system. Only a user who has not too much work to do in a system will be patient enough to carry through the currently available natural language interactions. Menus usually supplement direct manipulation, and there is no advantage to be gained from using menus alone, if the actions concern objects on the screen which can be moved or changed.

It will be interesting to watch how the trade-off between the easy-to-learn but specific and concrete direct manipulation interface and the more general and abstract command or menu-based interfaces will develop. Probably some border line will be drawn between tasks which are easier and more efficiently performed with the help of direct manipulation and those for which another communication style would be better suited. It is also quite probable that there will be a range of tasks which will be best suited by natural language interaction. Both communication styles are well suited to novices. Perhaps we may even find that some people prefer language to images and vice versa. Research on these questions is under way.

SUMMARY

Human–computer communication must be adopted to suit the task and to the user. Still there may be some general recommendations to be taken into account where interface design is concerned.

In the present chapter, the issue of communication style is discussed, where system designers need to consider both precise and general preferences of style. It is found, however, that the efficiency and adequacy of different styles depend on the circumstances and in particular on the task at hand. Commands, menus, natural language and direct manipulation, can all serve particular applications. Direct manipulation seems to be the preferred interaction style for tasks involving concrete objects and for users making intermittent use of a system. An empty screen to be handled by commands may be preferred for experts, working with complex problems. The interaction with natural language interfaces may cause users problems because the computer capacity may either be overestimated (at the start) or underestimated (after some vain attempts to get the computer to understand).

Chapter 13

Lexical and Syntactical Aspects of Communication

Let us now turn to the rules of communication, its lexicon and syntax. The lexical aspects of communication concern what the words—or icons—stand for (denotation), and what associations they evoke (connotation). Syntax refers to the rules for constructing and combining instructions.

We can start with the lexical aspects.

DENOTATION

The system's model of the task defines the concepts to be denoted. The words (or icons) to be used in order to instruct the system should be as closely related as possible to the task to be performed. When a direct relationship can be found (as is sometimes the case in direct manipulation systems) the action to be performed feels "natural" and the learning required is minimal. The interface "disappears". As have seen above, it is not possible to create direct correspondences with all conceptual objects in all tasks, or to create direct parallels to all conceptual operations.

As soon as we have to use a symbol to denote a concept, the question of the relationship between symbol and referent arises. In ordinary natural language the relationship is conventional but generally also quite arbitrary. The words denoting things differ from language to language. For instance, "computer" is denoted "dator" in Swedish, "Rechner" in German, and "ordinadeur" in French, which also refer to different concepts: data, calculation, and order respectively.

It might be thought that the denotation of things by pictures would be less arbitrary. Pictures can at least resemble the thing depicted. And yet pictures too can vary from one language, or at least from one culture to another. For instance it is by no means self-evident that the images in Figure 48 denote men and women respectively. There exist countries where men wear skirts, and certainly women wearing skirts are getting increasingly rare in other countries.

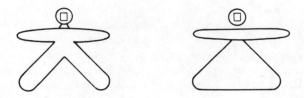

Figure 48 A seemingly straightforward representation of men and women.

A lot of work may be needed to find a relevant symbol for "erase", since a 2-D picture of an eraser as such is not very informative (Figure 49).

Figure 49 A picture of an eraser is not very informative.

That it is not easy to find generally comprehensible symbols for different concepts is confirmed by all the work that was needed to establish international traffic signs. In this case pictures do not always say more than a thousand words. The agreed sign for the command "stop!" is the one in Figure 50.

Figure 50 An international traffic sign for required halting.

even though the word on the sign does not mean "stop!" in all languages, not even if we constrain ourselves to European languages.

In attempting to find an agreed sign for "exit", the icon in Figure 51 has been used, but the best one was found to be the word "exit"! (Again a symbol (or word) which is not generally self-evident.)

Figure 51 An international sign for "Exit".

The situation in connection with computer use is more complex than this. First, there are so many more concepts to be covered by the symbols; secondly, many of the concepts are less familiar than the concepts necessary to traffic. A file directory may not be at all familiar to the novice user, and the concept of "zapping" which may appear in a menu probably even less so. The idea of scrolling to the left and right may seem very strange to a user who is accustomed to working on paper and who might have been able to accept the idea of a paper roll scrolling up and down. In all these cases the words are not self-explanatory, simply because the concepts are not known.

Even when concepts are known, there is still the question of choosing an acceptable name for particular concepts. It has been suggested that the semantic properties of words should be taken into consideration in choosing words for a system. Words which are more distinctive should be preferred to more general words which could refer to a lot of different situations. Studies supporting this suggestion have compared general and specific commands in different situations (Barnard et al., 1982, Scapin, 1982). Thus the words "search" and "display", for instance, are easier to remember in handling a computer system than "select" and "read".

The result of all this is a confusing lack of conformity between computer systems. The following are some examples.

Although most systems accept the log-out command "lo", some still fail to understand this and require the command "k" (for kill) instead. That "rm" means "remove" may be guessed by a shrewd and competent user (unless he guesses "read mail", "random movement", or "row margin" instead), but that "man" should mean "show" or "type" is difficult for a user to swallow who thinks that "man" should be short for "manual" (see also Norman, 1981).

One factor which makes the unconventional vocabulary and all the abbreviations still more confusing is that most systems work with menus or commands based on the English language. Since the systems will be used in different language communities, this means either that each new community has to translate the words and abbreviations used, or that they have to train their users in the English computerese of the system designers. Even professional people may be disturbed by the English used in the systems and manuals, as we saw in chapter 11.

As an example of the difficulty in translating English-based computerese into other languages, I can quote an inter-European study of Unix mail in which I was involved (van der Veer et al., 1987a). When we tried to translate the concept of "default" into Dutch, German and Swedish, we found that there was no equivalent single word in any of these languages. The closest we could come was a phrase which in English would have meant roughly "that which happens unless you do something else"—obviously rather a clumsy expression.

"Default" also provides us with an example of a concept that is useful in computer contexts but that has been borrowed from another context. The meaning of the word is not originally connected with computers at all. The original use of the word does not seem to be familiar in the other language communities. Of course, as has been said many times before, users learn. But how much has to be learnt, and at what price?

CONNOTATION

Words often mean much more than they directly denote. "Computer" literally means something which computes, but almost all who hear the word today are aware of other meanings. Some perceive it as something awful, something that intrudes into our privacy and threatens our jobs; others react with feelings of pleasure, thinking of the relief it offers from tedious corrections, rewriting and redrawings; others again see it as a challenge to invent new and intriguing problem solvers, waiting only for the problems to arise.

The words used in telling a computer system what to do can affect the ease with which a user learns the system, and the user's attitude towards the system. The usual "login" command for starting a system can sound pretty nonsensical to a novice user, but the "logout" command is perhaps easier to accept than words like "kill" and "abort", because of the absence of other connotations.

In a short study Lars Oestreicher (1987) asked novice computer science students to estimate how dangerous different commands were if they wanted to leave a session without changing their file. He found big individual differences in the connotations for different commands, but certain words were consistently considered more "dangerous" than others. Among these were "Finish", "Halt" and "Stop". More than half of the subjects, who were rather knowledgeable about computers, considered the commands "abort" and "break" to be fairly harmless.

It would be interesting to make similar studies of the connotations attached to icons.

THE SYNTACTICAL ASPECTS OF COMMUNICATION

By syntax is meant the rules underlying a certain language usage. In particular, syntax refers to the ordering of words to be used in forming acceptable sentences. In a computer situation Shneiderman (1980) described syntactical knowledge as varied and device-dependent. It is acquired by rote memorization and is easily forgotten.

This characterization of the syntactical aspect of computer languages does not correspond to the linguistic characterization of syntax. In a natural language, the syntax describes the underlying regularity, the rules on which "grammatical" sentences are built. Such rules do not have to be varied and "device-" (i.e. language-) dependent. They may rather be universal at a very general level in different languages (cf Chomsky, 1965).

However, the syntax proposed for specific computer languages has been developed not according to human characteristics, but to be able to handle particular aspects of the programming task. The syntactical rules of a programming language are thus much less general and conventional than those of a natural language.

Of course, between natural languages there are also big differences in the details of the grammar required to form acceptable sentences. Accidence, in particular, differs from language to language. The same is true of computer languages. The irritating colons required in COBOL do not fulfill the same mission as the full-stops which are so easy to forget in PROLOG, and the parentheses needed in LISP are easily disregarded by novice programmers.

In the following exposition I shall concentrate on the regularities, the syntactical aspects, of human–computer communication, and in particular on those aspects which concern the interface to "end users".

As we noted in our discussion of human cognition (Part I), human beings are very good at recognizing and utilizing regularities in the multitude of information they encounter. Even small children build up their own rules for the way words should be formed. We find "overregularization" in forms such as "seed" instead of "saw", "runned" instead of "ran" and "childs" instead of "children". Adults who turn into computer users do not lose this ability to find regularities. In fact they will insist on consistency and regularity, since this makes their task of learning the system easier.

Several studies confirm the hypothesis that human–computer communication is easier to learn, the fewer the rules behind it. Reisner (1982) compared different communication languages used in a graphics editing system, and found that it was possible to use formal grammar as a design tool. It has even been found that consistency *within* a particular command language is more helpful to a user than compatibility *between* the command language and the natural language (Barnard et al., 1981). This is certainly a challenge to systems designers involved in the design of natural language interfaces!

It may not always be easy to design consistent command strings based on natural language, as the Swedish conference system, COM, has shown. This system has been developed with the users in mind, and it should be suited to novice users, intermittent users, and expert users. Some examples are given in Table 11. It should be noted that COM can be used both like a menu, when several options are shown, or like a command, when only the option with the highest priority is shown. The users themselves can choose between the command or menu styles.

The problems involved in finding short telling commands (or menu names) based on natural language associations are amply demonstrated by these examples. All commands involve at least a predicate and an object. The word within the parentheses in Table 11 should not be written. The other words can be abbreviated. As we see sometimes the predicate and sometimes the object come into focus in order to distinguish between different instructions. Thus it is not

Table 11.   Some examples of commands to be used in COM

Writing	Comment
(Write new) Notice	Focus on object
(Send a) letter (to)	Focus on object
Comment (on entry)	Focus on predicate
Personal (answer)	Focus on adjective
Editing	
Erase (line above)	Focus on predicate
(Remove last) word	Focus on object
(Use) editor SOS	Focus on instrument
Change membership	
(Become) member (of)	Focus on object
Withdraw (permanently from)	Focus on predicate

possible to find consistent rules governing the choice of the appropriate word to use.

If systems designers cannot solve the problem of designing an optimal syntax for a user–computer dialogue, perhaps the user could do so? Some systems offer the users the opportunity of defining their commands themselves. In such cases, it might be expected that users would find an optimal set of commands to suit their particular task and communication style. However, users do not seem able to recognize what is a good communication style (see Grudin & Barnard, 1985). Grudin and Barnard compared various given command abbreviations with others created by the users themselves. Their conclusion is that creating an abbreviation is easier than remembering it once you have created it, and that people perform better with a good given set of abbreviations than with personally created abbreviations. What, then is "good"? The researchers believe it is important to find the "right" consistency. In their experiment the consistent rule was to use the first two letters in each command, (e.g. "fr" for "front" and "ba" for "back"), even though this might result in "inconsistent" combinations of consonants and vowels.

Since internal consistency appears to be such an important factor, we have to ask ourselves how consistency can be measured, and what type of consistency must be sought in developing useful communication languages.

Payne & Green (1983) suggested that grammar can best be described on two levels, one of which concerns the family resemblance between rules. The job of finding a grammar to describe the relation between task and action in computer systems is still being tackled, and some interesting attempts have been made to describe various existing systems (cf. Payne & Green, 1986; Green, Schiele & Payne, 1988). If this development continues we should aquire a good basis for describing systems in terms of their syntactical rules. Attempts are also being made to add some semantic aspects to the analysis of systems in the ETAG analysis proposed by Tauber (Tauber, 1988).

SUMMARY

In this chapter, the issues of lexical and syntactical aspects of human–computer communication are discussed.

The choice of words or icons to denote commands or menu options must be carefully considered. Familiar concepts often have a number of different conventional denotations, particularly if words are used. But computer concepts may not correspond exactly to everyday concepts, and the question of choosing denotations which are both informative and distinctive is an important one. There is some evidence that more specific denotations are to be preferred to the more general. Standardization of at least some denotations would benefit all those who use several different computer systems.

When it comes to syntax, human–computer communication must be consistent. The fewer the rules that have to be learnt to handle a particular interface, the quicker the learning will be. There is a trade-off between compatibility with natural language (which is not very consistent) and formal language in which consistency can be created. Users should not be expected to choose for themselves the most efficient way of communicating with the system. A systematic analysis of the task makes it easier to find consistent rules.

Chapter 14

Physical Aspects of Communication

The lexical and syntactical aspects of communication are related to the "higher" cognitive functions, as their dependence on comprehension and conceptual formation bears witness. The actual interaction with the computer in terms of input and output concerns more "low-level" aspects of human functioning, i.e. our perceptual and motor apparatus. In this context the perceptual and motorial restrictions of the human users must be taken into consideration. I shall not go into great detail here, since much has already been written on human requirements in connection with the physical design of computer screens and input devices. However, some general points should be noted to complete our picture of the interface.

RESPONSE TIME AND COMPUTER BREAKDOWN

Human beings seldom just fall silent in the middle of a conversation, without giving any other sign that something is wrong. Computers have the unpleasant habit of either breaking down without any prior warning, or (more often) of delaying their response at a point when the user cannot see any reason for the hesitation.

These breakdowns and response delays generally have quite natural physical causes, such as disturbances in the electrical system (breakdowns) or heavy load on the computer system (delayed response). However, since the computer as a physical entity is often far away from (and invisible to) the user, the natural causes cannot be easily related to their effects.

Studies of the use of computers in offices have shown the most common reason for stress and dissatisfaction with computers to be connected with the frequent breakdowns in the system. It should be remembered that these studies were performed some time ago, when computer systems were more unreliable than they are now. The reasons for stress are easy to understand: if the user is mainly working with data input or data search (for instance booking tickets in a travel agency), the whole job will come to a halt if the computer "breaks down". The work load accumulates. Yet the customers are still there and they cannot wait for their tickets.

The long and irregular response times, due perhaps to time-sharing in the big computer systems, are another frequent source of annoyance—and not just because the job does not get done fast enough. This time the stress is mainly cognitive: if the user is performing some cognitively demanding task, an interruption which is not related to the task itself will disturb the brittle situation in working memory. Since working memory only retains information for a few seconds, unexpected interruption can be fatal to the whole problem-solving process. It has been found that the most frequent complaint from designers working with CAD, concerns response times (Wærn, K-G., 1986).

In certain situations users can accept long response times. If they have requested some lengthy and involved calculations, they can also plan the operation so that the storage of transient information in working memory will be unnecessary. In such cases the computer tells them "please wait", and they can either wait patiently or get on with some other task. However, if the user does not know that the request will take time he will not be adequately prepared, and may thus risk losing information from working memory. It will be no help here if the computer gives the "please wait" message; the user may still lose the precious steps planned in his mind. One of the things that the expert users of particular computer systems learn, is which processes will take a long time, and when. Time-planning could mean working at nights, when the computer is less loaded than during the working hours, or avoiding heavy transactions interactively, or planning for interruptions by writing down intermediate plans and results.

Systematic studies of response times indicate that for simple tasks like text entry and editing, response times of about 2 seconds are acceptable (Shneiderman, 1987). This figure does not refer to the time before the appearance of each letter typed (that would be quite too long!). Rather it refers to major rearrangements of the text.

Other studies have looked at users' own choice of response time. Williams (1973) allowed subjects to indicate to the system when they wanted its attention by pressing an attention key. He studied a data entry task, in which the response times varied from 2 to 8 seconds. At 2-second response, the attention key was pressed only 1.5% of the times, whereas at 8-second responses time, the attention key was pressed as many as 83% of the times. In another study (Youmans 1981), subjects were allowed to reduce the response time for different commands in an editing task by pressing a button. Here, the users requested shorter response times as they got more proficient in the system. Commands such as inserting a line, deleting a line or turning a page were forced into the 0.3- to 0.5-second range, which seems more compatible with the working memory requirements than the 2-second duration suggested above. These seemingly conflicting results must be considered in light of the tasks concerned. Turning a page during reading is a task which obviously requires that some textual information be kept in working memory, whereas data entry can be performed without any internally stored information.

QUALITY OF VISUAL OUTPUT

Since so much of the human–computer interface consists of visual output, the problems of the quality of the screen image have been discussed at length.

Flicker

Early problems connected with human–computer interaction centered around the bad quality of the display units. To avoid irritating flicker, screens had to be rather dark (the probability of detecting flicker increases the lighter the display) and small (the probability also increases with the size of the display).

Nowadays there is an international recommendation for a standard that VDUs should be flicker-free. However, it is not clear how such a standard can be defined or under what conditions the critical flicker frequency or CFF (i.e. the frequency at which perceived flicker becomes fused) should be measured.

Different conditions may cause the CFF to vary a good deal which means that the conditions under which a standard can be imposed must be clearly defined (cf Kelly, 1972). During "normal" work on visual display units the variation has been found to lie between 50 Hz (small display, size 10 degrees and low luminance, 25 cd/square metre) and 75 Hz (display size 70 degrees and luminance 400 cd/square metre) (Eriksson & Bäckström, 1987).

Positive or negative display mode

A question that has been under some debate concerns ways of presenting the letters, digits or figures on the screen. Early praxis (again due to poor technology) consisted of providing the information on the display unit in a light shade and leaving the screen dark. This is still the best solution, if the refresh rate cannot be kept high enough to avoid flicker. And, as we have seen, the perception of flicker depends on both the size and the luminosity of the screen. For a flicker-free screen, on the other hand, a "positive" presentation with dark figures on a light screen is better, in terms of both objective measurements of visual fatigue and subjective measurements of discomfort (Takeda, Fukui & Iida, 1987). The positive presentation is to be preferred for other reasons too, since it is compatible with working on paper, and because this type of display is suited to normal office lighting conditions (cf Bauer, 1984).

Resolution and addressability

Another important question concerns the presentation of continuous figures on a display unit so that they really do look continuous, while narrow lines and fine details are also clearly visible. These two requirements correspond to the addressability and resolution of the display. High addressability facilitates the presentation of continuous figures, while a high resolution favours the separation of fine details.

The trade-off between these two requirements can be calculated by reference to our human visual apparatus. One example can suffice for the present purpose; readers interested in greater detail are referred to the calculations in Murch & Beaton (1987). Let us suppose that the resolution is 0.254 mm (measured as the width of a raster line at one half of its maximum luminance intensity). Then the pixel limits which are suitable for the detection of alternate lines are between 0.92 (adjacent pixel limit) and 1.84 (alternate pixel limit).

Colour

Ever since it became possible to use colours on visual display units, multicolour terminals have been steadily increasing in number. When and how can colour be used to advantage in human interaction with computers? The following recommendations are derived from van Nes (1987).

If colour is used for texts, it is important that the contrast between the text and its background is high enough for the text to be easily legible. Here the combination of colours is crucial. Bright colours such as white, yellow, cyan (a greenish blue) or green are best suited for rendering text against a dark background, whereas blue, red or magenta should be used against bright backgrounds.

Colours usually suggest to a reader that the parts of the text which have the same colour also belong together. Thus colour markings can be used to stress relevant associations and should be avoided where such associations do not exist. This principle can also be used to colour code different concepts. For instance, a red colour could be used for what is important and a neutral colour for the rest. (This recommendation applies to light screens only, since red on a dark screen has too low a luminance value to be easily detected.)

If a single deviant colour is used, it will inevitably catch the attention of the reader, and can thus be used for things that have to be attended to.

Finally, a warning should be issued about excessive use of colour. Some display designers seem to be so enthusiastic about the possibilities of colour, that they produce a clutter which is not only displeasing but also confusing. Aesthetic considerations should not be disregarded in screen design, since the stylish use of colour may be important to the efficiency and satisfaction of people who have to work with displays.

Quality of auditory output

Auditory output can sometimes be useful, or even preferable to visual output. Auditory signals can be used as warnings and attention-catching messages when a user is visually preoccupied, and they can also be used for giving verbal information. Let us look at some of the factors connected with the role of auditory signals in providing information.

First it should be noted that in normal conversation the actual words used are not the only means of conveying the content of the message; the way things are said, the speech rythms, the pauses and hesitations also convey information about the content of what is being said. A person's way of speaking can tell a listener something about his reliability and, consequently, how far his message can be trusted.

Another important aspect of speech concerns its sequentiality. A listener usually has no chance to get a spoken message repeated, as is the case when text is shown on a screen. Not only is full attention demanded during the speech, but the listener also has to store the information in memory.

Both these properties of speech perception affect the information quality of computer-generated speech, whether it be based on the concatenation of naturally spoken words or on synthetic speech.

Concatenation is used by the speaking clock, for example, or by announcements of time-tables, telephone numbers, etc. Such speech can usually have a very high perceived quality, although it still sounds artificial—an artificiality that can be softened by adding rhythm and pauses. But would we actually prefer a more natural-sounding speaker in such cases? It may even be better that the mechanical quality is preserved, so as not to confuse people who might want to ask further questions. Rather mechanic-sounding speech usually suggests to the listener that the speaker is not very intelligent, an inference that is not totally inappropriate in the case of the concatenated "speaker".

Memory capacity is another aspect that has to be considered. In this context some experiments with auditory menus have provided interesting illustrations (Waterworth, 1984). Short menus did not give rise to any problem, but an auditory version of the "Prestel" information system proved very difficult to handle. Users had difficulty in retaining the menu options, as their requests for menus to be repeated and their inability to understand the hierarchical structure of the menu system clearly demonstrated. These results can be compared to the comparative ease (but see also above) in handling visual menus, when the user is able to scan the menu several times.

Finally there is the question of synthetic speech. It has frequently been shown that information provided in synthetic speech is more difficult to remember than information given in normal speech. There are several possible explanations for this. One suggestion is that synthetic speech is more difficult to encode at input, which means that already at that stage less information is being stored (Waterworth & Thomas, 1985).

It has also been suggested that synthetic speech usually contains less redundancy than natural language between people (Waterworth, 1984). In ordinary speech we do not often give bare straightforward instructions like: "Input your account number"; rather we also try to explain what we want to have done, and maybe even why. Introducing such natural redundancy into synthetic speech might make it more comprehensible to naive synthetic-speech listeners and easier for them to encode.

It should also be pointed out that people who become accustomed to synthetic speech can use it quite efficiently. Thus, for instance, blind people can get their newspapers delivered electronically in synthesized speech. They learn to understand the stream of sound which is quite incomprehensible to us naive listeners, even enjoying the high-speed speech that makes a rapid scan through the newspaper possible—a speed that a non-expert listener definitely could not catch.

Output media–conclusions

The case of the blind listener goes to support the proverbial claim that "necessity knows no law", and confirms the repeated assertion that anything we have really learnt well will be easy to do. Thus it can always be claimed that an expert user will learn to work with any communication system, whatever it is like. However badly designed the interface may be, the expert will always find a way of handling it. Once the sheer physical limitations of the human user have been met, the appropriate questions for a system designer should be: How long does it take to achieve this level of performance efficiency, using a particular interface? And how transferable are the particular expert skills to other domains, other interfaces, and other computer systems?

INPUT DEVICES

Input devices range from traditional keyboards to the currently fashionable pointing devices; from the still-restricted speech input systems to fancier equipment such as datagloves, pedals, and fictive animals.

All these input devices have their own particular areas of application and their strengths and weaknesses must be seen in light of these. Several input devices overlap when it comes to applications, and many can certainly be used in combination.

Keyboards

Keyboards are used for the input of text and digits. It would be difficult to imagine a wordprocessing system without a keyboard, or a calculator without a numeric pad. What remains to be discussed though is the placement arrangement of the keys.

Most people are quite familiar with the particular layout of the alphanumeric keyboard on most typewriters and most terminals and personal computers. This keyboard is often called the "qwerty" keyboard, the name derived from the first letters in the uppermost row from left to right. This keyboard is certainly not the most efficient one in terms of input speed. In fact it was originally designed for a mechanical system in which it was essential that the letters were not typed too quickly, to avoid the risk of their sticking together. With the advent of the electronic media such considerations are no longer necessary, and it might well be thought that some other type of keyboard should be used. Why not an alphabetic keyboard that would eliminate the learning required for the "qwerty" version? Alphabetic keyboards are used in some systems for teaching children to spell, for instance. It has also been estimated that such a solution would speed up text input compared with the "qwerty" keyboard. However, attempts at introducing alphabetic keyboards have failed. The possible gain in input speed is not worth the cost of relearning the typing skill (which according to some reports takes about a week).

In Europe special problems arise regarding the location of keys for the particular letters required in different languages, for instance the accented vowels in French, cedilla in French and Spanish, the Spanish ñ, the å in Swedish and the ä and ö of German and Swedish, the Danish and Norwegian ø. These problems are somewhat ironically highlighted at the office of the European Commission, where there are terminals with different keyboards, so that no particular language community will be at an advantage. Let us hope that their users can at least use the same keyboard at different times! Languages with quite different alphabets, such as Greek, Bulgarian or Russian may cause less trouble, since everything has to be different in such cases.

Particularly intriguing problems are posed by Japanese (and probably also Chinese) ideographic writing (cf Komatsubara et al., 1986). Different kinds of text input are possible in Japan, one based on ideographs (Kanji), two on phonetic symbols (Katakana and Hiragana) and one on alphabetic symbols (Romanji). Wordprocessors cannot of course use the 2000 characters or more that are necessary to produce Kanji, and are therefore based either on the phonetic input of Katakana or Hiragana or on Romanji, which is then converted to Kanji by the wordprocessor's inbuilt lexicon. Ergonomically the most suitable design for the whole system means finding the best trade-off between number of keystrokes and amount of mental load. Fewer keystrokes can be produced if the operator learns by heart the specific rules based on Japanese grammatical rules for producing Kanji characters. But a greater mental load is then required to learn and use these rules. Japanese ergonomists will certanly be doing a great deal more work on this problem.

The arrangement of numbers is another subject of controversy. Pocket calculators start with the digits at the bottom left, whereas telephone dials start from the top left. Which standard should be adopted for computer input? It has been demonstrated that the telephone arrangement has some advantage. But despite the fact that telephones are much more common than pocket calculators, most computer keypads still have the bottom-upwards arrangement. Could it be that computer users do not dial telephone numbers very often? Perhaps they use automatic dialling services, or do they use the computer rather than the telephone to talk to other people?

The computer keyboard has several other keys as well. These are used for the quick deletion of a line, for instance, or to signal input from the screen to the computer, to expand the character set in text input, or to distinguish between different modes and different instructions. The arrangement and denotation of these keys are far from standardized, however, which is naturally a nuisance to people using different kinds of equipment. Standardization is being discussed, and it will be interesting to see how far and how soon it can be accomplished.

Pointing devices

It is always necessary when using computer systems to indicate where a particular input is to be made. This is done with the help of some kind of pointing device. The simplest kind of pointing is done by an automatic step-wise movement following the input of a letter, in the same way as on a typewriter. But active pointing by the user needs some other kind of pointing device in addition to the purely automatic one.

In order to perform direct manipulation and to use menus, the user must be able to point at the object to be manipulated or to select the option in the menu. This pointing can be done on the screen direct, or indirectly on some separate surface.

Lightpens and touchscreens have been used for direct pointing. Their advantage is that the user needs no extra training to direct his hand (or eye) to the right place. However, his hand may easily obscure the spot he is attending to, or the lightpen or finger may be too wide to allow for a fine enough grain on the screen. A further disadvantage of these devices is the physical effort involved in lifting the hand up to the screen. A display unit lying on the desk would remove at least that particular problem.

A direct pointer that is more elegant than efficient is the eye tracker, which catches the eye-movement of the user in order to select a particular target. Several people, for example Ware & Mikaelian (1987), have worked on devices of this kind. According to these inventors, the eye tracker "can be used as a fast selection device providing that the target size is not too small" (op cit. p.183). Knowing of the effort required to keep the eyes on a particular spot, I am not sure I would trust my own eyes to work with such a device!

Various devices such as the mouse (used extensively in direct manipulation systems), the trackball (used in videogames and air traffic control), the joystick (used in cars and aeroplanes) and the tablet (mostly used in graphic systems) have been used for indirect pointing. Nor should we forget foot controls (used in cars, weaving looms and organs, for instance). All indirect devices require some certain training so that the user learns the connection between the movement on the surface touched and the visual movement of the cursor on the screen. The speed and acceleration or deceleration of the movement can sometimes vary (for instance to make large movements more efficient), in which case extra training will be needed.

The efficiency of the devices depends on the task to be performed and the experience of the operator. Some studies have found the mouse to be faster than the joystick (Card, English & Burr, 1978), and others that the trackball is faster and more accurate than a joystick, while the graphics tablet is slightly faster but also slightly less accurate than the trackball (Albert, 1982). Keyboard control of the cursor is generally slower, except when the screen contains only a few targets to which the cursor can be made to jump by simple keystrokes (Albert, 1982, Card, English & Burr, 1978). It should also be noted that the pointing operation cannot be evaluated separately from the main task. If the main task involves extensive keyboard input, performance will be more efficient if the operator is able to stay within the keyboard range and to use the keys to move the cursor instead of having to lift his hand to grab a mouse (Karat, McDonald & Anderson, 1984).

Foot control—the so-called mole (Pearson & Weiser, 1986)—has not yet been used much in computer situations but has a long history in the home (weaving looms and pianos), on the road (cars), and in the air. Using the feet leaves the hands free to perform other tasks. Thus this kind of device could be useful in tasks that keep the hands busy, like wordprocessing or drawing. Some of the instructions now given by cursor keys or a mouse could be done by using the feet. Examples could be instructions for moving or deletion, or scrolling.

Direct manipulation devices

For direct manipulation other devices apart from pointing may be required. For instance, writing and drawing "by hand" might be preferred devices for annotating text, proof-reading or sketching. In such cases something as similar as possible to pen and paper would be desirable. Devices of this kind are still at an experimental stage, but progress can be expected.

Mouse-driven and even worse menu-driven, input for drawing is enough to make most designers agree—as one of them put it—that using a computer-aided design system for architectural purposes is like "playing the cello with a 6-foot-long bow".

To design something in three dimensions also raises the need of turning the object round so as to see it from different angles. When we are still children we learn to coordinate hand and eye efficiently, and a device which simulated natural hand–eye coordination would be the most efficient. The turning of the figure should be possible to perform in the same direction and at the same rate as it would be by hand. In some computer-aided design systems it is still not possible to follow visually the actual movement of turning. The designer orders a movement and is then left alone to think, while the system redraws the screen in a couple of seconds. By the time the object reappears, viewed from another angle, many designers have lost touch and sometimes have to mentally recreate the situation (cf also chapter 11).

A fancier and also more "direct" input device for three-dimensional input is the so-called "dataglove" presented by Zimmerman et al. (1987). This device is a glove, worn on the hand, with sensors which pick up the movements of hand and fingers and feed them into a projection of the hand on the screen. The dataglove can be used to move and turn virtual objects in real time in three dimensions. No studies of users have yet been published, but there is every reason to believe that such a three-dimensional input device would be perceived as much more direct than any other device used hitherto. However, it also seems likely that the accuracy of the device is too low to be acceptable for design work. In other applications, such as moving robot arms in an environment hostile to human beings, the dataglove could prove quite useful.

Speech input

The computer user might dream of a future in which he is freed from the keyboard, sitting instead in a comfortable chair or lying in his bed, with his hands and eyes quite free and simply talking straight to the computer. To feed instructions with a limited vocabulary into the computer by speaking to it is not such a distant dream as working with free, natural-language text input.

With the help of speech analysers combined with parsing systems and a lexicon, such a dream could be realized for certain well-defined applications. But not all applications would benefit from speech use. Moving a cursor by using the voice, for instance, is much slower and less popular even than cursor keys (Murray, van Praag & Gilfoil, 1983). Nor was text editing found to be quicker by this method, at least not during the first 90 minutes of use (Leggett & Williams, 1984).

The present technical limitations to speech analysis and automated speech comprehension mean that speech input into computers is too clumsy an instrument. Speakers have to "train" the system to identify the words spoken, and even so the system will still often confuse words like "three" and "repeat" and "1" and "5" (cf Waterworth, 1984). When the system fails to understand, a long dialogue is needed to sort out what was actually meant, to the considerable irritation of the users.

Although a lot of development is being done, for instance on the production of a "listening typewriter" which can take in a spoken text and produce a written one, the dreams still seems remote.

SUMMARY

On the physical level the first general question concerns response times and their effects. It seems that problem-solving tasks (like designing or freely composing a text) benefit from quick responses in any processes such as turning pages or rotating figures which interrupt the flow of thought.

Several output media and input devices have been suggested and tested. Visual media have to allow for the nature of the human eye, for instance regarding sensitivity to flicker and resolution requirements. Auditory output can consist of simple beeps as warnings or final signals, or of concatenated words to indicate the time, etc, or of synthesized speech for longer messages. At the present time synthesized speech is still difficult for inexperienced users to encode.

Input can vary from simple pointing to complex free production, and the requirements with regard to input devices vary accordingly. When it comes to the input of text or numbers, efficiency and familiarity both have to be considered in the design of keyboards and numeric pads. Users will not change their habits unless they see that a clear advantage is to be gained! Writing and drawing by hand have yet to wait for their appropriate input systems.

The special problems connected with direct manipulation in three dimensions have not yet been solved. Nor can hopes of using speech as a convenient way of communicating with the computer be fulfilled in the near future.

Chapter 15

Metacommunication

METACOMMUNICATION—DEFINITION AND MOTIVATION

Let us now leave the communication between user and system which aims at performing a task. Our next topic instead concerns the "metacommunication". This concept was introduced in chapter 7, and refers to all activities concerned with communication about the conceptual model underlying the design of the system (Tauber, 1986, Wærn, 1985). Metacommunication can have the following aims: to introduce a novice user to the system, to handle failures caused by the user, to provide reminders of system functions and commands, to give information about the current state of the system, to give information about present context and previous actions, or to give users the opportunity to change the state of the system.

All systems provide some sort of metacommunication, although some claim to have very little need for it. The direct manipulation systems, for instance, are proposed to be easy to learn without any explicit instruction. Since the user can manipulate some objects directly, and these manipulations reflect manipulations made in the real world, he should not need any instructions about how to perform the manipulations (cf chapter 12). But even in direct manipulation systems, some metacommunication is necessary. For instance, the user has to know how to use the buttons on the mouse (should one button be pressed in while the mouse is being moved and released while it performs, or the other way round, for example?). Hidden menus and implicit assumptions (like only being able to have one object at a time at the clipboard) also require some explication not contained in the direct manipulation. Also, when things go wrong or when the user wants to perform acts which cannot be performed by direct manipulation, some metacommunication is necessary.

In the following pages I shall analyse some of the requirements of good metacommunication. The designer must decide which medium is likely to be most suitable for different kinds of metacommunication. And he must also decide when to supply metacommunication and how it should be formulated.

267

Metacommunication inside and outside the system

There is a considerable difference between the kinds of metacommunication that can be handled outside or inside the system. Communication about the tasks that can and cannot be performed by the system, for example, would be best performed outside it. This metacommunication would tackle aspects such as misunderstandings on the part of the user, who perhaps believes that the system should be able to perform a task for which it is not in fact built. Such problems may become quite common as natural language facilities develop; the naive user is more likely to overestimate the capacities of computer systems that closely resemble human beings in their communication (cf chapter 12).

Some kinds of metacommunication, on the other hand, may be handled more efficiently within the system, for instance if the necessary help or error diagnosis depends upon an analysis of the user's actual attempts at solving a particular problem. Here it might be difficult for a human adviser to follow a user's sequence of commands, results, backtracking and new attempts. A system which keeps a "log" of the user's interactions, would be in a better position to give advice on the basis of the user's abortive attempts. This does not mean that a log necessarily contains all the information needed for giving good advice (as we have already seen in chapter 7); it may be necessary for the log to be read by a human adviser in order to obtain the best possible error diagnosis and recommendations for help.

Also we can expect a human expert adviser to be better at explaining the causes of error than any inbuilt help facilities. Human experts can adapt to the communicative needs of their partners to an extent which still seems impossible for computer systems. (At least in theory! In practice this will depend on the communicative capacity of the adviser in question—some systems experts are notoriously bad.)

When should metacommunication occur?

Every metacommunication intervenes in some way in the performance of the main task. We then have to consider whether the intervention should be active or passive. Active intervention prevents and guides; passive intervention is available on request only. Since users probably differ in their acceptance of intervention and their need for help, it may be necessary to let users switch from active to passive or vice versa, according to their cognitive styles or personalities.

Metacommunication at different communication levels

Metacommunication can be related to the different levels of the dialogue, as suggested earlier, i.e. the task, the semantic, the syntactic, and the physical interaction level. The requirements on the content of the metacommunication will vary, depending on the level concerned. So, too, may the demands that the users make on the metacommunication.

At the task level, we should remember that the "end user" always regards a computer system as a tool to be used in performing a task. This means that he not only wants a list of system functions when he seeks help; he also wants an explicit account of how these functions can help him in his envisaged task. The task in question may be an old familiar one, or a new one which has arisen because of the opportunities provided by the system. However that may be, the user wants to relate the system to a real task. At this level the designer of the metacommunication thus has to be well acquainted with the application side. In fact it may be even better to let someone who is an expert on the *task* try to understand how a system could best be used in the context of that particular task. The expert can then point out other possibilities or possible restrictions affecting the task. Such comments may be more useful to metacommunication at the task level than information about possible "features" of a system, but without any relation to particular tasks.

Information connected with the task level will be crucial at several different points in an end-user's encounters with a system. First, such information often appears in advertisements, intended to influence people in their assessment of systems and their decision about which one to buy. Some aspects in particular contribute to the quality of the information at this point, such as its validity and reliability, as well as opportunities for making real comparisons between systems. Secondly, the user must be able to understand the system in relation to the task when he confronts the system for the first time. Since the person who is going to have to use the system later is probably not the same as the person deciding to buy it now, the information required about the task in the system will differ in these two stages. When people are actually trying to use the system, it is crucial that the task referred to in metacommunication is the same as the task to be performed. If misunderstandings occur, these have to be diagnosed and treated before the task can be tackled correctly. In this case the user will need a human adviser, preferably one who knows both the system and the task.

The semantic level in the system is concerned with the objects which the system uses to perform the task, and the functions which are performed on those objects. Here the metacommunicative problem is how to explain these objects and functions so that the user can make the best use of them. Metacommunication at this level can take place in two ways: either by explaining the objects and functions separately, thus providing a comprehensive overview of the system, or by giving direct advice about how to proceed. In the second case, the direct advice should embrace the user's goal as well as the conditions for using the functions in the system. Recommendations may assume the following form, for example: "If you want to achieve x, then use the following functions in the system: ...". Or: "In order to use function y, check that condition x is fulfilled".

The best mix of comprehensive overview and direct procedural advice will depend on the nature of the task performed and on the user's personal learning style.

At this level it is possible to supply help messages of the kind exemplified above within the system. Error messages, however, are difficult to derive solely with the help of the system, at this level. Errors on the semantic level are generally due to misunderstandings. Thus, in order to diagnose errors at this level, the user's model of the task in the system must be known to the system. As we saw in chapter 7 it is difficult to diagnose this model on the sole basis of a log of the user's interactions with the system.

This type of diagnosis calls for higher-order information, which can only be obtained by asking the user. The questions should then concern what the user believes the system does, what he intends to do, and how he himself interprets the system's reactions to his errors. This information can easily be obtained by a human adviser who is then fairly well equipped to diagnose mistakes on the semantic level, to explain them and to suggest solutions for overcoming them. At present any system solution to these diagnostic problems would be too clumsy to be acceptable to a user, since it would be restricted to written questions and answers.

Metacommunication at the syntactic level of the system is concerned with how the user should understand the required syntax of commands and how he should interpret the contents of menu options. The syntax of commands refers to the order as well as the number of arguments, the use of delimiters such as blanks, points or slashes, etc.

Hitherto this kind of metacommunication has generally been included in manuals. But people are not very good at reading and using instructions (Wright, 1981) or manuals (Scharer, 1983), mainly because it is difficult to write comprehensible manuals for all users and user purposes (Wright, 1984). Questions of syntax may thus have to be answered either by human advisers or interactive help, by error handling or by tutorial systems.

Syntax problems are among the most common problems that face the novice. Coping with syntax often requires attention to detail and the memorizing of several independent (and often nonsensical) pieces of information by rote. We know that people have problems with attention and with rote memory. It is quite possibe to relieve people of attending to at least some details, for instance by spelling checks on commands (and automatic correction for obvious slips). Attempts to design help and error messages within the system are certainly worthwhile. Because the user may need a great number of messages, he will benefit most from selective help and comprehensible error messages. A human adviser is (again) the best solution. Where no human expert is available, online facilities may solve some of the problems.

The last and most detailed level of metacommunication comes in the actual physical interaction between system and user. At this point there is a plethora of details which the user must recognize, and where metacommunication may be helpful. There seems to be no hope of presenting all these details in a manual, nor in extensive online help lists. Instead, the details have to be learnt by doing. What kind of metacommunication is then required?

The first necessity is that the system should tell the user what is task-relevant in response to the user's action. In some cases, direct feedback will show what is wrong, as when a single keyyyyyyyy is depressed longer than a fraction of a second. In other cases, explicit help or error messages are the only way of communicating the interactive restrictions. This is the case, for instance, when the system does not "understand" what a user wants.

Sometimes, however, it is difficult for the system to give the user adequate feedback. In the most obvious case the system never receives the user's request at all. If the user fails to press the key on the mouse or the pen on the tablet, no message is transmitted and the system naturally cannot know what the user has done. But the user may believe he has put in a request. In a study of a CAD system, in which tablet and pen were used as input (Wærn, 1984), this proved to be a common difficulty.

Another quality necessary in metacommunication at the interactive level is that it should help users to attend to the relevant parts of the interface, particularly where output from the system is concerned. For instance, online metacommunication should always occur at a certain position on the screen; the main principle of communication is that the results of a user's request should always be given when and where the user expects it. However, this principle sometimes has to be set aside. The response time required for the system furnishes a good illustration. When the system requires more time to perform the task than the user expects it is good practice that the system tells not only that it is working but also announces that it is ready (this is often signalled by way of beeps). To take another example, the user may not know where the different results of a spread-sheet program will appear, in which case the positions of the new results should be clearly marked, and the marks retained until the user makes the next request.

The existence of multi-tasking and multi-windowing environments makes yet another kind of metacommunication necessary at the interactive level. The user has to know where he is at the moment, something which may easily be forgotten after an interruption, perhaps to take a telephone call. He might also want to know what is going on in the other tasks (windows), or at least when these calculations are complete. However, in a multi-task environment it is not as evident as in a single-task environment that the system should immediately signal the completion of the task. The user may be disturbed in performing one task if he is interrupted by the message that some other task is finished. The conditions for administering metacommunication in these environments call for further study. The system may have to "know" when a user has completed a major part of his other tasks, in order not to interrupt him in the middle of a train of thought. Users may have different preferences about the things they want to know straight away, perhaps to know immediately that a letter has arrived.

Where and when should metacommunication about interactions occur? Manuals are no good for this kind of information; too many details have to be covered. Tutorials within the system may cover some details, but in the long run will become tiresome. Good selective help and error messages might be able to compete in efficiency with human advisers. A human adviser may have difficulty in finding out what the user really has done. Details in interactions are not easy for an onlooker to spot. As already suggested, a system may keep a log, either for the use of the system itself or as an aid to the human adviser.

How can current metacommunication be improved?

From the examples and general points discussed above we can see that there is no single system which fulfills all the qualities that may be required of a good metacommunication system. At the same time we know that no system— nowadays at least—can survive if it is bad in all respects. Let us try to discover where the weak points lie, and where improvements could be made.

Manuals are often described as "illegible" or "verbose", depending upon the user. Since we now know (from the above analyis) that manuals can give some information that self-explanations in the system cannot, it might be a good idea to let manuals concentrate on the following types of information.

(a) What tasks the system is intended for, and what tasks are not suited to it. This last piece of information is very rarely included in any manual, but it is far from being unimportant, at least in the case of tasks which have functions in common. Example: Information retrieval and communication systems usually have very bad editing facilities. A natural piece of information would thus be concerned with editing—for instance: "You can only make some very minor alterations to anything you write in this system. If you want an elegant product, you had better edit it first in another system."

(b) How to enter and leave the system. Naturally a user cannot use a system if he does not know how to access it. This could become a major difficulty in the "open systems" now being developed. Or sometimes a user gets lost in a system, without being able to remember, or to find the "exit" command. This information is generally contained in current manuals, but it may become more difficult to find it as manuals become more extensive.

(c) How to enter and exit the help facilities of the system. It may be all right to exclude from the manual most information about commands, provided all the information is available on line. But the user must then know how to gain access to the information. If users still prefer to see this information written on paper (as beginners often do), the manual could instruct the user how to get the online information printed. (The same goes for users with slow terminals.)

At present a human adviser seems to be indispensable at most levels of learning. However, it is not necessary for the adviser to be available throughout the learning experience. Sometimes users want to be left on their own to explore the system in peace, making and correcting their own mistakes. Nor, of course, is there any guarantee that a human expert will be a good adviser. This brings us to the question of educating computer system advisers (and educators), but this is a problem which lies outside the scope of the present book.

When it comes to the self-explanatory facilities, it is easy to find weak points. Help facilities consisting of long lists of commands, for instance, are not really helpful. What a user might want is the chance to describe a goal and to be given a list of possible ways of attaining it. Help facilities should thus be very selective. Also, very few help facilities at present recognize that the users may need help at different levels. Most help is currently directed towards the syntax level.

Error messages may be the most difficult to adapt to users' needs. But it should often be possible, even without any intelligence in the system, to avoid messages which are meaningless to a non-expert user, such as "no information" or "file open". The message "fatal error in pass zero" would also be likely to scare a novice user.

Thus, common sense suggests several improvements that could be made with regard to metacommunication. However, in the actual task–system–user situation it is necessary to use more than common sense. Some research has been undertaken in this area, both on system problems (how can interactive metacommunication be implemented?) and on user problems (how do users comprehend different types of metacommunication in different situations?). However, the problems are by no means solved yet. More research is needed, and it should be remembered that the metacommunication is related to the topic of computer aided instruction. Advanced online metacommunication can be regarded as the equivalent of an intelligent computer tutor, whose subject matter is the computer system itself.

Some learning systems or tutorials for interactive systems have recently become available. However, these learning environments possess many poor features. For example, it is not possible to do things in an active way or to try out newly learned skills at the learning stage. The tutorials are strictly controlled. Most users like to try out something they have just learned, to achieve a certain competence and develop an adequate mental model. Another bad feature is that there is no possibility of looking back to refresh one's memory or to change a learning strategy. Contemporary systems do not consider the individual learning process.

Metacommunication would probably gain much from more contact with researchers in this area (see for example Sleeman & Brown, 1982).

SUMMARY

Communications between human users and computer systems will probably continue for the foreseeable future to include aspects which are difficult to learn and remember. Thus some method must be provided of explaining to the user how this communication takes place. This brings us to the question of metacommunication, which includes all kinds of communication about human–computer communication.

Metacommunication can be provided inside or outside the system. Most people prefer external sources in the shape of experienced people with enough time to answer questions. When no such people are available, manuals can help by indicating the purposes for which a system can be used, how to enter and exit it, and how to get access to (and exit from!) the help facilities of the system. Within the system help can be provided about the lexicon (command words) and syntax required. The most difficult task at present concerns the explanation of errors made by the user. Of course, some errors are easy to spot, particularly typing errors. But for syntax or even worse conceptual errors, the system has to "know" why the error was performed in order to give intelligible error messages. This is a task in which even a knowledgeable tutor may fail and is a great challenge to designers of different kinds of self-explaining systems.

Part IV. The Effects Perspective

Introduction

Nowadays, when computers intrude into the daily lives of so many people, we readily assume that they will affect our thinking in several ways.

In this respect, however, we must distinguish between the direct effects of the computers themselves and any side-effects which they may have. Computers give rise to structural problems on the labour market in the shape of unemployment for some people and an excess of work for others. This is due not to the intrinsic nature of computers, but to the functions computers can fulfil, to what they can do. It has often been pointed out that computers may lead to the impoverishment of many people's work. But this again is not due to any inherent quality in the computers themselves. We do not have to organize work in such a way that one person has to sit feeding data into the computer all day long. It is not an intrinsic feature of computers that people should be misused in this way. Another kind of misuse of people is requiring them to wait passively for the work to be automatically performed by computers, but still be at hand to supervise the work done by computers. When an error arises, people are responsible. I am not going to discuss organizational issues here; this is something which others can do far better. Instead, I shall present some ideas about the way in which intensive work with computers may affect our thinking habits and how computer-related ideas may invade our everyday thinking.

Speculations about the effects of new media on our thinking are nothing new. Plato, for instance, reflected upon the possible destructive effect of writing on human thought. In Phaedrus a dialogue is reported between the Egyptian god Theuth, the inventor of writing, and Thamos, a wiser if less inventive deity. Thamos points out that Theuth's invention "will encourage forgetfulness in the minds of your pupils, because they will not exercise their memories, relying on the external, written symbols rather than the process of reminiscence within themselves". Thamos concludes that writing simulates rather than represents wisdom.

In our time there are other fears related to modern technology, but still reflecting Thamos' line of reasoning. Will our children be incapable of doing "mental arithmetic" if they are given access to pocket calculators too early? Will their ability to read be destroyed by their TV viewing habits? And what will happen to our ability to reflect, if computers take over most thinking tasks?

277

What will happen to our own knowledge, when so much knowledge is stored in computers?

Behind these questions and fears there lies an implicit assumption: that the introduction of a new technology necessarily means that old ones will disappear. There is in fact no ground for such an assumption. The art of rote learning did not disappear altogether with the advent of writing, so why should we expect the art of mental arithmetic to disappear with the arrival of the pocket calculator? What is more likely to happen is that we will acquire more alternatives: we can choose between learning aurally (by going to lectures) or visually (by reading books). We can always choose to do mental arithmetic if we want to, or if for some reason it is more convenient to do sums in the head than to use a calculator.

Computers may help us to process numerical or other symbols but we must learn when *not* to use them as well as *how* to use them. Instead of speculating about what might happen if computers intruded into all our thinking situations, we should be asking ourselves how they can supplement our opportunities for information processing. What new thinking habits could the computer introduce us to? What new concepts might we acquire by familiarizing ourselves with the computer culture?

In the following pages I shall be discussing some ways in which computers may affect our thinking. The first effect concerns the more immediate consequences of working with computers. For instance, will the "language" required by the computer affect our ordinary language? Will the problem-solving methods provided or required by the computer affect our thinking habits in other situations?

Another effect which ranges a little further afield concerns our everyday concepts. What will happen when computers present us with new concepts and ideas? In particular it has been suggested that our previous concepts about human knowledge, and about human understanding and learning may be challenged.

What I shall not be considering here are all the intriguing opportunities and dangers that computers open up, because of the different functions they can fulfil. This topic would require another book, and in the present volume I will leave them to the imagination of the reader.

Chapter 16

Effects on Cognitive Performance

INTRODUCTION

Computers and computer-related work are of course linked in many ways to the outside world. In studying the possible effects of working with computers on human thinking and behaviour in the world outside, let us look first at the most direct effects, namely those that are connected with the nature of computer-related work as it is today.

What can we identify in computer work that is specific enough to distinguish it from other kinds of work? Since computers and computer work can vary so much, no general characterization can be made. However, we can identify two areas in which work on computers differs from other types of work: in the interaction with the computer, and in the problem-solving methods used by the computer.

As we have seen in earlier chapters, interaction with a computer differs in several ways from interactions with people. In particular, the language used to communicate with most computer systems differs heavily from our "natural" language. We will therefore have to consider the possible effects on communication in general, as well as on more specific aspects such as syntax or vocabulary.

Let us then consider the other area in which computers may differ from other information-processing tools, which is their problem-solving methods. The problem solving for which we use information-processing tools other than computers are mostly concerned with numerical information-processing. Using computers (note the denotation!) for numerical calculations should not thus be too foreign to our way of thinking about calculations in general. However, when problems cannot be solved by calculations (e.g. judgmental problems, the planning of action sequences, or the designing of tools), we have hitherto been restricted either to formal methods (e.g. logic, operational analysis) or to human intuition (e.g. the selection of "important" aspects, or heuristic methods).

Computers can be used in problem-solving, provided it is possible to describe the problem unequivocally and to find an algorithm with whose help it can be solved. This means people who work with computers in this way will learn to

279

describe problems formally and will learn different kinds of algorithms. This "formal" approach to problems may have implications for problem-solving in situations where computers are not involved.

Nowadays, however, it is also possible to find solutions at least to some problems with the help of a computer, even if an algorithm cannot be found, as shown by the various heuristic methods which are adopted in the field of artificial intelligence. People applying heuristic methods on a computer may acquire a kind of knowledge that differs from formal algorithms and which can be transferred to problem-solving situations outside the computer world.

Some speculations and empirical studies connected with the effect of computers on problem solving will be presented below.

COMPUTER LANGUAGE AND ITS EFFECTS ON EVERYDAY LANGUAGE

There are different ways of communicating with computer systems. In particular, there are different communication "styles" for special-purpose work aimed at tasks outside the computer and for general-purpose work aimed at tasks within the computer itself.

For special-purpose work with tasks not related to the computer, computer systems are generally designed nowadays so that the user can communicate with them in the "language" required by the task he wants to perform. This means that the user can employ the concepts relevant to the task (such as letters, words, lines, and paragraphs for a wordprocessing task), and that the designations of these concepts (in words or pictures) are easily comprehensible.

For general-purpose work, both the concepts and their designations may be rather arbitrary. For programming, it is more efficient to work with concepts such as "ordered lists", "arrays" or "matrices" than with concepts such as "words" and "lines". The operations to be performed are also different from those performed in the task the program is intended to serve. Thus the designations of the concepts and operations can be much more arbitrary than those employed in an application task.

In both cases, the language used to handle the computer is much more restricted than the everyday language used outside the computer world. Can these restrictions have any effect on people who work a great deal with computers? Will their language in the everyday world be influenced by the poverty of the computer language?

Ingela Josefson is a Swedish researcher who has addressed the question of the possible effects of computers on language. She has not carried out any empirical studies aimed particularly at investigating this problem, but she draws conclusions from a more general consideration of the central role of our language. She suggests that the restricted language of computer commands (restricted vocabulary and poor syntax) is also likely to intrude the user's language even in other contexts (Josefson, 1985).

To what extent is such an effect plausible? There are two factors which might be expected to lead to negative effects on computer-users' language. The first is the transfer effect, the second is connected with "competition".

These factors should be analysed one at a time. For transfer effects, the computer world and the world outside computers should be similar enough in order that habits acquired in one world be transferable to the other. In reality, though, most contexts outside the computers, such as home, shops, buses, factories, are radically different from the computer world. Not only are activities and purposes different, but so are the topics talked about. Ordinary weather conversations with neighbours, talks about school with the children at dinner, or arguments about political issues are unlikely to be included in the range of situations similar enough to the computer situation to trigger transfer effects.

Is there any situation which is similar enough so that transfer effects could be expected to occur? Perhaps when we ask an assistant to perform some very simple task for us, the situation may be similar to a computer situation. And yet even such situations are not really alike at all: we know that the assistant is a human being, and we will thus probably expect him or her to possess a good deal of prior knowledge, which means we do not have to spell out everything that has to be done. We need not mention "obvious" actions. If we ask a hairdresser to cut our hair, we do not have to specify the use of comb and scissors. We do not have to specify that the hair is on our head, either. If we use a computer to "cut" and "paste" in our manuscript, however, all equivalent things will have to be specified, either by us as users or by the programmer. In many programs we will have to give a name to the thing we want to move (equivalent to us telling the comb that the thing we want to be moved from the left to the right is called hair).

A possible transfer effect springing from the continuous use of instructions to get computers to perform their tasks could be that computer users start to express themselves much more explicitly even in the context of ordinary everyday tasks. However, I have never heard anybody complain that computer users are more explicit than other people. Rather the opposite (this is another effect which will be discussed later).

And what about the second possibility, the "competition" effect? This effect would arise because computer users had become so preoccupied by their computer activities, that they have no time to develop other talents. The computer "hacker" is regarded as an unsocial being, totally absorbed in his own affairs and without any interest in other people. But again nobody has yet been able to demonstrate such a competition effect. Another explanation for the apparent "oddity" of at least some computer hackers may come nearer the mark, namely that working with computers encourages the development of a special "computer culture".

"Computer culture" effects on language

Computer activities geared to applied tasks, such as wordprocessing, database registering or search, at least preserves contact with the world outside computers. But what happens to the people who are mainly concerned with the "inside" world of the computer?

I define "computer culture" as the "culture" developed in computer departments in businesses, at universities or in schools. A common idea of such departments is that they are full of unsociable people sitting on their own and gazing at the computer screen, mumbling incomprehensibly to themselves. In fact, we would find groups of people linked together by close common bonds of knowledge, experience, jokes and games. These people may not be able to communicate their particular knowledge to others, but they certainly have no difficulty in communicating with one another and having fun together. To illustrate an application of their special common knowledge, I have listed in Table 12 some examples from the hacker jargon dictionary, compiled by "hackers" at MIT, together with other interested contributors.

Table 12. Some examples of computer-related expressions from the "hacker jargon", found in an online dictionary

The -p convention:	Turning a word into a question by appending the letter "p"; from the LISP convention of appending the letter "p" to denote a predicate (a Boolean-values function). The question should expect a yes/no answer, though it needn't. At dinnertime: "Foodp?"
	One of the best of these is a Gosperism (i.e. due to Bill Gosper). When we were at a Chinese restaurant, he wanted to know whether someone wanted to share the soup with him. His inquiry was: "Split-p soup?"
CDR (ku'der):	From LISP. Used with "down" to trace down a list of elements.
CONS:	From LISP. v. 1. To add a new element to a list. 2. CONS UP: To synthesize from smaller pieces: "to cons up an example".
GC:	From LISP terminology (garbage collection). 1. To clean up and throw away useless things. "I think I'll GC the top of my desk today". 2. To recycle, reclaim or put to another use.
NIL:	From LISP terminology for "false". No. Usage: used in reply to a question, particularly one asked using the "-P convention".
T:	From LISP terminology for "true". Yes. Usage: Used in reply to a question, particularly one asked using the "-P-convention".

But hacker jargon does not only contain computer-related words; the dictionary includes at least as many examples of words borrowed from the "natural" world. For example:

SOFTWARE ROT Hypothetical disease, the existence of which has been deduced from the observation that unused programs or features will stop working after sufficient time has passed, even if "nothing has changed".

Hacker jargon also launches marvellous combinations of influences from the hacking situation and the hacker jargon itself. For example:

SAGA

A cuspy but bogus raving story dealing with N random broken people.

These examples were chosen to illustrate the intentional use of computer jargon in natural situations. They reflect a common characteristic of an "in-group", namely the wish to emphasize their togetherness. The sharing of knowledge over the terminals (the online dictionary) is typical for this desire. Many other professions play with a specialized vocabulary for the same reason. That hackers intentionally speak a language different from the language used by ordinary computer users cannot be denied. But they are almost certainly capable of controlling their use of hacker jargon. There is no reason to believe that they could not express themselves more "naturally" in "natural" situations.

It cannot of course be denied that it is sometimes difficult to talk to computer experts. This is not due to their jargon only, but rather to the fact that they do not know how much (or how little) we "outsiders" (or "lusers") know about their favourite topic. Since they probably use the technical terms in their thoughts about technical problems, they will have to "translate" these terms to outsiders to make them understand. There is no self-evident measure of the amount of extra information necessary to make things comprehensible. And sometimes, the use of "computerese" may reflect a wish to keep others off sacred ground. But with these reflections we have moved a long way from the eventual effects of computers on language!

COMPUTER INTERVENTION EFFECTS ON PROBLEM SOLVING

I have now covered some of the possible effects of computers on language. But what about possible effects on human problem solving? Computer problem solving may be very different from human problem solving. Using a computer program system for a particular task may also be very different from solving the problem on one's own.

Computer intervention in problem solving does not always take the same shape. In some cases the computer may be used to replace the human agent altogether; in others it is used in collaboration with him; in yet others the role of the computer may be very small and the user is obviously using the computer as a tool. And the effects of these different types of computer use are also quite different.

When a human agent is replaced, the effect will naturally be that the person replaced forgets his or her previous skills and knowledge in the area where the computer has taken over. If computers take over some but not all the work which is necessary if the human agents are to perform their whole task satisfactorily, the effect will be to reduce the opportunities for exercising important cognitive skills.

A Swedish study (Göranzon, 1984) illustrates this kind of situation. A system was built to help to calculate health insurance payments. All the regulations were taken into account and the rights of the applicant were automatically calculated. All the social insurance employee had to do was to tell the system which different categories the applicant belonged to. Since this system is still in operation, it provides a good test of the possible effects on the social workers' problem-solving ability.

According to the social workers themselves, they soon found that they lost their ability to remember and interpret the various regulations. Since the computer system just provided them with a ready-made solution, without any explanation, they had no chance of checking it. Also, the classification required by the system did not always quite fit the individual applicant. Before the present system was introduced, the social worker had an opportunity to find an appropriate description of the particular applicant's problems, so that the best possible outcome (for the applicant) would result. Now, it was very difficult to see how the chosen classification affected the actual outcome.

This undesirable and unintended outcome can be blamed on the old-fashioned style of the computer system. The system was developed in the early 1970s, and good solutions were difficult or even impossible to implement due to technical limitations. However, it is possible to learn from this system in order to avoid similar mistakes in the future.

First, why was it decided that all decisions should be automated? It might well have been better to automate decisions referring to run-of-the-mill cases, leaving more time for the more complicated problems. But then we could ask: what is "run-of-the-mill?" The social worker's experience decides whether or not a case falls into this category. A novice social worker would certainly need information about classifications and feedback about the effects of different choices. A fully automated procedure would effectively prevent the novice from learning anything from practice. The implication of this is that training would not include any practice—something which goes against almost everything we know about effective education.

Although it might be useful for social workers to have part of their decision-making automated, they would certainly feel much more at ease if they had some sort of control over the situation. The situation would be more satisfying if they could at least ask for some kind of explanation as soon as they were in doubt about the rightness of a decision. When people are given advice which they do not quite trust in ordinary life, they probably refuse to follow it unless they receive some satisfactory explanation for it. In the system we are discussing the social workers had no chance to refuse. In a real-life situation of this kind people feel patronized and helpless, and soon give up trying to understand.

A final difficulty relates to the classification of the clients. The classifications were not always able to fit individual cases in any clearcut way. (This is one of the most difficult problems to solve in computerizing a "natural" task.) Previously, the social workers had tried out different classifications and tested the effects. In the computerized system the effect of a classification cannot be directly assessed. The system provides answers but no reasons. Different classifications mean that different rules are applied and different outcomes are reached. If an applicant declares that another result had been obtained on another occasion, there is now no chance of finding out what classification had been made and which rules applied in that earlier instance.

This analysis suggests that the substitution of computer systems for human judgments should be approached with caution. More research is needed to identify the kind of circumstances in which people can benefit from the automation of certain parts of their thought processes. It could be argued that crucial elements needed to preserve personal competence should be retained—but what are these? I have spoken above as though explanations are the solution to the problem. But this might not be the case at all. Is it possible to provide explanations which people with little training can understand? Can we compensate for a lack in training by good explanations?

COMPUTER PROGRAMMING EFFECTS ON PROBLEM SOLVING

Let me now turn to another popular topic—the possible effects on thinking of work with the computer itself. The development of computer systems requires some very special knowledge and skills, and offers some very special challenges. It is therefore natural to suppose that people doing such work will transfer some of these skills to situations outside the computer world as well. What special challenges arise? What special knowledge is acquired?

Computer management (programming, systems development and the like) involves analysing the problem to be solved, finding a method to solve it (algorithmic or heuristic), translating the problem and method into a computer language, and debugging the program.

This means that anyone who has worked a lot with computer management will have learnt various methods for solving subproblems and one or more computer languages, and will have spent a good many vain hours debugging programs. He may also have acquired a general strategy for analysing a problem before trying to solve it, and for dividing the problem into independent subproblems which can be tackled one at a time.

What kind of situations can be tackled in this sort of way? Many common natural problem-solving situations require decision-making, planning and figuring out the effects of different actions. It may be a question of deciding which car to buy, how to plan the rebuilding of a garage, or how to rescue a car stuck in the snow on a lonely road.

Several enthusiasts (mainly people engaged in computer work themselves) argue persuasively that computer work is beneficial not only to thinking related to computer activities but also to problem-solving situations outside this field. In particular, it is claimed that programming work has a positive effect on problem-solving strategies.

Before speculating further, we should ask ourselves whether people who are trained for programming work think in a particular way. Is there any difference between computer workers and "ordinary people" when it comes to the approach to problems?

This question was posed in a preliminary study which I undertook together with some of my students. We examined the way in which different students—computer science students and psychology students—solved different problems. The problems were difficult, but did not require any particular mathematical knowledge.

You can check your own approach to the following task which is one of the five used in the investigation (Copi, 1961):

"Of three prisoners in a certain jail, one had normal vision, the second had only one eye, and the third was totally blind. All were of at least average intelligence. The jailer told the prisoners that from three white hats and two red hats he would select three and put one on each prisoner's head. Each was prevented from seeing what color hat was placed on his own head. They were brought together, and the jailer offered freedom to the prisoner with normal vision if he could tell what color hat was on his head. The prisoner confessed that he couldn't tell. Next the jailer offered freedom to the prisoner with only one eye if he could tell what color hat was on his head . The second prisoner confessed that he couldn't tell. The jailer did not bother making the offer to the blind prisoner, but agreed to extend the same terms to him when he made the request. The blind prisoner then smiled broadly and said:

" I do not need to have my sight;

From what my friends with eyes have said,

I clearly see my hat is _____ !".

The correct answer is that the blind man has a white hat.

The main result was that more computer science students than psychology students adopted a "formal" approach to the problem. By "formal" is meant an approach which does not take the content of the particular problem into account. Subjects using non-formal approaches might wonder, for instance, whether the blind man would be able to understand the question at all: "Since he was blind he could not possibly understand what "colour" means" (quotations from the think-aloud protocols of our study). Or they might consider probabilities: "Since there are more white hats than red ones, the probability that the blind man has a white hat is greater". The next interesting result was that more computer students than psychology students made a systematic listing of alternatives. The psychology students started instead often from some hypothesis, and tested its consequences. Since many hypotheses are possible, this strategy generally led to confusion.

These results cannot tell us whether computer training *per se* has a beneficial effect. In this particular case, the systematic approach did not help the subject to reach the solution. There were too many alternatives that had to be considered. Nor can the results support the hypothesis that computer education *induces* systematic thinking. It is equally possible that people who enjoy or are used to systematic approaches are more likely to choose a computer education than more unsystematically inclined people. But the results can be used to support our hypothesis that programming activity and problem solving are related in some way. It seems as though problem-solving strategies which are typical in programming (in this case formal, systematic) will also be used by people used to programming even when they are tackling other kinds of problems.

This conclusion can be compared to the findings of another study, concerned with approaches to problem solving (Schoenfeld & Herrman, 1982). This study addressed the question of whether training in problem solving would affect problem-solving performance in mathematical contexts. As this study was a longitudinal study, it is possible to draw some conclusions about the effects of the training in question. Students partaking in a computer-programming course acted as controls.

The following is an example of a mathematical problem used:

Let *G* be a (9 × 12) rectangular grid. How many different rectangles can be drawn on *G*, if the sides of the rectangles must be grid lines? (Squares are included, as are rectangles whose sides are on the boundaries of G.)

The investigators did not only study actual problem performance. They were also interested in problem perception. In order to study this, they gave the subjects different mathematical problems. They were then asked, not to solve the problems, but to tell which problems belonged together. Some clusters of problems could be formed by looking at superficial similarites, others could be formed by using deeper mathematical considerations. Some examples are the following:

Task 1
Show that the sum of consecutive odd
numbers, starting with 1, is always a square. For
example,

$1 + 3 + 5 + 7 = 16$

Task 3
Find and verify the sum,

$$\frac{1}{1 \cdot 2} + \frac{2}{1 \cdot 2 \cdot 3} + \frac{3}{1 \cdot 2 \cdot 3 \cdot 4} + \ldots \frac{n}{1 \cdot 2 \cdot 3 \ldots (n+1)}$$

Task 32
Show that a number is divisible by 9 if and
only if the sum of its digits is divisible by 9. For
instance, consider 12345678: $1 + 2 + 3 + 4 + 5 + 6 + 7 + 8 = 36 = 4 \times 9$, so 12345678 is divisible by 9.

Tasks number 1 and 3 share a "deep" similarity, whereas tasks number 1 and 32 share a "superficial" similarity.

It was found that problem solving training affected mathematical problem solving much more than the computer programming course did. It was also found that the students enrolled on the problem-solving course perceived the mathematical problems in terms of their "deep" relationships, as indicated above. The control subjects were more likely to sort the problems according to superficial similarities.

This study shows the extent to which transfer effects are related to the similarity between the source and the target of the transfer. According to the authors, the problem-solving course "focused on general mathematical problem-solving strategies ... and stressed a systematic, organized approach to solving problems. Problems studied in the course were similar to, but not identical to, those used in the sort [problem perception measurement, my comment]. ... " The control course "taught a structured, hierarchical, and orderly way to solve nonmathematical problems using the computer." (Quotations from Schoenfeld & Herrmann, 1982, p. 486.)

It can thus be said that the difference between the students in the problem-solving course and in the computer course consisted mainly of the extra training in mathematical problem solving that was part of the problem-solving course. The students on the computer course did show some improvement in mathematical problem solving, but this positive effect was not significant. Any transfer from this course to mathematical problem solving is thus, at best, slight.

In computer programming there is rarely any great effort to train people in problem-solving strategies. Any transfer effect can thus only be due to un-intentional transfer. This kind of transfer is much less efficient than intentional transfer. Only if the programming training is intensive, and if the situations covered vary widely (to allow for the creation of more general strategies), can we expect any effect on problem-solving strategies in other situations not related to programming. We should not thus expect any drastic change in general problem-solving strategies to emerge after a single programming course.

If courses concentrate on general problem-solving strategies, we might expect some effect on people's approaches to new problems, something which has been illustrated by the many courses that are now held in general problem solving. Some positive results have been reported for instance by Belmont, Butterfield & Ferretti (1982), Palinscar & Brown (1984), and Schoenfeld, 1979. We can therefore conclude that programming practice *per se* may not affect problem solving as much as explicit training in problem solving does.

But programming does more than just only encourage the analysis of problems and the systematic approach to them. Another important characteristic of programming is that it requires a certain amount of self-inspection. People engaged on programming make a lot of mistakes, which have to be corrected by reflecting on the thoughts that led to the incorrect solution. This reflection can be referred to as "metacognition"—i.e. cognition about one's own cognition (cf Flavell, 1979).

Since we know that children's metacognitive abilities are rather weak (see e.g. Brown, 1978), we would expect that training in programming would also improve a child's metacognition. This improved metacognition could then be applied to other situations as well. This is one of the claims made by the enthusiastic mathematician Seymourt Papert in his charming book *Mindstorms* (Papert, 1980). Papert presents a number of persuasive examples to show how young children benefit from having to express their ideas clearly. The children instructed a "turtle" (by the simple programming language LOGO, constructed by Papert) to perform various activities, among other things to draw lines, and in this way they produced the most wonderful drawings. Sometimes the lines did not come out as the children expected, but they soon learnt from their mistakes how to instruct the turtle to produce the intended result. Papert's data are illustrative and persuasive, but should perhaps be checked against data from less charismatic researchers.

One study of 6-year-old children supports Papert's claims (Clements & Gullo, 1984). In this case children were given extensive training in LOGO. After this training it was found that the children were more flexible (i.e. produced more ideas in an idea-fluency test) and also had better metacognition (measured by an instruction comprehension test). These results support the hypothesis that programming training affects metacognition. The "idea-fluency effect" was attributed to LOGO's ability to facilitate divergent thinking (several different solutions were always possible to the same problem).

Other studies of LOGO have not revealed any transfer effects, either in tasks related to programming, or in tasks not so related (Pea & Kurland 1983, Kurland, Clement, Mawby & Pea, 1986). The tasks consisted of planning, which is one of the ingredients of programming in LOGO.

Again we must conclude that it is not easy to predict transfer effects where thinking is concerned. Why should there be more transfer from programming in LOGO to an idea-fluency test than to a planning test? The similarity between planning and programming seems greater than between idea fluency and programming. Maybe the idea of "similarity" is far too simple to be useful: transfer of more general skills such as metacognition may occur without any similarity whatsoever. If this last contention is correct, we will have to separate "general" effects from "particular" effects. But even this is not sufficient to explain the difference between the studies: who would venture to say that "metacognition" is more general than "planning"? The solution must lie in a more detailed analysis of both tasks: the source and the target tasks in the transfer situation.

A well-defined and much studied task related to programming concerns the handling of logic. From most studies of logically "naive" persons we know that people do not handle logical conclusions in a way that is compatible with the laws of propositional calculus or first order predicate logic. We may then ask ourselves whether computer programmers, who have to battle with logical formulations in their daily work, would handle natural language formulations of logic in a different way from others who are not computer trained.

This question was posed in a study carried out at my own laboratory (Wærn, El-Khouri, Olofsson & Scherlund, 1986). It is interesting to compare the results in connection with two particular tasks: the judgment of conclusions from implicational sentences, and the Wason selection task. (The latter task requires the subjects to select evidence to prove (or disprove) a particular logical statement; see Chapter 7). The subjects studied were students on a computer science course with particular training in logic (referred to below as computer science students), others on a systems design course with no particular logical training (referred to below as systems design students), and lastly students on a psychology course. The psychology students had been given an extensive demonstration and explanation of the Wason selection task, but no particular training in general logic. Their course material contained some illustrations of the "deficiencies" which have been found in people's logical reasoning.

For the judgment of the conclusions it was found that the computer science students produced the highest number of correct judgments, followed by the system design students and that the psychology students ranked lowest. This difference was significant. For the Wason selection task, the psychology students and the computer science students produced the greatest number of correct answers.

This pattern of results indicates that the particular training to which the students had been exposed did have some effect. The psychology students were good at the selection task, as expected, but the benefit of this training did not transfer to their judgment of conclusions; the psychology students made more errors than the other subjects in the conclusion tasks. The computer science students with particular logical training were expected to be better at the conclusion task, but not at the selection task. The first expectation was met by the data, and it may therefore be suggested that some transfer effects are responsible for their fairly high performance level compared with the system design students.

Programming contains more than logic. Iteration or recursion is another important concept. The creator of the LOGO language, Seymour Papert, holds that the language not only encourages children to "debug" their attempts to accomplish a particular task, but also that the children can learn new "powerful" concepts with the help of the language. One of these "powerful" concepts is the concept of recursion. According to Papert this concept was acquired quite easily by the children he has observed. (It should be noted that this concept is one of the most difficult to learn for adult students, for instance when learning the LISP programming language.)

As we have seen, Papert's claims rest on anecdotal evidence from children working in a very stimulating environment. Other researchers have failed to find such marked effects. Pea & Kurland (1983) found that children's handling of different concepts, including recursion, did not transfer to other contexts (and even seemed difficult to acquire in the LOGO situation).

In two studies carried out at my own laboratory we used a problem which would be likely to invite an iterative thinking among people who were acquainted with this mode of thinking. The problem is derived from Carroll (1885) and has been slightly reformulated as follows:

> An oblong garden, half a yard longer than wide, consists entirely of a
> gravel-walk, a yard wide, which starts at one corner of the garden. Then
> it continues to the next corner, where it turns along the sides of the
> garden until it meets itself. It then continues on the inside, winding in

and in, till it has used up the whole of the area. The total length of the gravel-walk is 3.630 yards.

Find the dimensions of the garden.

In both studies it was found that computer science students were more inclined to use an iterative approach than psychology students (Wærn, 1986). However, most of the computer science students solved the problem in a way that shows more insight and is more efficient, i.e. they considered the length of the gravel-walk as indicating the area of the garden. This was also the solution arrived at by the (rather few) psychology students who understood the problem. We can thus say that people without any training in a particular method will not try to apply that method, even if the situation favours it. We can also say that some people may try to utilize methods they have learnt in a particular situation in other situations where they seem applicable, but they do not necessarily cling to these methods, and are also capable of changing to methods which are more adequate.

Conclusion about the effects of programming on thinking

It is clearly impossible to make any general claims about the specific effects of computers on thinking. We have found that different types of training produce different results. This may be due to the amount and type of computer training. Perhaps more intensive or more explicit training on a greater variety of problems would generate stronger transfer effects. It seems likely that very specific training would be necessary to yield very specific results. We cannot say that computer training "in general" is detrimental or beneficial. Rather, we need to formulate some more specific questions such as: what kind of training will have what effects on what kind of activity outside the computer world?

SUMMARY

This chapter was intended to provoke the reader into considering possible effects of computers on human thinking. It is probably impossible to predict all the effects that the functioning of the computer can have. No more than it was possible to predict the drastic change in our living habits that followed by the introduction of cars, trains and aeroplanes, is it possible now to predict the long-range effects of computers.

However, if we start from a transfer analysis, it is possible to analyse the possible effects that working with computer systems can have on our language and our approach to problem solving. We have seen that the effects of computer work on thinking in the world outside the computer is intimately related to the similarity between the computer situation and the outside world. It is unlikely that transfer effects occur when the similarity is slight.

Thus, fears that people who work with computers will neglect natural language and change to "computerese" are probably exaggerated. Also hopes that people who work with computers would apply computer-based problem-solving methods to problems outside the computer world seem equally unwarranted. Transfer from one area (the computer world) to another (the real world) is just not so simple to achieve!

Chapter 17

Conceptual Effects

INTRODUCTION

The transfer effects of computer activities do not seem very remarkable—not, at least, if we go by the empirical studies that have been carried out. Empirical studies often help to cool down overheated speculation. Perhaps computers have other effects on our thinking, rather than these very restricted transfer effects?

Longer range effects relate to our conception of the world. If the media define our message, the computer medium defines our concepts.

Computers represent versatile tools for most of our information-processing requirements. In the computer world "nothing is impossible", it may just be more or less difficult to implement. This element of power in computer information-processing will of course affect our thinking. We soon start to believe that if we could only put our problem to the computer it would be solved. This line of thought is already revealing itself in attempts to build computer systems for planning and decision-making in businesses. And it is blossoming in the (probably exaggerated) hope of utilizing human knowledge in the so-called "expert systems".

Computers will certainly affect our concepts because of *what* they can do; but a more basic conceptual change is concerned with *how* they do it. Let us start by examining this aspect of their operations.

CONSEQUENCES OF THE RULE-BASED MODEL

The power of computers lies in their ability to manipulate symbols according to predefined rules. This power allows us to compute the solution to every possible problem that we can express in unambiguous symbols and provided that we can formulate rules for handling these symbols. The symbols form the data and the rules form the program for solving the problem. This program is a strong candidate for "explaining" the solution to the problem, providing us with a computational explanation. This kind of explanation is rather different from the sort we have been used to hitherto. Our "why" questions have been answered ever since we were small in the shape of a few causes only: "Why does my snowman die?" "The snow melts, because the sun shines, and the sun is hot". Or the answers have stated some simple purpose: "Why do I have to eat spinach?" "So that you'll grow up healthy and strong".

As adults we continue to use these ways of understanding or explaining reality. These "natural explanations" seem to have some characteristic features: we prefer simplicity, i.e. a small number of influential factors; these should preferably be independent of each other; further, the factors should preferably emanate from something "outside" the situation to be explained. For example: we try to understand why certain people are more creative than others. Some research has been done on brain lateralization, which is often used as an argument for a causal explanation. It is claimed that creativity arises because the right celebral hemisphere dominates over the left. The research does not provide any good grounds for propounding this causal effect, but many people accept the explanation anyhow. It satisfies their idea of what an explanation should look like. It presents a single cause, and the cause lies "outside" the domain they want to have explained.

In contrast to a simple causal explanation in terms of independent factors, the computer offers an explanation in terms of a system. The system is described by states, a mechanism that reads those states, and a set of rules which change the states as regards both their present value and the present situation. If as a non-computer trained reader you found this description difficult, you will readily understand that the systems way of describing things is difficult to cope with in terms of our "common sense" reasoning. A system refuses to let itself be reduced to a bunch of independent factors. Instead it works through symbols used to define the world, and through the rules for processing them. The common sense difficulties notwithstanding, systems are as valid a means of explanation as "factors". But we are simply not used to thinking in such terms. How would a system explanation work?

The factor view of explanation separates the world into an effect and a set of factors which may be responsible for that effect (Figure 52). The weight ascribed to this factorial responsibility can vary. The situation is described by its values in the different factors. Different situations will give rise to different effects, depending on the factors involved and their weight of importance in the situation.

The systems view of explanation is as concerned with the process by which the effect is achieved as with the effect itself (Figure 52). The process is derived from the application of rules in the order that they are relevant. A control mechanism (here depicted by the eye) determines which rule should be applied at any single instance. Each application of the rules can change the situation, whereby another rule may be applicable in the next step. This means that different processes will result, either when different rules are defined or when different conditions prevail.

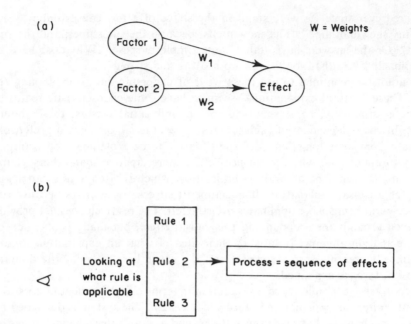

Figure 52 The difference between a factor view of explanation (a) and a systems view of explanation (b).

The systems view of explanation is similar to the calculation of an equation, where the steps taken cannot be regarded as factors but where they do rely on explicit rules. It can also be compared to the derivation of a proof from a set of logical formulae. Here no simple combination of factors can be used to derive the result, but the result is derived by a process using different rules at different stages in the derivation.

There is nothing new in principle about the computational basis of computers, they still rely on simple two-value logic. However, in practice their computational power makes a big difference. The number of rules now possible to use as a basis for calculation far exceeds the number which can be handled conveniently and within a limited time by way of paper and pencil only. Moreover, the requirement of patience and unerring attention in following the rules suits an automaton much better than a human being.

This means that the computer can be used as a toolkit or a paintbox, with whose help we can create any set of rules we can imagine within the limits of our programming ability. The implications of our creation can then be calculated by running the program.

The idea of construction can now be used in explaining reality. If we can construct a set of rules which, as a result, reflects the phenomena that we observe in reality, then we have derived an explanation of reality which is alternate to the common causal one. The nature of reality poses some very definite limits on the rules that can be used, and the system can be used to test the implications of the chosen rule set.

Computational explanation in science

The "construction view" of understanding and explanation may add new aspects to sciences which have had difficulty in establishing causal relationships in the physical sense. When causes cannot be found by experiment, we can instead start from certain assumptions (formulated in rules) and derive the consequences from "running" the rules on existing or hypothetical data.

We have already mentioned pure logic as an example of a computational science that works out deductions from a set of propositions. But pure logic is based upon a few well-established context-free rules. When context has to be taken into account, many more rules are necessary. Here computers offer themselves as tools to keep track of the rules and process the data according to them. Still logic can form a basis to ensure consistency and validity.

Context-bound rules may be tested in scientific fields where the sources of evidence are uncertain and conflicting, such as history or psychopathology. Hitherto these sciences have relied mainly on our human capacity to obey rules and to check derivations from them, now, however, more complex systems of rules and derivations can be proposed because we have access to a mechanism which is not constrained by the limits of working memory and which sticks strictly to the definitions provided. This mechanism makes it much easier to check the effects of different gap-filling assumptions. Imperfections can be detected in the verbally formulated theories that flourish in economics, sociology, education, and psychology. Implicit assumptions will now have to creep out into the open, no longer hidden and sheltered by informally specified concepts. (Note: This does not mean that vagueness and fuzziness has to be abandoned altogether. Informal and fancy ideas also have their place, particularly for the creative leaps in the development of a science. It should be acknowledged, however, that the attempts to specify the vague ideas can also lead to creative insights.)

Up to now the striving for computational theories in sciences beyond computer science has been most marked in the interdisciplinary field known as cognitive science. It is interesting to note that the successes are not as easily achieved as was hoped to start with. Let us therefore look closer at some requirements for the use of computational theories.

Computational theories—the requirements

If we take cognitive science as a prototype for the way in which computational theories may develop in other sciences too, we find that certain particular requirements obtain, and that they are not very different from the requirements that mathematical or logical theories are expected to fulfil. The biggest difference lies in the greater permissiveness of the computational theories: we do not have to represent our problems in terms of context-free mathematical or logical formulae. Instead we can work on a context-bound conceptual level, more fitted to the particular problem at hand.

The first requirement is related to the need for formalization. Formalization means that each conceptual object and each operation on this object must be clearly defined. "Clearly" means that the definition must preserve all the relevant distinctions which have to be made in the theory, and it means that the definition should be expressible in the language that is used later for the computation.

The clarity requirement is beneficial to the field of science as such: every science gains from every attempt to render concepts that are explicit and precise. The requirement that concepts be defined in terms of a particular formalism will introduce a restriction. Every formal language restricts the possibility of describing concepts. There seems to exist an unavoidable trade-off between richness, in the sense of distinctions retained in concepts, and the efficiency of the formalism. For instance, if we decide to describe the world in terms of black or white, true or false, we will have all the power of predicate calculus. If we want to keep all the nuances that we use in our natural life, for instance by employing fuzzy logic, a good deal of the power of calculation is lost. For instance we will not be able to prove that conclusions are false by showing that a contradiction exists.

In order to formulate a computational theory, we thus have to decide how far we can go in accepting the loss of descriptive nuances in order to gain some calculational power. It should perhaps be mentioned that this trade-off argument applies not only to attempts to formulate theories in terms of computer programs; every formalization will include the same decision problems.

It is perhaps also worth pointing out that in sciences which have no previous tradition of unequivocal concept definition, this first step will be very time-consuming. From cognitive science we learn that the concepts have to be laboriously described from the lowest-level distinctions necessary for each concept, via relations between concepts, relations between relations, and up to the highest structure necessary to preserve the relevant distinctions. In cognitive science such definitions have been applied to very simple and well-defined objects, such as Terry Winograd's (1972) program which can understand instructions to move different blocks in a very constrained world. It has also been proved possible to expand the definitions to more complex concepts, such as Roger Schank's scripts (Schank & Abelson, 1977) representing people's knowledge of connected facts in particular situations, as for instance a visit to a restaurant. For our everyday reasoning such complex units of knowledge are needed just as much as the tiny details about the object, actors and action involved in representing the fact that "John gives a book to Jane".

Sciences which adopt the computational approach will have to cope in some way with the precision requirements. This can be done either by restricting the domain to very simple concepts or by devoting a great deal of time to the definition of the conceptual entities. Thus the possible effect of the computational idea will probably not lie in substituting new ways of looking at a field for old ones. Rather, old informal conceptual analyses will be supplemented by more formal analyses, the products of people with enough patience to work through an uninterestingly simplified problem to embrace its necessary, often laborious details.

Computational practice in everyday life

Researchers will always be able to benefit from the use of new tools. But what about the layman? A non-scientific explanation can range from an intuitive appeal to something well known, to a full argument based upon careful reasoning, often in terms of causal explanations. However, it is rather rare for an everyday explanation to be based on a constructive argument, which consists of rules to be read by a mechanism, and which changes the state of the thing to be explained in complex ways. Such explanations are simply too demanding for the capacity of our working memory. Even a small set of premises to be worked out in a logical argument will overtax us.

History is full of examples of the use of intellectual tools to support activities whose intellectual requirements were too heavy. The simplest examples are writing, invented to support memory, and pocket calculators to support mental arithmetic. What kind of analogous support could we find in the computer tool?

In fact, any imaginable situation which we could describe in terms of a set of rules can be handled by the computational approach. It is easy enough to envisage small expert systems to help us diagnose faults in our cars, and to tell us whether we can fix it ourselves or whether we need professional service. The same applies to diagnosing faults in the TV set, or mistakes in our children's maths tests, or even in a marital quarrel that we now regret.

We should note, however, that the requirement on formulating rules may exclude some of the more interesting and perhaps even more important problems. Some authors (e.g. Dreyfus, 1972, Dreyfus & Dreyfus, 1986), argue persuasively that no part of human thinking can be described by rules. The early optimism concerning the topic of "artifical intelligence" has been supplemented by sceptisism, making the picture more balanced. Since we cannot prove by a computational argument that a problem is impossible to solve, we shall have to rely on our human reasoning. In constrained problems and artificial worlds, it will be possible to solve problems computationally. We do not yet know how far we can stretch the limits of the constraints and artificiality.

Construction games

Computational power can also be exploited in constructing and testing rules of our own, instead of using rules devised by other people. This use of computers already has a long tradition among people involved in programming. The advent of simple programming languages makes this computer power available to almost everybody. A multitude of applications, serious and trivial, can be envisaged.

Anyone with a hobby, be it flowers, gardening, knitting or hiking, could try to formulate an expert system for his or her domain of expertise. New intriguing relationships might be detected in the existing observations, and new observations could lead to the formulation of new rules and expectations.

New games could be invented, for our own and other people's entertainment. Why should computer experts be the only ones to enjoy computers? Simple rule-formulations should make the fun available to everybody!

Why should we allow ourselves to be confined to the imagination of video game constructors, when we could construct video games for ourselves? In future computer programming should be as easy as building models from a construction kit. A computer construction kit can be used for fun and for education. Children will learn the implications of different assumptions by creating fantastic monsters. They will learn the necessity of explicitness and consistency by trying to make their monsters move. It is no easy task to get six legs to move without their stepping on one another!

Computers have already been used to create pictures and music by novices in art and music as well as by professionals. In future, we can readily envisage other more abstract creations. Why not create new, secret languages (as children always have done)? It is easy to make them sound really foreign by following a couple of simple rules! And what about new rules in nature? What would happen if the law of gravity worked in the opposite direction? What if the velocity of light was not the greatest? What if ...? You can make up your own games, test your own hypotheses, either sophisticated or simple. The "what if ..." questions stimulate imagination, and may now be easier to answer than they used to be before the computer.

COMPUTERS CHALLENGE OUR CONCEPTION OF OURSELVES

Obviously it is very easy to get carried away by the opportunities for creating computer systems. Once intelligent talking computers belonged to science fiction, but there is no doubt that the power of existing computers has already affected our conception of ourselves. This has been delightfully illustrated in Sherry Turkle's book: *The Second Self* (1984). Prior to the advent of computers we conceived ourselves, the human race, as *Homo sapiens*. Our most important gift was our intelligence. It is intelligence which has made it possible for us to survive despite our physical weakness. It is intelligence which distinguishes us from other animals, in particular the apes, whom physically we so much resemble. The power of computers, particularly the so called "artificial intelligence" programs has changed our view of ourselves. There are many problems that we consider require intelligence that the computer solves more efficiently than us. In terms of intelligence we are no longer so remarkable.

It was not very long ago that the dividing line between human beings and computers was drawn at the level of learning: people could learn, while computers were bound by the set of instructions given to them. Nowadays there are computer programs which learn from experience, and nobody stresses our particular learning ability any longer. (Nonetheless the designers of learning systems believe they have a lot to learn from human learning.)

If computers can perform the same intellectual tasks as us, then there must be something else which distinguishes us from them. We despise the idea of being compared to a "rule-following mechanism" however flexible and powerful it may be. But perhaps it is our idea of "the mechanism" that is wrong? Hitherto the mechanism has been defined as a fixed device, whose actions are predetermined and which can only perform the actions prescribed for it. However, the idea of a computational mechanism differs radically from that old deterministic, fixed machine: not only is computability powerful, but it also allows for a very high degree of flexibility. Would we refute the idea of being compared with a mechanism, if the mechanism were powerful as well as flexible?

In fact there is something in the mechanistic idea which still disturbs us. As human beings we feel there is a big difference between being "determined" and having "intentional" control over our actions. We may not believe that we always exercise intentional control, but we like to imagine that we can sometimes act as masters. This very human distinction between "deterministic" and "intentional" actions has been invalidated by the computer. Control over a program may come from within as well as without. The program may set new goals of its own, then let these goals as well as the original input given at the start govern its further activities. We would like to think that the computer's actions are always determined by the programmer, a human being. However, programmers often report how astonished they have been by the functioning of programs that they themselves have written. We still do not want to describe this experience as though the computer had acquired intentional control over its own workings.

In future we may change our ideas about machines to include something which has a will of its own over which we have only partial control, as we have over a child. And yet we may still feel reluctant to accept a computational explanation of our own human behaviour, even if we restrict the explanation to the intellectual domain. Is it really possible to separate mind from matter, to consider thinking in isolation from its biological source? Surely a board of printed circuits must result in "thinking" of quite a different kind, compared with that of a biological brain, however complex the board might be?

Of course we are being unscientific if we reject the idea of a computational explanation of our thinking just because we do not like it. There must be other reasons if we, as serious researchers, are to consider the possible refutation of the computational view of human intellect.

Hubert Dreyfus suggests one reason. As a Professor of Philosophy he denies the possibility that all the intellectual actions performed by men and women are manageable within the confines of a computer, however efficient it may be (Dreyfus, 1972). The knowledge used by human beings even in processing the most simple inference in language can never be captured by a computer. Even if we have big computers and fast processing, it will not be possible to represent all the knowledge used, for one simple reason: we just do not know what knowledge we employ. Much of our knowledge is not amenable to explicit representation. Everyday common reasoning cannot be captured by simple concepts on which principled rules can operate. Instead common-sense reasoning relies on vague associations and intuitive feelings. Moreover, everybody's knowledge contains elements of "tacit" knowledge, self-evident experience, which can never be communicated to other people. We have already encountered this problem in chapter 10, when discussing expert systems.

According to this argument we can see that our distinctly human gifts have been lifted out of the explicit, rational, and logical domain into the realm of mystic, intuitive, tacit knowledge, where no conscious or even intentional mental activity goes on.

Does the solution to the problem—i.e. preserving the special dignity of the human being—lie in reserving for ourselves only the mystical and little understood features of thinking? Perhaps we do not value an intellectual performance as highly once we understand it? In the same way that poetry, when analysed, loses its poetic flavour?

Let us consider the claim that human beings are creative, whereas computers never can be. Computers can only work according to rules specified by human beings, whereas human beings can play, or "jump out of" the system of predefined concepts, and so come up with totally new ideas. When it was found that computers did not play chess as well as the human chess masters, it was suggested that this was because the computer program could not find the "creative", "new" solutions.

This explanation may be true. But it could also be relevant to suggest that the definition of "creativity" must be changed, if we want to exclude the possibility of computer programs producing creative results. Computer programs have already been designed which invent new concepts; there are computer programs which write poetry and music (perhaps not of a very high quality but still new) and there are programs which create art. If we want to reserve "creativity" as an exclusively human quality, it must be circumscribed to such an extent that only the most outstanding artists, writers or thinkers will rank as "creative".

Yet we want creativity to be a virtue common to most human beings, do we not?

Another solution to the human/machine dilemma is to redefine human virtues as belonging to the emotional rather than the intellectual sphere. Human beings may be as special as we think they are because they experience emotions, because they can feel empathy with other human beings without having to analyse the rules behind their feelings. An emotion such as "fear" may be described by a computer program and its effects may be computed, but a computer will never "feel" the emotion. The emotion is fake. Just as a hurricane simulated in a computer cannot lift the smallest flake of dust from your desk, the simulated emotion cannot shake any circuits or get any tapes wet with tears.

Since experience can only be described but not conveyed to a computer the phenomenon of empathy cannot even be simulated: the computer will never be able to understand anybody's headache, because it has never experienced a headache itself. A human being, however, can almost feel what it is like for his friend to have a headache, even if he hasn't actually "got" one himself. The same applies to most feelings: we understand people who are suffering the experiences familiar to us; we can share another's joy which we have already known ourselves.

Emotions and empathy can be regarded as "unique" to human beings, because they require that we share similar experiences. The experience of possessing a body with physical restrictions, pains, and desires has not (yet) been programmed into a computer.

Let us now go back to consider intellectual activities. The arguments pertaining to emotions can also be applied to these. We do not have to rely on emotions or empathy only in defining the difference between our own thinking and thinking as produced by a computer program. Let us instead rethink our thinking about thinking.

Searle (1980) teaches us that the intellectual activity simulated by a computer program is not thinking, just as a simulated hurricane is not a real hurricane. In a computer, symbols are isolated from the real world. We may mistake the symbol manipulation in the computer for the symbol manipulation that occurs within ourselves, because they can be described in a similar way. But the difference is as great as that between differential equations describing a somersault and my performing one.

Cognitive researchers isolate intelligent problem solving from perception, emotion and motor activities in the common scientific desire to keep non-studied factors under control. But they never deceive themselves into believing that thinking can be separated from its relations with these other modes, and even less from its relations with the outer world.

An "intelligent" computer program exhibits a "free floating" intelligence. It works with symbols which may stand for anything. The symbols have no "meaning" in themselves, they may be exchanged for other symbols and produce corresponding results, only by changing the symbols. The results follow inevitably from the given rules. They have nothing to do with the relation between the symbols and the outer world.

This is unlike human thinking. In most human thinking the relation to the outer world is central. Human intelligence is related to the receiving and making sense of sensory information, as well as adjusting this information by way of actions. The thinking "in between" can never be separated from perception and action. We create "meaning" as a bridge between the perceived outer world and the experienced inner knowledge related to that perception. The meaning of the problem to be solved is central. If we change the meaning of a symbol, the rules for working with that meaning will change as well. If reality changes, or the symbols are related to reality in new ways, the meaning will change. When a person misinterprets a problem, the expression of the problem has conveyed a meaning which is different from that intended by the person who posed it. For the problem solver the symbols in the expression have pointed to a reality which was not intended by the person posing the problem. When someone experiences a sudden insight into the meaning of a problem, he has recognized that the symbols contained in it can be related to the outer world in a way he had not considered before.

The computer is "fed" with symbols whose meaning has already been processed by human beings. The computer does not have to bother with bridging the gap between reality and symbols. A computer program will therefore "misunderstand" reality only to the extent that the person bridging the gap feeds it the wrong symbols. It will give rise to new insights only to the extent that the translator of meaning into symbols can feed it with alternative descriptions of the same reality.

The reader may now ask: what about robots? Surely they relate their actions to perceptions of the outer world? Surely they can think with reference to their perceptions and their actions? These questions represent another example of how the computer affects our thinking: we have to analyse and redefine our concepts. I shall leave this example for readers to think out for themselves (or to look for the solution in Searle's book).

Conclusion

Computers have the power to shake our fundamental ideas about science as well as about ourselves. Once upon a time, our conception of the world was founded on magic. Since then, rationality has been the trademark of Western culture. Computers offer us the power to test a range of "ifs", which opens up quite a new dimension in human thinking—a new kind of magic, coupled with a powerful rationality.

The use of computers will also necessitate a change in some of our concepts. In particular most concepts related to "thinking" and "intelligence" have to be redefined. Not only will they aquire new meanings; they will also have to be supplemented by new words which can refer to the different realities of computers and human beings. The advent of computers has not only made it necessary to distinguish between "natural" and "artifical" intelligence, it has also made the distinction betwen different kinds of representations more pertinent than ever.

As long as we still use the same words to describe different realities, we will have to live with the resulting confusion. It is as confusing to talk about "artifical intelligence" as to talk about a "living stone". And yet there was once a time when philosophers explained why a dropped stone fell to the ground by talking about its inner striving to return to its home.

SUMMARY

In this chapter, some conceptual effects of computers are discussed.

First, the consequence of the rule-based model on which the computer relies is discussed. It could be expected that a model of this kind might give rise to a new concept of explanation—a computational or constructive explanation, which differs from the more commonly employed causal explanation. A constructive explanation can be useful in scientific fields where causal factors are difficult to find, such as economy or history. Examples from cognitive science show the power but also the strict requirements of computational explanations.

Computational rules can also be used in everyday life, both as defined by others, and as constructed by the user himself. The given rules may take the form of simple "expert" systems, such as troubleshooting. Self-designed rules can be used for serious business as well as for leisure. Computational rules can be tried out in art or music, for constructing games or developing insights in hobby contexts. But it is important to remember that all these uses of computers for intellectual support must be coupled to a sound scepticism regarding the feasibility to use a rule-based approach.

Finally, we have discussed the effects of computer ideas and computer ways of functioning on our conception of ourselves as thinking and feeling beings. It is obvious that to the same extent as the computer develops its information-processing capacity, so may we have to revise our concepts of "thinking", "communicating" or even "feeling". Artificial intelligence challenges our conception of human intelligence.

References

Albert, A.E. (1982). The effect of graphic input devices on performance in a cursor positioning task. *Proceedings from the Human Factors Society*, 26th Annual Meeting, 54–58.

Anderson, J.R. (1980). Acquisition of cognitive skill. *Psychological Review*, **89**, 369–406.

Anderson, J.R. (1983). *The Architecture of Cognition*. Cambridge, MA: Harvard University Press.

Anderson, J.R. (1985). *Cognitive Psychology and its Implications*. Second Edition. New York W.H. Freeman and Company.

Andersson, K. & Helldén, H. (1987). Maskinkonstruktion med produktmodeller och AI. Unpublished manuscript. (Machine design with product models and AI. In Swedish).

Anzai, Y. & Simon, H. (1979). The theory of learning by doing. *Psychological Review*, **86**, 2, 124–140.

Bariff, M.L. & Lusk, E.J. (1977). Cognitive and personality tests for the design of management information systems. *Management Science*, **23**, 820–829.

Barnard, P., Hammond, N., Morton, J. & Long, J. (1981). Consistency and compatibility in human–computer dialogue. *International Journal of Man–Machine Studies*, **15**, 87–134.

Barnard, P., Hammond, N., MacLean, A. & Morton, J. (1982). Learning and remembering interactive commands in a text-editing task. *Behaviour and Information Technology*, **1**, 347–358.

Bartlett, F. (1932). *Remembering*. London: Cambridge University Press.

Bauer, D. (1984). Improving VDT workplaces in offices by use of a physiologically optimized screen with black symbols on a light background: basic considerations. *Behaviour and Information Technology*, **3**, 363–369.

Bayman, P. & Mayer, R.E. (1984). Instructional manipulation of users' mental models for electronic calculators. *International Journal of Man–Machine Studies*, **20**, 189–199.

Beishuizen, J.J. (1988). Search strategies in internal and external memories. In: G.C. van der Veer & G. Mulder (Eds.), *Human–Computer Interaction. Psychonomic Aspects*, Heidelberg, London, N.Y., Tokyo: Springer, 374–391.

Belkin, N.J. (1978). Information concepts for information science. *Journal of Documentation*, **34**, 55–85.

Belmont, J.M., Butterfield, E.C. & Ferretti, R.P. (1982). To secure transfer of training instruct self-management skills. In: D.K. Detterman & R.J. Sternberg (Eds.), *How and How Much Can Intelligence be Increased?* Norwood, NJ: Ablex.

Bernouilli, D. (1954). Specimen theoriae novae de mensura sortis. *Econometrica*, **22**, 23–36.

Bisseret, A. (1987). Towards Computer-aided Text Production. Paris: INRIA.

307

Bocker, H.D., Fischer, G. & Nieper, H. (1986). The enhancement of understanding through visual representations. In: M. Mantei & P. Orbeton (Eds), *Human Factors in Computing Systems*, CHI '86. New York: ACM, 44–50.

Boden, M. A. (1977). *Artificial Intelligence and Natural Man*. New York: Basic Books.

Bower, G.H. (1978). Contacts of cognitive psychology with social learning theory. *Cognitive Therapy and Research*, **2**, 123–146.

Brehmer, B. (1979). Preliminaries to a psychology of inference. *Scandinavian Journal of Psychology*, **20**, 155–158.

Brehmer, B. (1980). In one word: Not from experience. *Acta Psychologica*, **45**, 223–241.

Brosey, M. & Shneiderman, B. (1978). Two experimental comparisons of relational and hierarchical database models. *International Journal of Man–Machine Studies*, **10**, 625–637.

Brown, A.L. (1978). Knowing when, where, and how to remember: A problem of metacognition. In: R. Glaser (Ed.), *Advances in instructional psychology*, Vol. 1, Hillsdale, NJ: Lawrence Erlbaum Assoc., 77–165.

Bubenko, J. A. Jr. (1981). On concepts and strategies for information and requirements analysis. The Systems Development Laboratory, Stockholm and Göteborg, Sweden, SYSLAB report No 4.

Bubenko, J. Jr. & Lindencrona, E. (1984). *Konceptuell modellering—Informationsanalys*. (Conceptual modelling—information analysis. In Swedish.) Lund: Studentlitteratur.

Card, S. K., English, W.K. & Burr, B.J. (1978). Evaluation of mouse, rate-controlled isometric joystick, step keys and task keys for text selection on a CRT. *Ergonomics*, **21**, 601–613.

Card, S.K., Moran, T. P. & Newell, A. (1983). *The Psychology of Human–Computer Interaction*. Hillsdale, NJ: Lawrence Erlbaum Assoc.

Card, S.K., Roberts, J.M. & Keenan, L.N. (1984). On-line composition of text. *Proceedings from INTERACT '84* (First IFIP Conference on Human–Computer Interaction), London: Imperial College.

Carroll, J.M. & Thomas, J.C. (1980). Metaphor and the cognitive representation of computing systems. Report RC 8302, IBM Watson Research Center.

Carroll, L. (1885). *A Tangled Tale*. London: Macmillan and Company, Ltd.

Chapanis, A. (1961). Men, machines, and models. *American Psychologist*, **3**, 113–131.

Chase, W.G. & Simon, H.A. (1973). The mind's eye in chess. In: W.G. Chase (Ed.), *Visual Information Processing*. New York: Academic Press.

Chomsky, N. (1965). *Aspects of the Theory of Syntax*. Cambridge, MA: MIT Press.

Clancey, W.J. (1983). The epistemology of a rule-based expert system: A framework for explanation. *Artificial Intelligence*, **20**, 215–251.

Clements, D.H. & Gullo, D.F. (1984). Effects of computer programming on young children's cognition. *Journal of Educational Psychology*, **76**, 1051–1058.

Collier, R.M. (1983). The word processor and revision strategies. *College Composition and Communication*, **34**.

Cooke, N.M. & McDonald, J.E. (1987). The application of psychological scaling techniques to knowledge elicitation for knowledge-based systems. *International Journal of Man–Machine Studies*, **26**, 533–550.

Cooley, M.J.E. (1981). *The impact of CAD on the designer and the design function*. Ph.D. dissertation, London: North East London Polytechnic.

Copi, I.M. (1961). *Introduction to Logic*. Second Edition. New York: Macmillan.

Craik, K. (1943). *The Nature of Explanation*. Cambridge: Cambridge University Press.

Daiute, C. & Kruidenier, J. (1985). A self-questioning strategy to increase young writers' revising processes. *Applied Psycholinguistics*, **6**, 307–318.

Danielsson, W.A. (1985). The writer and the computer. *Computers and Humanities*, **19**, 85–88.

Date, C.J. (1977). *An Introduction to Database Systems*. Reading, MA: Addison-Wesley.

Davies, D.R. & Tune, G.S. (1970). *Human Vigilance Performance*. London: Staples Press.

De Bono, E. (1977). *Lateral Thinking*. Harmondsworth: Penguin (reprinted 1979).

De Leeuw, L. (1983). Teaching problem solving: an ATI study of the effect of teaching algorithmic and heuristic solution methods. *Instructional Science*, **12**, 1–48.

De Leeuw, L. & Welmers, H. (1978). The need for help during problem solving instruction in relation to task complexity and personality variables. *Proceedings of the XIXth International Congress of Applied Psychology*, München.

Desmarais, M.C. & Pavel, M. (1987). User knowledge evaluation: An experiment with UNIX. In: H.-J. Bullinger & B. Shackel (Eds), *Human–Computer Interaction—INTERACT '87*. Amsterdam: North-Holland, pp.151–156.

Desmarais, M.C., Larochelle, S. & Giroux, L. (1987). The diagnosis of user strategies. In: H.-J. Bullinger & B. Shackel (Eds), *Human–Computer Interaction—INTERACT '87*. Amsterdam: North-Holland, pp.185–189.

diSessa, A., Models of Computation. In: D.A. Norman & S.W. Draper (Eds.) *User Centered System Design. New Perspectives on Human–Computer Interaction*, Hillsdale, New Jersey: Lawrence Erlbaum Assoc., 201–218.

Dornic, S. (1977). Mental load, effort, and individual differences. *Report from the Department of Psychology*, University of Stockholm, No. 509.

Dornic, S. (1986). Information processing, stress, and individual differences. *Le Travail Humain*, **49**, 61–73.

Douglas, S.A. & Moran, T.P. (1983). Learning operator semantics by analogy. *Proceedings of the National Conference on Artificial Intelligence*, Washington, D.C.

Dray, S.M., Ogden, W.G. & Vestewig, R.E. (1981). Measuring performance with a menu-selection human–computer interface. *Proceedings of the Human Factors Society*, 25th Annual Meeting, 746–748.

Dreyfus, H. L. (1972). *What Computers Can't Do: A Critique of Artificial Reason*. New York: Harper & Row.

Dreyfus, H.L. & Dreyfus, S. E. (1986). *Mind over Machine. The Power of Human Intuition and Expertise in the Era of the Computer*. Oxford: Blackwell.

Du Boulay, B., O'Shea, T. & Monk, J. (1981). The black box inside the glass box: presenting computing concepts to novices. *International Journal of Man–Machine Studies*, **14**, 237–280.

Durding, B.M., Becker, C.A. & Gould, J.D. (1977). Data organization. *Human Factors*, **19**, 1–14.

Dörner, D., Kreutzig, H., Reither, F. & Stäudel, T. (1983). *Lohausen. Von Umgang mit Unbestimmtheit und Komplexität*. Bern: Huber.

Eason, K.D., Harker, S.D.P., Raven, P.F., Brailsford, J.R. & Cross, A.D. (1987). A user centred approach to the design of a knowledge based system. In: H.-J. Bullinger & B. Shackel (Eds.), *Human–Computer Interaction—INTERACT '87*. Amsterdam: North-Holland, 341–346.

Easterbrook, J.A. (1959). The effect of emotion on cue utilization and the organization of behaviour. *Psychological Review*, **66**, 183–201.

Ebbinghaus, H. (1885). *Memory: A Contribution to Experimental Psychology* (translated by Ruger, H.A. & Bussenues, C.E., 1913) New York: Teachers College, Columbia University.

Ebel, K.-H. & Ulich, E. (1987). Social and labour effects of computer-aided design/computer-aided manufacturing (CAD/CAM). Sectorial Activities Programme, International Labour Office, Geneva, No. 6.1/WP.9

Edwards, P. (1967). *The Encyclopaedia of Philosophy*. New York: Crowell Collier and Macmillan Inc.

Ehrenreich, S.L. (1981). Query language: design recommendations derived from the human factors literature. *Human Factors*, 13, 709.

Einhorn, H. H. & Hogarth, R.M. (1978). Confidence in judgment: Persistence of the illusion of validity. *Psychological Review*, 85, 395–416.

Ericsson, K. A. & Simon, H. A. (1984). *Protocol Analysis: Verbal Reports as Data*. Cambridge, MA: MIT Press.

Eriksson, S. & Bäckström, L. (1987). Temporal and spatial stability in visual displays. In: B. Knave & P.-G. Widebäck (Eds.), *Work with Display Units*. Amsterdam: North-Holland, 461–473.

Eysenck, M.W. (1967). *The biological basis of personality*. Springfield, Ill.: American lecture series.

Eysenck, M.W. (1977). *Human Memory: Theory, Research and Individual Differences*. Oxford: Pergamon Press.

Eysenck, M.W. (1982). *Attention and Arousal*. Cognition and Performance. Berlin: Springer.

Feigenbaum, E.A. (1980). Knowledge Engineering: The Applied Side of Artificial Intelligence. Stanford, Ca: Stanford University, Heuristic Programming Project.

Filkes, R.E. (1982). A commitment-based framework for describing co-operative work. *Cognitive Science*, 6, 331–347.

Finne, H. (1982). Mellom tegnebrett og terminal. Konstruktörers arbeidsmiljö og organisering av datamaskinassistert konstruksjon. (Between drawing board and terminal. Designers' work environment and the organization of computer aided design. In Norwegian). Trondheim: Institutt for industriell miljöforskning. IFIM rapport, No STF82 A 82002.

Finne, H. (1988). Organizational alternatives in the integration of CAD/CAM. In: M. Rader, B. Wingert & U. Riehm (Eds.), *Social Science Research on CAD/CAM*. Heidelberg: Physical-Verlag, 195–205.

Fischoff, B., & Beyth-Marom, R. (1983). Hypothesis evaluation from a Bayesian perspective. *Psychological Review*, 90, 239–260.

Fischoff, B. & MacGregor, D. (1987). *Journal of the American Society for Information Science*, 37, 222–233.

Flavell, J.H. (1970). Developmental studies of mediated memory. In: H.W. Reese & L.P. Lipsitt (Eds.), *Advances in Child Development and Behavior*. Vol. 5, New York: Academic Press, pp.181–211.

Flavell, J. H. (1979). Metacognition and cognitive monitoring: A new era of psychological inquiry. *American Psychologist*, 34, 906–911.

Flavell, J.H. & Wellman, H.M. (1977). Metamemory. In: R.V. Kail, Jr. & J.W. Hagen (Eds.), *Perspectives on the Development of Memory and Cognition*. Hillsdale, NJ: Lawrence Erlbaum Assoc., pp.3–33.

Flower, L. & Hayes, J.R. (1980). Plans and the cognitive process of composing. In: C. Frederiksen, M. Whiteman, & J. Dominic (Eds.), *Writing: The Nature, Development and Teaching of Written Communication*. Hillsdale, NJ: Lawrence Erlbaum Assoc.

Gentner, D. & Stevens, A. (Eds.) (1983). *Mental models*, Hillsdale, NJ: Lawrence Erlbaum Assoc.

Gerstendörfer, M. & Rohr, G. (1987). Which task in which representation on what kind of interface? In: H-J. Bullinger & B. Shackel (Eds.), *Human–Computer Interaction—*

INTERACT '87. Amsterdam: North-Holland, pp.513–518.

Göranzon, B. (1984). *Datautvecklingens filosofi*. (The Philosophy of Computer Development. In Swedish). Stockholm: Carlsson & Jönsson.

Gould, J.D., Conti, J. & Hovanyecz, T. (1983). Composing letters with a simulated listening typewriter. *Communications of the ACM*, **26**, 4, 295–308.

Green, T.R.G. Schiele, F. & Payne, S.J. (1988). Formalizable models of user knowledge. In: T.R.G. Green, J-M. Hoc, D.M. Murray & G.C. van der Veer (Eds.), *Working with Computers: Theory versus Outcome*. London: Academic Press.

Grudin, J., & Barnard, P. (1985). When does an abbreviation become a word? And related questions. In: L. Borman & B. Curtis (Eds.), *Human Factors in Computing Systems*, CHI '85. New York: ACM, pp.121–125.

Hagert, G. (1986). *Logic modeling of conceptual structures: Steps towards a computational theory of reasoning*. Doctoral dissertation, Uppsala Theses in Computing Science No. 3, UPMAIL.

Halasz, F. & Moran, T.P. (1982). Analogy considered harmful. In: *Human Factors in Computing Systems*, CHI '82, New York: ACM, pp.383–386.

Halasz, F.G., Moran, T.P. & Trigg, R.H. (1987). Note Cards in a Nutshell. In: J.M. Carroll & P.P. Tanner (Eds.), *Human Factors in Computing Systems and Graphics Interface*. New York: ACM, pp.45–52.

Hart, P.E. (1980). What's preventing the widespread use of expert systems? Position paper, Expert Systems Workshop, San Diego, Ca., pp.11–14.

Haugeland, J. (1981). *Mind design*. Montgomery, VT: Bradford/MIT Press.

Hauptmann, A.G. & Green, B.F. (1983). A comparison of command, menu-selection and natural language computer programs. *Behaviour and Information Technology*, **2**, 163–178.

Hayes-Roth, F. (1984). The knowledge-based expert system: A tutorial. IEEE, *Computer*, 11–28.

Hayes-Roth, F., Waterman, D.A. & Lenat, D.B. (Eds.) (1983). *Building expert systems*. Reading, MA: Addison-Wesley.

Hecking, M. (1987). How to use plan recognition to improve the abilities of the intelligent help system SINIX consultant. In: H-J. Bullinger & B. Shackel (Eds.), *Human–Computer Interaction—INTERACT '87*. Amsterdam: North Holland, pp.657–662.

Helldén, H. (1987). Design based on product modelling. Report from the Royal Institute of Technology. Stockholm: Department of Machine Design.

Henderson, D.A. (1986). The Trillium User Interface Design Environment. In: M. Mantei & P. Orbeton (Eds.) *Human Factors in Computing Systems*, N.Y.: ACM, 221–227.

Hershey, W. (1985). Idea processors. *Byte*, June, 337–350.

Hoffman, P.J. & Blanchard, W.A. (1961). A study of the effects of varying amounts of predictor information on judgment. Oregon Research Institute Research Bulletin.

Hubel, D.H. & Wiesel, T.N. (1962). Receptive field, binocular interaction and functional architecture in the cat's visual cortex. *Journal of Physiology*, **160**, 106–154.

Hutchins, E.L., Hollan, J.D. & Norman, D.A. (1986). Direct manipulation interfaces. In: D.A. Norman & S.W. Draper (Eds.) *User Centered System Design. New Perspectives on Human–Computer Interaction*. Hillsdale, NJ: Lawrence Erlbaum Assoc., pp.87–124.

Johansson, G. & Sandén, P.-O. (1982). Mental belastning och arbetstillfredsställelse i kontrollrumsarbete. (Mental stress and work satisfaction in supervisory work. In Swedish). Stockholm: Rapporter från Psykologiska Institutionen, Stockholms Universitet, Nr. 40.

Johnson, C.K. & Jordan, S.R. (1983). Emergency management of inland oil and hazardous chemical spills: a case study in knowledge engineering. In: F. Hayes-Roth, D.A. Waterman & D.B. Lenat, *Building Expert Systems*. London, Amsterdam, Don Mills, Ontario, Sydney, Tokyo: Addison-Wesley, 349-397.

Johnson-Laird, P.N. (1983). *Mental Models*. Cambridge: Cambridge University Press.

Josefson, I. (Ed.) (1985). *Språk och erfarenhet*. (Language and Experience. In Swedish). Stockholm: Carlsson Bokförlag.

Kahnemann, D. (1973). *Attention and Effort*. Englewood Cliffs, NJ: Prentice Hall.

Kahneman, D., Slovic, P. & Tversky, A. (1982). *Judgment under Uncertainty: Heuristics and Biases*. London: Cambridge University Press.

Karat, J., McDonald, J. & Anderson, M. (1984). A comparison of selection techniques: Touch panel, mouse and keyboard. *Proceedings from INTERACT '84*, 149-153.

Katzeff, C. (1986a). Dealing with a database query language in a new situation. *International Journal of Man–Machine Studies*, **25**, 1-17.

Katzeff, C. (1986b). Logical reasoning, models, and database query writing—the effect of different conceptual models upon reasoning in a database query writing task. HUFACIT reports, The Department of Psychology, University of Stockholm, No. 10.

Katzeff, C. (1988). The effect of different conceptual models upon reasoning in a database query writing task. *International Journal of Man–Machine Studies*, **29**, 37-62.

Kelly, D.H. (1972). Flicker. In: D. Jameson & L.M. Hurvich (Eds.), *Handbook of Sensory Physiology*. Vol VII/4. Berlin: Springer Verlag.

Kelly, G.A. (1955). *The Psychology of Personal Constructs*. New ˉ ork: Norton.

McKeown, K.R. (1985). Discourse strategies for generating natural-text. *Artificial Intelligence*, **27**, 1-41.

Kidd, A.L. & Cooper, M.B. (1985). Man–machine interface issues in the construction and use of an expert system. *International Journal of Man–Machine Studies*, **22**, 91-102.

Kiger, J.I. (1984). The depth/breadth trade-off in the design of menu-driven user interfaces. *International Journal of Man–Machine Studies*, **20**, 201-213.

Kinney, G.C., Marsetta, M. & Showman, D.J. (1966). Studies in Display Symbol Legibility, Part XII. The Legibility of Alphanumeric Symbols for Digitalized Television. Bedford, MA: The Mitre Corporation, ESD-TR-66-117.

Kjellberg, T. (1982). *Integrerat datorstöd för mänsklig problemlösning och mänsklig kommunikation inom verktadsteknisk produktion, begränsat till produktutveckling, produktionsberedning, konstruktion och tillverkningsberedning. En systemansats baserad på produktmodeller.* (Integrated computer aids to support human problem solving and human communication for mechanical production within the limits of product development, production planning, design and planning for manufacturing. In Swedish). Doctoral dissertation, Department of Manufacturing Systems, The Royal Institute of Technology: Stockholm.

Kjellberg, T. (1984). The integration of CAD/CAM based on product modelling for better communication. Tokyo: CIRP.

Kjellberg, T. (1986). Some aspects on human factors in CAD. In: Proceedings from the conference Work with Display Units, Stockholm, pp.652-656.

Komatsubara, A., Nakajima, N., Yokoyama, S. & Yokomizo, Y. (in press). Evaluation of Japanese text input systems on mental load. Paper presented at the conference Work with Display Units, Stockholm. To be published in: F. Klix, H. Wandke, N. Streitz & Y. Wærn (Eds.), *MACINTER-2*. Amsterdam: North-Holland (in press).

Koriat, A., Lichtenstein, S. & Fischoff, B. (1980). Reasons for confidence. *Journal of Experimental Psychology: Human Learning and Memory*, **6**, 107-118.

Kosslyn, S.M., Ball, T. & Reiser, B.J. (1978). Visual images preserve metric spatial information: Evidence from studies of image scanning. *Journal of Experimental Psychology: Human Perception and Performance*, 4, 47–60.

Kurland, M.D., Clement, C., Mawby, R. & Pea, R.D. (1986). Mapping the cognitive demands of learning to program. In: J. Bishop, J. Lochhead & D.N. Perkins (Eds.), *Thinking: Progress in research and Teaching*. Hillsdale, NJ: Lawrence Erlbaum Assoc.

Landauer, T.K. & Nachbar, D.W. (1985). Selection from alphabetic and numeric menu trees using a touch screen: Breadth, depth, and width. In: L. Borman & B. Curtis (Eds.), *Human Factors in Computing Systems*, CHI '85. New York: ACM, pp.73–78.

Lawler, R.W., duBoulay, B., Hughes, M. & Macleod, H. (1986). *Cognition and Computers*. Studies in Learning. Chichester: Ellis Horwood Series in Cognitive Science.

Leggett, J. & Williams, G. (1984). An empirical investigation of voice as an input modality for computer programming. *International Journal of Man–Machine Studies*, 20, 493–520.

Lehner, P.E. (1987). Cognitive factors in user/expert-system interaction. *Human Factors*, 29, 97–109.

Liberman, A.M., Cooper, F.S., Shankweiler, D.P. & Studdert-Kennedy, M. (1967). Perception of the speech code. *Psychological Review*, 74, 431–461.

Lichtenstein, S. & Fischhoff, B. (1980). Training for calibration. *Organizational Behavior and Human Performance*, 26, 149–171.

Linde, L. (1986). What is domain skill: frames in information seeking. *Behavioral Science*, 31, 89–102.

Linde, L. & Bergström, M. (1988). Impact of prior knowledge of informational content and organization on learning search principles in a database. *Contemporary Educational Psychology*, 90–101.

Linde, L. & Wærn, Y. (1985). On search in an incomplete database. *International Journal of Man–Machine Studies*, 22, 563–579.

Lochovsky, F.H. & Tsichritzis, D.C. (1977). User performance considerations in DBMS selection. Proceedings from the ACM SIGMOD, 128–134.

Löwstedt, J. (1986). *Automation eller kunskapsproduktion? Om ingenjörsarbetets organisation och innehåll vid införandet av datorstödd konstruktion (CAD).* (Automation or knowledge production? On the organization and content of engineering work by the introduction of computer aided design (CAD). In Swedish). Stockholm: EFI.

Magnusson, D. & Heffler, B. (1969). The generality of behavioral data III: Generalization potential as a function of the number of observation instances. *Multivariate Behavioral Research*, 4, 29–42.

Malone, T.W., Grant, K.R. & Turbak, F.A. (1986). The information lens: An intelligent system for information sharing in organizations. In: M. Mantei & P. Orbeton (Eds.), *Human Factors in Computing Systems*, CHI '86. New York: ACM, pp.1–8.

Martin, J. (1982). *Viewdata and the Information Society*. Englewood Cliffs, NJ: Prentice-Hall.

Mayer, R.E. (1981). The psychology of how novices learn computer programming. *Computer Surveys*, 13, 121–141.

McCracken, D.L. & Akscyn, R.M. (1984). Experience with the ZOG human–computer interface system. *International Journal of Man–Machine Studies*, 21, 293–310.

Meehl, P.E. (1954). *Clinical versus statistical prediction*. Minneapolis, MN: University of Minnesota Press.

Miller, G.A. (1956). The magical number seven, plus or minus two: Some limits on our capacity for processing information. *Psychological Review*, 63, 81–97.

Miller, G.A., Galanter, E. & Pribram, K. (1960). *Plans and the Structure of Behavior*. New York: Holt, Rinehart & Winston.

Minsky, M. (1975). A framework for representing knowledge. In: P.H. Winston (Ed.), *The Psychology of Computer Vision*. New York: McGraw-Hill.

Montgomery, H. (1983). Decision rules and the search for a dominance structure: Towards a process model of decision making. In: P. Humphreys, O. Svenson & A. Vari (Eds.), *Analyzing and Aiding Decision Processes*. Budapest: Akade'mia Kiado' and Amsterdam: North-Holland.

Moran, T.P. (1981). The command language grammar: a representation for the user interface of interactive computer systems. *International Journal of Man–Machine Studies*, **15**, 3–50.

Moran, T. (1983). Getting into a system: External–internal task mapping analysis. A. Janda (Ed.), *Human Factors in Computing Systems*, CHI '83. New York: ACM, pp.45–49.

Moran, T. (1987). Where is the action in human–computer interaction? Invited lecture at the conference: Work with Display Units, Stockholm, 1986. A summary is given in: B. Knave & P.-G. Widebäck (Eds.), *Work with Display Units*. Amsterdam: North-Holland.

Murch, G.M. & Beaton, R.J. (1987). Matching display characteristics to human visual capacity. In: B. Knave & P.-G. Widebäck (Eds.), *Work with Display Units*. Amsterdam: North-Holland, pp.407–411.

Murphy, A.H. & Winkler, R.L. (1977). Can weather forecasters formulate reliable probability forecasts of precipitation and temperature? *National Weather Digest*, **2**, 2–9.

Murray, D. M. (1987). Embedded user models. In: H-J. Bullinger & B. Shackel (Eds.), *Human–Computer Interaction—INTERACT '87*. Amsterdam: North-Holland, pp.229–235.

Murray, J.T., van Praag, J. & Gilfoil, D. (1983). Voice versus keyboard control of cursor motion. *Proceedings from the Human Factors Society*, 27th Annual Meeting, 103.

Nelson, T. (1980). Interactive systems and the design of virtuality. *Creative Computing*, **6**, 56 ff. and 94 ff.

Newell, A. & Simon, H. (1956). The Logic Theory Machine: a complex information processing system. *IRE Transactions on Information Theory*, IT-2, 61–79.

Newell, A. & Simon, H.A. (1961). GPS, a program that simulates human thought. In: H. Billing (Ed.), *Lernende Automaton*, pp.109–124.

Newell, A. & Simon, H.A. (1972). *Human Problem Solving*. Englewood Cliffs, NJ: Prentice-Hall.

Nisbett, R.E. & Ross, L. (1980). *Human Inference: Strategies and Shortcomings of Social Judgment*. Englewood Cliffs, NJ: Prentice-Hall.

Nisbett, R.E. & Wilson, T.D. (1977). Telling more than we can know: verbal reports on mental processes. *Psychological Review*, **8**, 231–259.

Norman, D. (1981). The trouble with UNIX. *Datamation*, **27**, 556–563.

Norman, D. (1986). Cognitive Engineering. In: D.A. Norman & S.W. Draper (Eds.), *User Centered System Design*. New Perspectives on Human–Computer Interaction. Hillsdale, NJ: Lawrence Erlbaum Assoc., pp.31–62.

Oestreicher, L. (1987). The human computer interface. A user's guide? M.Sc. Thesis, Department of Computer Science, Uppsala University.

Ogden, W.C. & Sorknes, A. (1987). What do users say to their natural language interface? In: H.-J. Bullinger & B. Shackel (Eds.), *Human–Computer Interaction—INTERACT '87*. Amsterdam: North-Holland.

O'Malley, C., Draper, S. & Riley, M. (1984). Constructive Interaction: A method for studying user–computer–user interaction. *INTERACT '84*, IFIP, Part II, 1–5.

O'Shea, T. & Eisenstadt, M. (Eds.) (1984). *Artificial Intelligence: Tools, Techniques, and Applications*. New York: Harper & Row.

Pahl, G. & Beitz, W. (1984). *Engineering Design*. The Design Council, London.

Paivio, A. (1971). *Imagery and Verbal Processes*. New York: Holt, Rinehart and Winston.

Palinscar, A.S. & Brown, A.L. (1984). Reciprocal teaching of comprehension-fostering and comprehension-monitoring activities. *Cognition and Instruction*, **1**, 117–175.

Papert, S. (1980). *Mindstorms: Children, Computers, and Powerful Ideas*. New York: Basic Books.

Pask, G. (1976). Styles and strategies of learning. *British Journal of Educational Psychology*, **46**, 128–148.

Payne, S. & Green, T.R.G. (1983). The user's perception of the interaction language: A two-level model. In: A. Janda (Ed.), *Human Factors in Computing Systems, CHI '83*. New York: ACM, pp.202–206.

Payne, S.J. & Green, T.R.G. (1986). Task-action grammars: A model of the mental representation of task languages. *Human–Computer Interaction*, **2**, 93–133.

Pea, R.D. & Kurland, D.M. (1983). On the cognitive and educational benefits of teaching children programming: A critical look. In: *New Ideas in Psychology*, Vol. 1. Elmsford, NY: Pergamon.

Pearson, G. & Weiser, M (1986). Of moles and men: The design of foot controls for workstations. In: M. Mantei & P. Orbeton (Eds.), *Human Factors in Computing Systems, CHI '86*. New York: ACM, pp.333–339.

Pelz, W.H. & Wittstock, M. (1986). Methodological study to develop a taxonomy of userfriendliness for application software. Paper presented at the conference Work with Display Units, Stockholm.

Piaget, J. (1957). *Logic and Psychology*. New York: Basic Books.

Polanyi, M. (1969). *Personal Knowledge*. Chicago: University of Chicago Press.

Polson, P. G. & Kieras, D.E. (1985a). A quantitative model of the learning and performance of text editing knowledge. In: L. Borman & B. Curtis (Eds.), *Human Factors in Computing Systems, CHI '85*. New York: ACM, pp.207–212.

Polson, P. G. & Kieras, D.E. (1985b). An approach to the formal analysis of user complexity. *International Journal of Man–Machine Studies*, **22**, 365–394.

Polson, P., Muncher, E. & Engelbeck, G. (1986). A test of a common elements theory of transfer. In: M. Mantei & P. Orbeton (Eds.), *Human Factors in Computing Systems, CHI '86*. New York: ACM, pp.78–83.

Poltrock, S.E., Steiner, D.D & Tarlton, P.M. (1986). Graphic interfaces for knowledge-based system development. In: M. Mantei & P. Orbeton (Eds.), *Human Factors in Computing Systems, CHI '86*. New York: ACM, pp.9–15.

Potosnak, K.M. (1984). Choice of Interface Modes by Empirical Groupings of Computer Users. In: *Interact '84*, IFIP, 262–267.

Poulson, D.F., Johnson, C.A. & Moulding, J. (1987). The use of participative exercises in human factors for education and design. In: H.-J. Bullinger & B. Shackel, (Eds.), *Human–Computer Interaction—INTERACT '87*. Amsterdam: North-Holland, pp.469–472.

Pratt, J.M. (1987). The social impact of user models. In: H.-J. Bullinger & B. Shackel (Eds.), *Human–Computer Interaction—INTERACT '87*. Amsterdam: North-Holland, pp.473–478.

Preece, J. (1982). Graphs are not straightforward. Proceedings of the Conference on Cognitive Engineering, Amsterdam.

Price, H.E. (1985). The allocation of functions in systems. *Human Factors*, **27**, 33–45.

Pylyshyn, Z.W. (1984). *Computation and Cognition. Toward a Foundation for Cognitive Science*. Cambridge, MA., MIT Press.

Ray, H.N. (1985). A study of the effect of different data models on casual users performance in writing database queries. *International Journal of Man–Machine Studies*, **23**, 249–262.

Reisner, P. (1977). Use of psychological experimentation as an aid to development of a query language. *IEEE Transactions of Software Engineering*, SE-3, 218–229.

Reisner, P. (1981). Human factors studies of database query languages: a survey and assessment. *Computing Surveys*, **13**, 13–31.

Reisner, P. (1982). Further developments toward using formal grammar as a design tool. In: *Human Factors in Computing Systems, CHI '82*. New York: ACM.

Robertson, G., McCracken, D. and Newell, A. (1981). The ZOG approach to man–machine communication. *International Journal of Man–Machine Studies*, **14**, 461–488.

Rosch, E. & Lloyd, B.B. (1978). *Cognition and Categorization*. Hillsdale, NJ: Lawrence Erlbaum Assoc.

Rumelhart, D.E. (1975). Notes on a schema for stories. In: D.G. Bobrow & A.M. Collins (Eds.), *Representation and Understanding*. New York: Academic Press, 211–236.

Rumelhart, D.E. & Ortony, A. (1977). The representation of knowledge in memory. In: R.C. Anderson, R.J. Spiro & W.E. Montague (Eds.), *Schooling and the Acquisition of Knowledge*. Hillsdale, NJ: Lawrence Erlbaum Assoc.

Rutkowski, C. (1982). An introduction to the human applications standard computer interface, Part I: Theory and principles. *Byte*, **11**, 291–310.

Sääf, J. (1984). Can experience be a disadvantage in computer programming? B.A. thesis, Department of Psychology, University of Stockholm.

Scapin, D.L. (1982). Generation effect, structuring, and computer commands. *Behaviour & Information Technology*, **1**, 401–410.

Schank, R. C. & Abelson, R. (1977). *Scripts, Plans, Goals, and Understanding*. Hillsdale, NJ: Lawrence Erlbaum Assoc.

Scharer, L.L. (1983). User training: Less is more. *Datamation*, July, 175–182.

Schoenfeld, A.H. (1979). Can heuristics be taught? In: J. Lochhead & J. Clement (Eds.) *Cognitive Process Instruction*. Philadelphia, Pa.: Franklin Institute Press.

Schoenfeld, A.H. & Herrman, D.J. (1982). Problem Perception and Knowledge Structure in Expert and Novice Mathematical Problem Solvers. *Journal of Experimental Psychology: Learning, Memory, and Cognition*, **8**, 484–494.

Searle, J. R. (1980). Minds, brains, and programs. *The Behavioural and Brain Sciences*, **3**, 417–424. (Reprinted in Haugeland (1981) 282–306.)

Severinsson-Eklundh, K. & Sjöholm, C. (1987). Textförfattande med datorstöd. En enkät- och intervjuundersökning på KTH. (Text writing with computer support. In Swedish) Report from the IPLab-project, The Department of Numerical Analysis and Computer Science, The Royal Institute of Technology, Stockholm.

Shepard, R.N. (1967). Recognition memory for words, sentences, and pictures. *Journal of Verbal Learning and Verbal Behavior*, **6**, 156–163.

Shepard, R.N. & Metzler, J. (1971). Mental rotation of three-dimensional objects. *Science*, **171**, 701–703.

Shneiderman, B. (1980). *Software Psychology: Human Factors in Computer and Information Systems*. Boston, MA: Little, Brown and Co.

Shneiderman, B. (1987). *Designing the User Interface. Strategies for Effective Human–Computer Interaction*. Reading, MA., Addison-Wesley,

Simon, H.A. (1974). How big is a chunk? *Science*, **183**, 482–488.

Singleton, W.T. (1974). *Man–Machine Systems Design*. London: Penguin.

Singley, M.K. & Anderson, J.R. (1985). The transfer of text-editing skill. *International Journal of Man–Machine Studies*, **22**, 403–423.

Sleeman, D. & Brown, J.S. (1982). *Intelligent tutoring systems*. London: Academic Press.

Small, D. & Weldon, L. (1983). An experimental comparison of natural and structured query languages. *Human Factors*, **25**, 253–263.

Smith, R.B. (1986). The alternate reality kit: An animated environment for creating interactive simulations. *Proceedings of the 1986 IEEE Computer Society Workshop on Visual Languages*, pp.99–106.

Sprowl, J., Balasubramanian, O., Chinwalla, T., Evend, M. & Klawans, H. (1984). An expert system for drafting legal documents. In: D.J. Frailey & R.K. Brown (Eds.), *AFIPS Conference Proceedings*. National Computer Conference, 1984, July 9–12. AFIPS Press.

Streitz, N. A., Lieser, A. & Wolters, A. (1989). User-initiated versus computer-initiated dialogue modes: A comparative analysis of cognitive processes based on differences in user models. In: F. Klix, N. Streitz, Y. Wærn & H. Wandke (Eds.), *MACINTER2*. Amsterdam: North-Holland, 75–88.

Suh, N.P., Bell, A.C. & Gossard, D.C. (1978). On an axiomatic approach to manufacturing and manufacturing systems. *Journal of Engineering for Industry*, **2**, 100.

Suh, N.P. & Kim, S.H. (1985). Mathematical foundations of manufacturing science: theory and implications. Laboratory for Manufacturing and Productivity. Cambridge, MA: MIT Press.

Swartout, W.R. (1981). Explaining and justifying expert consulting programs. *IJCAI-81*, 815–821.

Takeda, T., Fukui, Y., & Iida, T. (1987). Influence of CRT Refresh Rates on Accommodation Aftereffects. In: B. Knave & P-G. Widebäck (Eds.) *Work with Display Units '86*. Amsterdam: North-Holland, 474–482.

Tauber, M.J. (1986). An approach to metacommunication in human–computer interaction. In: F. Klix & H. Wandke (Eds.), *MACINTER1*. Amsterdam: North-Holland, pp.35–49.

Tauber, M. (1988). On mental models and the user interface. In: T. Green, J.-M. Hoc, D. Murray & G.C. van der Veer (Eds.), *Working with Computers. Computers and People Series*. London: Academic Press.

Treisman, A.M. (1960). Verbal cues, language and meaning in selective attention. *Quarterly Journal of Experimental Psychology*, **12**, 242–248.

Tucker, Jr. A.B. & Nirenburg, S. (1984). Machine Translation: A contemporary view. In: M.E. Williams (Ed.), *Annual Review of Information Science and Technology*, Vol. 19. White Plains, NY: Knowledge Industry Publications Inc., for the American Society for Information Sciences, pp.127–160.

Turkle, S. (1984). The Second Self. *Computers and the Human Spirit*. New York: Simon & Schuster.

Tversky, A. (1972). Elimination by aspects: A theory of choice. *Psychological Review*, **79**, 281–299.

Van der Veer, G.C. & Beishuizen, J.J. (1987). Learning styles in conversation—a practical application of Pask's Learning Theory to human–computer interaction. In: F. Klix & H. Wandke (Eds.), *MACINTER1*. Amsterdam: North-Holland.

Van der Veer, G. C., Guest, S., Innocent, P., McDaid, E., Oestreicher, L., Tauber, M.J., Vos, U. & Wærn, Y. (1987a). Human factors in Telematics. A progress report to COST-11-ter. Available from Gerrit van der Veer, Free University, Amsterdam.

Van der Veer, G. C., Guest, S., Haselager, W. Innocent, P., McDaid, E., Oestreicher, L., Tauber, M.J., Vos, U. & Wærn, Y. (1987b). An interdisciplinary approach to human factors in telematic systems—a review of the problems and possible solutions by a COST-11 ter working group. Paper presented at the workshop Mental Models in Computer Systems, Schärding. To be published in D. Ackerman & M. Tauber (Eds.), *Mental Models in Computer Systems*.

Van der Veer, G.C., Tauber, M.J., Wærn, Y. & van Muylwijk, B. (1985). On the interaction between system and user characteristics. *Behaviour and Information Technology*, **4**, 289–308.

van der Veer, G.C. & van de Wolde, T. (1982). Psychological aspects of problem solving with the help of computer languages. *Computers and Education*, **6**, 229–234.

van der Veer, G.C., Wijk, R. & Felt, M.A.M. (in press). Metaphors and metacommunication in the development of mental models. In: P. Falzon, J-M. Hoc, N. Streitz & Y. Wærn (Eds.), *Psychological Foundations of Human Computer Interaction*. Academic Press.

van Muylwijk, B., van der Veer, G.D., & Wærn, Y. (1983). On the implications of user variability in open systems. An overview of the little we know and the lot we have to find out. *Behaviour and Information Technology*, **2**, 212–326.

Van Nes, F. L. (1987). Colour on displays—boon or curse? In: B. Knave & P.-G. Widebäck (Eds.) *Work with Display Units*, Amsterdam: North-Holland, pp.438–440.

Vossen, P.H., Sitter, S. & Ziegler, J. (1987). An empirical validation of cognitive complexity theory with respect to text, graphics and table editing. In: H.-J. Bullinger & B. Shackel (Eds.), *Human–Computer Interaction—INTERACT '87*. Amsterdam: North-Holland, pp.71–78.

Wærn, K.-G. (1985). CAD som arbetsinstrument. En förstudie inom projektet "Kompetensutveckling i CAD/CAM". (CAD as work took. A pilot study within the project "Competence development in CAD/CAM. In Swedish). *HUFACIT reports*, The Department of Psychology, University of Stockholm, No. 1.

Wærn, K.-G. (1986). CAD-användares synpunkter. (CAD-users' opinions. In Swedish). HUFACIT report, Department of Psychology, The University of Stockholm, No. 9.

Wærn, K.-G. & Haglund, N. (1985). CAD-rutin och rutin-CAD. (CAD-routine and routine-CAD. In Swedish). HUFACIT report, Department of Psychology, The University of Stockholm, No. 3.

Wærn, K.-G. (1988a). Cognitive aspects of computer aided design. In: M. Helander (Ed.), *Handbook of Human–Computer Interaction*. Amsterdam: North-Holland.

Wærn, K-G. (1988b) Competence Development in CAD/CAM. HUFACIT report, Department of Psychology, The University of Stockholm, No. 18.

Wærn, Y. (1984). To predict difficulties in using a computerised drawing system. HUFACIT Reports, Department of Psychology, University of Stockholm, No. 4.

Wærn, Y. (1985). Learning computerized tasks as related to prior task knowledge. *International Journal of Man–Machine Studies*, **22**, 441–455.

Wærn, Y. (1986). Understanding learning problems in computer aided tasks. In: F. Klix, & H. Wandke (Eds.), *MACINTER1*. Amsterdam: North-Holland.

Wærn. Y. (1987). Does computer interest induce mechanical thinking? In: H.-J. Bullinger & B. Shackel (Eds.), *Human–Computer Interaction—INTERACT '87*. Amsterdam: North-Holland, pp.43–50.

Wærn, Y. (1989). Mental effort and mental mood in human–computer interaction. In: F. Klix, N. Streitz, Y. Wærn & H. Wandke (Eds.), *MACINTER II*. Amsterdam: North-Holland.

Wærn, Y. (1989). Learning a word-processing task by doing. In: F. Klix, N. Streitz, Y. Wærn & H. Wandke (Eds.), *MACINTER II*. Amsterdam: North-Holland.

Wærn, Y. & Askwall, S. (1981). On some sources of metacomprehension. *Scandinavian Journal of Psychology*, **22**, 17–25.

Wærn, Y. & Rabenius, L. (1985). Metacognitive aspects of learning difficult texts. Working Papers from The Cognitive Seminar, Department of Psychology, University of Stockholm, No. 18, 1985. Also in: E. de Corte, H. Lodewijks, R. Parmentier & P. Span (Eds.), *Learning and Instruction. European Research in an International Context: Volume 1.* Pergamon Press/Leuven University Press, pp.349–357.

Wærn, Y., El-Khouri, B., Olofsson, M. & Scherlund, K. (1986). Does computer education affect problem solving strategies? Paper presented at the conference "Work With Display Units". Stockholm, May, 1986.

Wærn, Y. & Rabenius, L. (1987). On the role of models in the instruction of novice users of a word processing system. *Zeitschrift fuer Psychologie*, Suppl. 9

Wærn, Y., van der Veer, G.C., Guest, S., Haselager, W., Hjalmarsson, A., Innocent, P., McDaid, E, Oestreicher, L., Svärd, P-O & Tauber, M.J. (1988). Does transparency matter in learning UNIX Mail? In: R. Speth (Ed.), *Research into Networks and Distributed Applications. EUTECO '88.* Amsterdam: North-Holland, pp.429–442.

Waltz, D.L. (1976). An English language question answering system for a large relational database. *Communications of the ACM*, 21, 526–539.

Ware, C. & Mikaelin, H.H. (1987). An evaluation of an eye tracker as a device for computer input. In: L. Borman & B. Curtis (Eds.), *Human Factors in Computing Systems, CHI '85.* New York: ACM, pp.183–188.

Warren, C. & Whitefield, A. (1987). The role of task characterisation in transferring models of users. The example of engineering design. In: H.J. Bullinger & B. Shackel (Eds.), *Human–Computer Interaction—INTERACT '87*, Amsterdam: North-Holland, pp.237–243.

Wason, P.C. & Johnson-Laird, P.N. (1972). *The Psychology of Reasoning: Structure and Content.* Cambridge, MA: Harvard University Press.

Waterworth. J. (1984). Speech: How to use it. In: A. Monk (Ed.), *Fundamentals of Human–Computer Interaction.* London: Academic Press, pp.221–236.

Waterworth, J.A. & Thomas, C.M. (1985). Why is synthetic speech harder to remember than natural speech? In: L. Borman & B. Curtis (Eds.), *Human Factors in Computing Systems, CHI '85.* New York: ACM.

Weizenbaum, J. (1966). ELIZA—a computer program for the study of natural language communications between man and machine. *Communications of the ACM*, 9, 36–45.

Welford, A.T. (1968). *Fundamentals of Skill.* London: Methuen.

Welty, C. & Stemple, D.W. (1981). Human factors comparison of a procedural and a nonprocedural query language. *ACM Transactions for Database Systems.*

Wertheimer, M. (1945). *Productive Thinking.* Chicago: The University of Chicago Press.

Whitehead, A.N. & Russell, B. (1935). *Principia Mathematica*, Cambridge, The University Press. (Vol. 1, second edition, reprinted).

Williams, C.M. (1973). System response time: A study of users' tolerance. Yorktown Heights, NY: IBM Advanced Systems Development Division Technical Report, 17–272.

Wingert, B., Duus. W., Rader, M. & Riehm, U. (1984). *CAD im Maschinenbau. Wirkungen, Chancen, Risken.* Berlin: Springer Verlag,

Winograd, T. (1982). *Understanding Natural Language.* New York: Academic Press.

Winograd, T. & Flores, F. (1986). *Understanding Computers and Cognition. A New Foundation for Design.* Norwood, New Jersey: Ablex.

Witkin, H.A., Dijk, R.B., Paterson, H.F., Goodenough, D.R., & Karp, S.A. (1962). *Psychological Differentiation: Studies of Development.* New York: Wiley.

Wright, P. (1981). 'The instructions clearly state...' Can't people read? *Applied Ergonomics*, 12, 131–141.

Wright, P. (1984). Designing the documentation that explains how IT works. *Design Studies*, **5**, 2.

Yankelovich, N., Meyrowitz, N. & vanDam, A. (1985). Reading and writing the electronic Book. *Computer*, October, **18**, 15–30.

Yerkes, R.M. & Dodson, J.D. (1908). The relation of strength of stimulus to rapidity of habit-formation. *Journal of Comparative Neurology and Psychology*, **18**, 459–482.

Youmans, D.M. (1981). User requirements for future office workstations with emphasis on preferred response times. IBM United Kingdom Laboratories, Hursley Park.

Young, R.M. & Hull, A. (1982). Cognitive aspects of the selection of Viewdata options by casual users. Pathways to the Information Society. *Proceedings of the 6th International Conference on Computer Communication*, London, pp.571–576.

Young, R.M. (1983). Surrogates and mappings: Two kinds of conceptual models for interactive devices. In: Gentner, A. & Stevens, D. (Eds.) *Mental models*. Hillsdale, NJ: Lawrence Erlbaum Assoc., 35–52.

Zelniker, T. & Oppenheimer, L. (1973). Modification of information processing of impulsive children. *Child Development*, **44**, 445–450.

Zimmerman, T.G., Lanier, J., Blanchard, C., Bryson, S. & Harvill, Y. (1987). A hand gesture interface device. In: J.M. Carroll & P.P. Tanner (Eds.), *Human Factors in Computing Systems, and Graphic Interface, CHI '87*. New York: ACM, pp.189–192.

Author Index

Subject Index

325